FROM SEA TO SEA

AND OTHER SKETCHES

FROM SEA TO SEA

AND OTHER SKETCHES

Letters of Travel

BY

RUDYARD KIPLING

VOLUME II

London
MACMILLAN AND CO., LIMITED
1904

First Edition February 1900
Reprinted March 1900, 1901, 1904

CONTENTS

FROM SEA TO SEA

CONTENTS

XXXV

THE CITY OF DREADFUL NIGHT

I

III

THE SMITH ADMINISTRATION

FROM SEA TO SEA

CONTINUED

No. XXV

TELLS HOW I DROPPED INTO POLITICS AND THE TENDERER SENTIMENTS. CONTAINS A MORAL TREATISE ON AMERICAN MAIDENS AND AN ETHNOLOGICAL ONE ON THE NEGRO. ENDS WITH A BANQUET AND A TYPE-WRITER.

I HAVE been watching machinery in repose after reading about machinery in action. An excellent gentleman who bears a name honoured in the magazines writes, much as Disraeli orated, of 'the sublime instincts of an ancient people,' the certainty with which they can be trusted to manage their own affairs in their own way, and the speed with which they are making for all sorts of desirable goals. This he called a statement or purview of American politics. I went almost directly afterwards to a saloon where gentlemen interested in ward politics nightly congregate. They were not pretty persons. Some of them were bloated, and they all swore cheerfully till the heavy gold watch-chains on their fat stomachs rose and fell again; but they talked over their liquor as men who had power and unquestioned access to places of trust and profit. The magazine-writer discussed theories of government; these men the practice. They had been there. They knew all about it. They banged their fists on the table and spoke of political 'pulls,' the vending of votes, and so forth. Theirs was not the talk of village babblers reconstructing the affairs of the nation, but of strong, coarse, lustful men fighting for spoil and thoroughly understanding the best methods of reaching it. I listened long and intently to speech I could not understand, or only in spots. It was the speech of business, however. I had sense enough to know *that*, and to do my laughing outside the door. Then I began to understand why my pleasant and well-educated hosts in San Francisco spoke with a bitter scorn of such duties of citizenship as voting and taking an interest in the distribution of offices. Scores of men have told me with no false pride that they would as soon concern themselves with the public affairs of the city or State as rake muck. Read about politics as the cultured writer of the magazines regards 'em, and then, and not till then, pay your respects to the gentlemen who run the grimy reality.

I'm sick of interviewing night-editors, who, in response to my demand for the record of a prominent citizen, answer: 'Well, you see, he began by keeping a saloon,' etc. I prefer to believe that my informants are treating me as in the old sinful days in India I was used to treat our wandering Globe-trotters. They declare that they speak the truth, and the news of dog-politics lately vouchsafed to me in groggeries incline me to believe—

but I won't. The people are much too nice to slangander as recklessly as I have been doing. Besides, I am hopelessly in love with about eight American maidens—each perfectly delightful till the next one comes into the room. O-Toyo was a darling, but she lacked several things; conversation, for one. You cannot live on giggles. She shall remain unmoved at Nagasaki while I roast a battered heart before the shrine of a big Kentucky blonde who had for a nurse, when she was little, a negro 'mammy.' By consequence she has welded on to Californian beauty, Paris dresses, Eastern culture, Europe trips, and wild Western originality, the queer dreamy superstitions of the negro quarters, and the result is soul-shattering. And she is but one of many stars. *Item*, a maiden who believes in education and possesses it, with a few hundred thousand dollars to boot, and a taste for slumming. *Item*, the leader of a sort of informal salon where girls congregate, read papers, and daringly discuss metaphysical problems and candy—a sloe-eyed, black-browed, imperious maiden. *Item*, a very small maiden, absolutely without reverence, who can in one swift sentence trample upon and leave gasping half a dozen young men. *Item*, a millionairess, burdened with her money, lonely, caustic, with a tongue keen as a sword, yearning for a sphere, but chained up to the rock of her vast possessions. *Item*, a typewriter-maiden earning her own bread in this big city, because she doesn't think a girl ought to be a burden on her parents. She quotes Théophile Gautier, and moves through the world manfully, much respected, for all her twenty inexperienced summers. *Item*, a woman from Cloudland who has no history in the past, but is discreetly of the present, and strives for the confidences of male humanity on the grounds of 'sympathy.' (This is not altogether a new type.) *Item*, a girl in a 'dive' blessed with a Greek head and eyes that seem to speak all that is best and sweetest in the world. But woe is me! —she has no ideas in this world or the next, beyond the consumption of beer (a commission on each bottle), and protests that she sings the songs allotted to her nightly with no more than the vaguest notion of their meaning.

Sweet and comely are the maidens of Devonshire; delicate and of gracious seeming those who live in the pleasant places of London; fascinating for all their demureness the damsels of France clinging closely to their mothers, and with large eyes wondering at the wicked world; excellent in her own place and to those who understand her is the Anglo-Indian 'spin' in her second season; but the girls of America are above and beyond them all. They are clever; they can talk. Yea, it is said that they think. Certainly they have an appearance of so doing. They are original, and look you between the brows with unabashed eyes as a sister might look at her brother. They are instructed in the folly and vanity of the male mind, for they have associated with 'the boys' from babyhood, and can discerningly minister to both vices, or pleasantly snub the possessor. They possess, moreover, a life among themselves, independent of masculine associations. They have societies and clubs, and unlimited tea-fights where all the guests are girls. They are self-possessed without parting with any tenderness that is their sex-right; they understand; they can take care of themselves; they are superbly independent. When you ask them what makes them so charming, they say: 'It is because we are better educated than your girls and—and we are more sensible in regard to men. We have good times all round, but we aren't taught to regard every man as a possible husband. Nor is he expected to marry the first girl he calls on regularly.' Yes, they have good times, their freedom is large, and they do not abuse it. They can go driving with young men, and receive visits from young men to an extent that would make an English mother wink with horror; and neither driver nor drivee have a thought beyond the enjoyment of a good time. As certain also of their own poets have said—

> Man is fire and woman is tow,
> And the Devil he comes and begins to blow.

In America the tow is soaked in a solution that makes it fire-proof, in absolute liberty and large knowledge; consequently accidents do not exceed the regular percentage arranged by the Devil for each class and climate under the skies. But the freedom of the young girl has its drawbacks. She is—I say it with all reluctance—irreverent, from her forty-dollar bonnet to the buckles in her eighteen-dollar shoes. She talks flippantly to her parents and men old enough to be her grandfather. She has a prescriptive right to the society of the Man who Arrives. The parents admit it. This is sometimes embarrassing, especially when you call on a man and his wife for the sake of information; the one being a merchant of varied knowledge, the other a woman of the world. In five minutes your host has vanished. In another five his wife has followed him, and you are left with a very charming maiden doubtless, but certainly not the person you came to see. She chatters and you grin; but you leave with the very strong impression of a wasted morning. This has been my experience once or twice. I have even said as pointedly as I dared to a man: 'I came to see you.' 'You'd better see me in my office, then. The house belongs to my women-folk—to my daughter, that is to say.' He spoke with truth. The American of wealth is owned by his family. They exploit him for bullion, and sometimes it seems to me that his lot is a lonely one. The women get the ha'pence; the kicks are all his own. Nothing is too good for an American's daughter (I speak here of the moneyed classes). The girls take every gift as a matter of course. Yet they develop greatly when a catastrophe arrives and the man of many millions goes up or goes down and his daughters take to stenography or type-writing. I have heard many tales of heroism from the lips of girls who counted the principals among their friends. The crash came; Mamie or Hattie or Sadie gave up their maid, their carriages and candy, and with a No. 2 Remington and a stout heart set about earning their daily bread.

'And did I drop her from the list of my friends? No, Sir,' said a scarlet-lipped vision in white lace. 'That might happen to me any day.'

It may be this sense of possible disaster in the air that makes San Franciscan society go with so captivating a rush and whirl. Recklessness is in the air. I can't explain where it comes from, but there it is. The roaring winds off the Pacific make you drunk to begin with. The aggressive luxury on all sides helps out the intoxication, and you spin for ever 'down the ringing grooves of change' (there is no small change, by the way, west of the Rockies) as long as money lasts. They make greatly and they spend lavishly; not only the rich but the artisans, who pay nearly five pounds for a suit of clothes and for other luxuries in proportion. The young men rejoice in the days of their youth. They gamble, yacht, race, enjoy prize-fights and cock-fights—the one openly, the other in secret—they establish luxurious clubs; they break themselves over horse-flesh and—other things; and they are instant in quarrel. At twenty they are experienced in business; embark in vast enterprises, take partners as experienced as themselves, and go to pieces with as much splendour as their neighbours. Remember that the men who stocked California in the Fifties were physically, and as far as regards certain tough virtues, the pick of the earth. The inept and the weakly died *en route* or went under in the days of construction. To this nucleus were added all the races of the

Continent—French, Italian, German, and, of course, the Jew. The result you shall see in large-boned, deep-chested, delicate-handed women, and long, elastic, well-built boys. It needs no little golden badge swinging from his watch-chain to mark the Native Son of the Golden West—the country-bred of California. Him I love because he is devoid of fear, carries himself like a man, and has a heart as big as his boots. I fancy, too, he knows how to enjoy the blessings of life that his world so abundantly bestows upon him. At least I heard a little rat of a creature with hock-bottle shoulders explaining that a man from Chicago could pull the eye-teeth of a Californian in business. Well, if I lived in Fairyland, where cherries were as big as plums, plums as big as apples, and strawberries of no account; where the procession of the fruits of the seasons was like a pageant in a Drury Lane pantomime and where the dry air was wine, I should let business slide once in a way and kick up my heels with my fellows. The tale of the resources of California—vegetable and mineral—is a fairy tale. You can read it in books. You would never believe me. All manner of nourishing food from sea-fish to beef may be bought at the lowest prices; and the people are well developed and of a high stomach. They demand ten shillings for tinkering a jammed lock of a trunk; they receive sixteen shillings a day for working as carpenters; they spend many sixpences on very bad cigars, and they go mad over a prize-fight. When they disagree, they do so fatally, with firearms in their hands, and on the public streets. I was just clear of Mission Street when the trouble began between two gentlemen, one of whom perforated the other. When a policeman, whose name I do not recollect, 'fatally shot Ed. Kearney,' for attempting to escape arrest, I was in the next street. For these things I am thankful. It is enough to travel with a policeman in a tram-car and while he arranges his coat-tails as he sits down, to catch sight of a loaded revolver. It is enough to know that fifty per cent of the men in the public saloons carry pistols about them. The Chinaman waylays his adversary and methodically chops him to pieces with his hatchet. Then the Press roars about the brutal ferocity of the Pagan. The Italian reconstructs his friend with a long knife. The Press complains of the waywardness of the alien. The Irishman and the native Californian in their hours of discontent use the revolver, not once, but six times. The Press records the fact, and asks in the next column whether the world can parallel the progress of San Francisco. The American who loves this country will tell you that this sort of thing is confined to the lower classes. Just at present an ex-judge who was sent to jail by another judge (upon my word, I cannot tell whether these titles mean anything) is breathing red-hot vengeance against his enemy. The papers have interviewed both parties and confidently expect a fatal issue.

Now let me draw breath and curse the negro waiter and through him the negro in service generally. He has been made a citizen with a vote; consequently both political parties play with him. But that is neither here nor there. He will commit in one meal every *bêtise* that a scullion fresh from the plough-tail is capable of, and he will continue to repeat those faults. He is as complete a heavy-footed, uncomprehending, bungle-fisted fool as any *memsahib* in the East ever took into her establishment. But he is according to law a free and independent citizen —consequently above reproof or criticism. He, and he alone, in this insane city will wait at table (the Chinaman doesn't count). He is untrained, inept, but he will fill the place and draw the pay. Now God and his father's Kismet made him intellectually inferior to the Oriental. He insists on pretending that he serves tables by accident —as a sort of amusement. He wishes you to understand this little fact. You wish to eat your meals, and if possible to have them properly served. He is a big, black, vain baby and a man rolled into one. A coloured gentleman who insisted on getting me pie when I wanted something else, demanded information about India. I gave him some facts about wages. 'Oh hell,' said he cheerfully, 'that wouldn't keep me in cigars for a month.' Then he fawned on me for a ten-cent piece. Later he took it upon himself to pity the natives of India—'heathen' he called them, this Woolly One whose race has been the butt of every comedy on the Asiatic stage since the beginning. And I turned and saw by the head upon his shoulders that he was a Yoruba man, if there be any truth in ethnological castes. He did his thinking in English, but he was a Yoruba negro, and the race type had remained the same throughout his generations. And the room was full of other races—some that looked exactly like Gallas (but the trade was never recruited from that side of Africa), some duplicates of Cameroon heads, and some Kroomen, if ever Kroomen wore evening dress. The American does not consider little matters of descent, though by this time he ought to know all about 'damnable heredity.' As a general rule he keeps himself very far from the negro and says unpretty things about him. There are six million negroes more or less in the States, and they are increasing. The Americans once having made them citizens cannot unmake them. He says, in his newspapers, they ought to be elevated by education. He is trying this: but it is like to be a long job, because black blood is much more adhesive than white, and throws back with annoying persistence. When the negro gets a religion, he returns, directly as a hiving bee, to the first instincts of his people. Just now a wave of religion is sweeping over some of the Southern States. Up to the present, two Messiahs and one Daniel have appeared; and several human sacrifices have been offered up to these incarnations. The Daniel managed to get three young men, who he insisted were Shadrach, Meshach, and Abednego, to walk into a blast furnace; guaranteeing non-combustion. They did not return. I have seen nothing of this kind, but I have attended a negro church. The congregation were moved by the spirit to groans and tears, and one of them danced up the aisle to the mourners' bench. The motive may have been genuine. The movements of the shaken body were those of a Zanzibar stick-dance, such as you see at Aden on the coal boats; and even as I watched the people, the links that bound them to the white man snapped one by one, and I saw before me—the *hubshi* (the Woolly One) praying to the God he did not understand. Those neatly dressed folk on the benches, the grey-headed elder by the window, were savages —neither more nor less. What will the American do with the negro? The South will not consort with him. In some States miscegenation is a penal offence. The North is every year less and less in need of his services. And he will not disappear. He will continue as a problem. His friends will urge that he is as good as the white man. His enemies . . . it is not good to be a negro in the land of the free and the home of the brave.

But this has nothing to do with San Francisco and her merry maidens, her strong, swaggering men, and her wealth of gold and pride. They bore me to a banquet in honour of a brave Lieutenant—Carlin, of the *Vandalia*—who stuck by his ship in the great cyclone at Apia and comported himself as an officer should. On that occasion—'twas at the Bohemian Club—I heard oratory with the roundest of *o*'s; and devoured a dinner the memory of which will descend with me into the hungry grave. There were about forty speeches delivered; and not one of them was average or ordinary. It was my first introduction to the American Eagle screaming for all it was worth. The Lieutenant's heroism served as a peg from which those silver-tongued ones turned themselves loose and kicked. They ransacked the clouds of sunset, the thunderbolts of Heaven, the deeps of Hell, and the splendours of the Resurrection, for tropes and metaphors, and hurled the result at the head of the guest of the evening. Never since the morning stars sang together for joy, I learned, had an amazed creation witnessed such superhuman bravery as that displayed by the American navy in the Samoa cyclone. Till earth rotted in the phosphorescent star-and-stripe slime of a decayed universe that God-like gallantry would not be forgotten. I grieve that I cannot give the exact words. My attempt at reproducing their spirit is pale and inadequate. I sat bewildered on a coruscating Niagara of—blatherumskite. It was magnificent—it was stupendous; and I was conscious of a wicked desire to hide my face in a napkin and grin. Then, according to rule, they produced their dead, and across the snowy tablecloths dragged the corpse of every man slain in the Civil War, and hurled defiance at 'our natural enemy' (England, so please you!) 'with her chain of fortresses across the world.' Thereafter they glorified their nation afresh, from the beginning, in case any detail should have been overlooked, and that made me uncomfortable for their sakes. How in the world can a white man, a Sahib of Our blood, stand up and plaster praise on his own country? He can think as highly as he likes, but his open-mouthed vehemence of adoration struck me almost as indelicate. My hosts talked for rather more than three hours, and at the end seemed ready for three hours more. But when the Lieutenant—such a big, brave, gentle giant!—rose to his feet, he delivered what seemed to me as the speech of the evening. I remember nearly the whole of it, and it ran something in this way: 'Gentlemen—It's very good of you to give me this dinner and to tell me all these pretty things, but what I want you to understand—the fact is—what we want and what we ought to get at once is a navy—more ships—lots of 'em—' Then we howled the top of the roof off, and I, for one, fell in love with Carlin on the spot. Wallah! He was a man.

The Prince among merchants bade me take no heed to the warlike sentiments of some of the old Generals. 'The sky-rockets are thrown in for effect,' quoth he, 'and whenever we get on our hind-legs we always express a desire to chaw up England. It's a sort of family affair.'

And indeed, when you come to think of it, there is no other country for the American public speaker to trample upon.

France has Germany; we have Russia; for Italy, Austria is provided; and the humblest Pathan possesses an ancestral enemy. Only America stands out of the racket; and therefore, to be in fashion, makes a sand-bag of the mother-country, and bangs her when occasion requires. 'The chain of fortresses' man, a fascinating talker, explained to me after the affair that he was compelled to blow off steam. Everybody expected it. When we had chanted 'The Star-Spangled Banner' not more than eight times, we adjourned. America is a very great country, but it is not yet Heaven with electric lights and plush fittings, as the speakers professed to believe. My listening mind went back to the politicians in the saloon who wasted no time in talking about freedom, but quietly made arrangements to impose their will on the citizens. 'The Judge is a great man, but give thy presents to the Clerk,' as the proverb saith.

And what more remains to tell? I cannot write connectedly, because I am in love with all those girls aforesaid and some others who do not appear in the invoice. The type-writer girl is an institution of which the comic papers make much capital, but she is vastly convenient. She and a companion rent a room in a business quarter, and copy manuscript at the rate of six annas a page. Only a woman can manage a type-writing machine, because she has served apprenticeship to the sewing-machine. She can earn as much as a hundred dollars a month, and professes to regard this form of bread-winning as her natural destiny. But oh how she hates it in her heart of hearts! When I had got over the surprise of doing business and trying to give orders to a young woman of coldly clerkly aspect, intrenched behind gold-rimmed spectacles, I made inquiries concerning the pleasures of this independence. They liked it—indeed, they did. 'Twas the natural fate of almost all girls,—the recognised custom in America,—and I was a barbarian not to see it in that light.

'Well, and after?' said I. 'What happens?'

'We work for our bread.'

'And then what do you expect?'

'Then we shall work for our bread.'

'Till you die?'

'Ye-es—unless—'

'Unless what? A man works till he dies.'

'So shall we.' This without enthusiasm—'I suppose.'

Said the partner in the firm audaciously: 'Sometimes we marry our employers—at least that's what the newspapers say.' The hand banged on half a dozen of the keys of the machine at once. 'Yes, I don't care. I hate it—I *hate* it—I hate it, and you needn't look so!'

The senior partner was regarding the rebel with grave-eyed reproach.

'I thought you did,' said I. 'I don't suppose American girls are much different from English ones in instinct.'

'Isn't it Théophile Gautier who says that the only differences between country and country lie in the slang and the uniform of the police?'

Now in the name of all the Gods at once, what is one to say to a young lady (who in England would be a Person) who earns her own bread, and very naturally hates the employ, and slings out-of-the-way quotations at your head? That one falls in love with her goes without saying; but that is not enough.

A mission should be established.

No. XXVI

TAKES ME THROUGH BRET HARTE'S COUNTRY, AND TO PORTLAND WITH 'OLD MAN CALIFORNIA.' EXPLAINS HOW TWO VAGABONDS BECAME HOMESICK THROUGH LOOKING AT OTHER PEOPLE'S HOUSES.

> I walked in the lonesome even,
> And who so sad as I,
> As I saw the young men and maidens
> Merrily passing by?

SAN FRANCISCO has only one drawback. 'Tis hard to leave. When like the pious Hans Breitmann I 'cut that city by the sea' it was with regrets for the pleasant places left behind, for the men who were so clever, and the women who were so witty, for the 'dives,' the beer-halls, the bucket-shops, and the poker-hells where humanity was going to the Devil with shouting and laughter and song and the rattle of dice-boxes. I would fain have stayed, but I feared that an evil end would come to me when my money was all spent and I descended to the street corner. A voice inside me said: 'Get out of this. Go north. Strike for Victoria and Vancouver. Bask for a day under the shadow of the old flag.' So I set forth from San Francisco to Portland in Oregon: and that was a railroad run of thirty-six hours.

The Oakland railway terminus, whence all the main lines start, does not own anything approaching to a platform. A yard with a dozen or more tracks is roughly asphalted, and the traveller laden with handbags skips merrily across the metals in search of his own particular train. The bells of half a dozen shunting engines are tolling suggestively in his ears. If he is run down, so much the worse for him. 'When the bell rings, look out for the locomotive.' Long use has made the nation familiar and even contemptuous towards trains to an extent which God never intended. Women who in England would gather up their skirts and scud timorously over a level crossing in the country, here talk dress and babies under the very nose of the cow-catcher, and little children dally with the moving car in a manner horrible to behold. We pulled out at the wholly insignificant speed of twenty-five miles an hour through the streets of a suburb of fifty thousand, and in our progress among the carts and the children and the shop fronts slew nobody; at which I was not a little disappointed.

When the negro porter bedded me up for the night and I had solved the problem of undressing while lying down,—I was much cheered by the thought that if anything happened I should have to stay where I was and wait till the kerosene lamps set the overturned car alight and burned me to death. It is easier to get out of a full theatre than to leave a Pullman in haste.

By the time I had discovered that a profusion of nickel-plating, plush, and damask does not compensate for closeness and dust, the train ran into the daylight on the banks of the Sacramento River. A few windows were gingerly opened after the bunks had been reconverted into seats, but that long coffin-car was by no means ventilated, and we were a gummy grimy crew who sat there. At six in the morning the heat was distinctly unpleasant, but seeing with the eye of the flesh that I was in Bret Harte's own country, I rejoiced. There were the pines and madrone-clad hills his miners lived and fought among; there was the heated red earth that showed whence the gold had been washed; the dry gulch, the red, dusty road where Hamblin was used to stop the stage in the intervals of his elegant leisure and superior card-play; there was the timber felled and sweating resin in the sunshine; and, above all, there was the quivering pungent heat that Bret Harte drives into your dull brain with the magic of his pen. When we stopped at a collection of packing-cases dignified by the name of a town, my felicity was complete. The name of the place was something offensive,—Amberville or Jacksonburgh,—but it owned a cast-iron fountain worthy of a town of thirty thousand. Next to the fountain was a 'hotel,' at least seventeen feet high including the chimney, and next to the hotel was the forest—the pine, the oak, and the untrammelled undergrowth of the hillside. A cinnamon-bear cub—Baby Sylvester in the very fur—was tied to the stump of a tree opposite the fountain; a pack-mule dozed in the dust-haze, a red-shirted miner in a slouch-hat supported the hotel, a blue-shirted miner swung round the corner, and the two went indoors for a drink. A girl came out of the only other house but one, and shading her eyes with a brown hand stared at the panting train. She didn't recognise me, but I knew her—had known her for years. She was M'liss. She never married the schoolmaster, after all, but stayed, always young and always fair, among the pines. I knew Red-Shirt too. He was one of the bearded men who stood back when Tennessee claimed his partner from the hands of the Law. The Sacramento River, a few yards away, shouted that all these things were true. The train went on while Baby Sylvester stood on his downy head, and M'liss swung her sun-bonnet by the strings.

'What do you think?' said a lawyer who was travelling with me. 'It's a new world to you; isn't it?'

'No. It's quite familiar. I was never out of England; it's as if I saw it all.'

Quick as light came the answer: '"Yes, they lived once thus at Venice when the miners were the kings."'

I loved that lawyer on the spot. We drank to Bret Harte who, you remember, 'claimed California, but California never claimed him. He's turned English.'

Lying back in state, I waited for the flying miles to turn over the pages of the book I knew. They brought me all I desired—from the Man of no Account sitting on a stump and playing with a dog, to 'that most sarcastic man, the quiet Mister Brown.' He boarded the train from out of the woods, and there was venom and sulphur on his tongue. He had just lost a lawsuit. Only Yuba Bill failed to appear. The train had taken his employment from him. A nameless ruffian backed me into a corner and began telling me about the resources of the country, and what it would eventually become. All I remember of his lecture was that you could catch trout in the Sacramento River—the stream that we followed so faithfully.

Then rose a tough and wiry old man with grizzled hair and made inquiries about the trout. To him was added the secretary of a life-insurance company. I fancy he was travelling to rake in the dead that the train killed. But he, too, was a fisherman, and the two turned to meward. The frankness of a Westerner is delightful. They tell me that in the Eastern States I shall meet another type of man and a more reserved. The Californian always speaks of the man from the New England States as a different breed. It is our Punjab and Madras over again, but more so. The old man was on a holiday in search of fish. When he discovered a brother-loafer he proposed a confederation of rods. Quoth the insurance-agent, 'I'm not staying any time in Portland, but I will introduce you to a man there who'll tell you about fishing.' The two told strange tales as we slid through the forests and saw afar off the snowy head of a great mountain. There were vineyards, fruit orchards, and wheat fields where the land opened out, and every ten miles or so, twenty or thirty wooden houses and at least three churches. A large town would have a population of two thousand and an infinite belief in its own capacities. Sometimes a flaring advertisement flanked the line, calling for men to settle down, take up the ground, and make their home there. At a big town we could pick up the local newspaper, narrow as the cutting edge of a chisel and twice as keen —a journal filled with the prices of stock, notices of improved reaping and binding machines, movements of eminent citizens—'whose fame beyond their own abode extends—for miles along the Harlem road.' There was not much grace about these papers, but all breathed the same need for good men, steady men who would plough, and till, and build schools for their children, and make a township in the hills. Once only I found a sharp change in the note and a very pathetic one. I think it was a young soul in trouble who was writing poetry. The editor had jammed the verses between the flamboyant advertisement of a real-estate agent —a man who sells you land and lies about it —and that of a Jew tailor who disposed of 'nobby' suits at 'cut-throat prices.' Here are two verses ; I think they tell their own story :—

God made the pine with its root in the earth,
 Its top in the sky ;
They have burned the pine to increase the worth
 Of the wheat and the silver rye.

Go weigh the cost of the soul of the pine
Cut off from the sky;
And the price of the wheat that grows so fine
And the worth of the silver rye!

The thin-lipped, keen-eyed men who boarded the train would not read that poetry, or, if they did, would not understand. Heaven guard that poor pine in the desert and keep 'its top in the sky'!

When the train took to itself an extra engine and began to breathe heavily, some one said that we were ascending the Siskiyou Mountains. We had been climbing steadily from San Francisco, and at last won to over four thousand feet above sea-level, always running through forest. Then, naturally enough, we came down, but we dropped two thousand two hundred feet in about thirteen miles. It was not so much the grinding of the brakes along the train, or the sight of three curves of track apparently miles below us, or even the vision of a goods-train apparently just under our wheels, or even the tunnels, that made me reflect; it was the trestles over which we crawled, —trestles something over a hundred feet high and looking like a collection of match-sticks.

'I guess our timber is as much a curse as a blessing,' said the old man from Southern California. 'These trestles last very well for five or six years; then they get out of repair, and a train goes through 'em, or else a forest fire burns 'em up.'

This was said in the middle of a groaning, shivering trestle. An occasional plate-layer took a look at us as we went down, but that railway didn't waste men on inspection-duty. Very often there were cattle on the track, against which the engine used a diabolical form of whistling. The old man had been a driver in his youth, and beguiled the way with cheery anecdotes of what might be expected if we fouled a young calf.

'You see, they get their legs under the cow-catcher, and that'll put an engine off the line. I remember when a hog wrecked an excursion-train and killed sixty people. 'Guess the engineer will look out, though.'

There is considerably too much guessing about this large nation. As one of them put it rather forcibly: 'We guess a trestle will stand for ever, and we guess that we can patch up a washout on the track, and we guess the road's clear, and sometimes we guess ourselves into the deepot, and sometimes we guess ourselves into Hell.'

. . . . .

The descent brought us far into Oregon and a timber and wheat country. We drove through wheat and pine in alternate slices, but pine chiefly, till we reached Portland, which is a city of fifty thousand, possessing the electric light of course, equally, of course, devoid of pavements, and a port of entry about a hundred miles from the sea at which big steamers can load. It is a poor city that cannot say it has no equal on the Pacific coast. Portland shouts this to the pines which run down from a thousand-foot ridge clear up to the city. You may sit in a bedizened bar-room furnished with telephone and clicker, and in half an hour be in the woods.

Portland produces lumber and jig-saw fittings for houses, and beer and buggies, and bricks and biscuits; and, in case you should miss the fact, there are glorified views of the town hung up in public places with the value of the products set down in dollars. All this is excellent and exactly suitable to the opening of a new country; but when a man tells you it is civilisation, you object. The first thing that the civilised man learns to do is to keep the dollars in the background, because they are only the oil of the machine that makes life go smoothly.

Portland is so busy that it can't attend to its own sewage or paving, and the four-story brick blocks front cobble-stones and plank sidewalks and other things much worse. I saw a foundation being dug out. The sewage of perhaps twenty years ago, had thoroughly soaked into the soil, and there was a familiar and Oriental look about the compost that flew up with each shovel-load. Yet the local papers, as was just and proper, swore there was no place like Portland, Oregon, U.S.A., chronicled the performances of Oregonians, 'claimed' prominent citizens elsewhere as Oregonians, and fought tooth and nail for dock, rail, and wharfage projects. And you could find men who had thrown in their lives with the city, who were bound up in it, and worked their life out for what they conceived to be its material prosperity. Pity it is to record that in this strenuous, labouring town there had been, a week before, a shooting-case. One well-known man had shot another on the street, and was now pleading self-defence because the other man had, or the murderer thought he had, a pistol about him. Not content with shooting him dead, he squibbed off his revolver into him as he lay. I read the pleadings, and they made me ill. So far as I could judge, if the dead man's body had been found with a pistol on it, the shooter would have gone free. Apart from the mere murder, cowardly enough in itself, there was a refinement of cowardice in the plea. Here in this civilised city the surviving brute was afraid he would be shot—fancied he saw the other man make a motion to his hip-pocket, and so on. Eventually the jury disagreed. And the degrading thing was that the trial was reported by men who evidently understood all about the pistol, was tried before a jury who were versed in the etiquette of the hip-pocket, and was discussed on the streets by men equally initiate.

But let us return to more cheerful things. The insurance-agent introduced us as friends to a real-estate man, who promptly bade us go up the Columbia River for a day while he made inquiries about fishing. There was no overwhelming formality. The old man was addressed as 'California,' I answered indifferently to 'England' or 'Johnny Bull,' and the real-estate man was 'Portland.' This was a lofty and spacious form of address.

So California and I took a steamboat, and upon a sumptuous blue and gold morning steered up the Willamette River, on which Portland stands, into the great Columbia—the river that brings the salmon that goes into the tin that is emptied into

that California owned timber ships and dealt in lumber, had ranches too, a partner, and everything handsome about him; in addition to a chequered career of some thirty-five years. But he looked almost as disreputable a loafer as I.

'Say, young feller, we're going to see scenery now. You shout and sing,' said California, when the bland wooded islands gave place to bolder outlines, and the steamer ran herself into a hornet's nest of black-fanged rocks not a foot below the boiling broken water. We were trying to get up a slue, or back-channel, by a short cut, and the stern-wheel never spun twice in the same direction. Then we hit a floating log with a jar that ran through our system, and then, white-bellied, open-gilled, spun by a dead salmon—a lordly twenty-pound Chinook salmon who had perished in his pride. 'You'll see the salmon-wheels 'fore long,' said a man who lived 'way back on the Washoogle,' and whose hat was spangled with trout-flies. 'Those Chinook salmon never rise to the fly. The canneries take them by the wheel.' At the next bend we sighted a wheel—an infernal arrangement of wire-gauze compartments worked by the current and moved out from a barge inshore to scoop up the salmon as he races up the river. California swore long and fluently at the sight, and the more fluently when he was told of the weight of a good night's catch—some thousands of pounds. Think of the black and bloody murder of it! But you out yonder insist in buying tinned salmon, and the canneries cannot live by letting down lines.

About this time California was struck with

madness. I found him dancing on the fore-deck shouting, 'Isn't she a daisy? Isn't she a darling?' He had found a waterfall—a blown thread of white vapour that broke from the crest of a hill—a waterfall eight hundred and fifty feet high whose voice was even louder than the voice of the river. 'Bridal Veil,' jerked out the purser. 'D—n that purser and the people who christened her! Why didn't they call her Mechlin-lace Falls at fifty dollars a yard while they were at it?' said California. And I agreed with him. There are many 'bridal veil' falls in this country, but few, men say, lovelier than those that come down to the Columbia River. Then the scenery began—poured forth with the reckless profusion of Nature, who when she wants to be amiable succeeds only in being oppressively magnificent. The river was penned between gigantic stone walls crowned with the ruined bastions of Oriental palaces. The stretch of green water widened and was guarded by pine-clad hills three thousand feet high. A wicked devil's thumbnail of rock shot up a hundred feet in midstream. A sand-bar of blinding white sand gave promise of flat country that the next bend denied; for, lo! we were running under a triple tier of fortifications, lava-topped, pine-clothed, and terrible. Behind them the white dome of Mount Hood shot fourteen thousand feet into the blue, and at their feet the river threshed among a belt of cottonwood trees. There I sat down and looked at California half out of the boat in his anxiety to see both sides of the river at once. He had seen my note-book, and it offended him. 'Young feller, let her go—

and you shut your head. It's not you nor anybody like you can put this down. Black, the novelist, he could. He can describe salmon-fishing, *he* can.' And he glared at me as though he expected me to go and do likewise.

'I can't. I know it,' I said humbly.

'Then thank God that you came along this way.'

We reached a little railway, on an island, which was to convey us to a second steamer, because, as the purser explained, the river was 'a trifle broken.' We had a six-mile run, sitting in the sunshine on a dummy waggon, whirled just along the edge of the river-bluffs. Sometimes we dived into the fragrant pine woods, ablaze with flowers; but we generally watched the river now narrowed into a turbulent mill-race. Just where the whole body of water broke in riot over a series of cascades, the United States Government had chosen to build a lock for steamers, and the stream was one boiling, spouting mob of water. A log shot down the race, struck on a rock, split from end to end, and rolled over in white foam. I shuddered because my toes were not more than sixty feet above the log, and I feared that a stray splinter might have found me. But the train ran into the river on a sort of floating trestle, and I was upon another steamer ere I fully understood why. The cascades were not two hundred yards below us, and when we cast off to go upstream, the rush of the river, ere the wheel struck the water, dragged us as though we had been towed. Then the country opened out, and California mourned for his lost bluffs and crags, till we struck a rock wall four hundred feet high, crowned by the gigantic figure of a man watching us. On a rocky island we saw the white tomb of an old-time settler who had made his money in San Francisco, but had chosen to be buried in an Indian burying-ground. A decayed wooden 'wickyup,' where the bones of the Indian dead are laid, almost touched the tomb. The river ran into a canal of basaltic rock, painted in yellow, vermilion, and green by Indians and, by inferior brutes, adorned with advertisements of 'bile beans.' We had reached The Dalles—the centre of a great sheep and wool district, and the head of navigation.

When an American arrives at a new town it is his bounden duty 'to take it in.' California swung his coat over his shoulder with the gesture of a man used to long tramps, and together, at eight in the evening, we explored The Dalles. The sun had not yet set, and it would be light for at least another hour. All the inhabitants seemed to own a little villa and one church apiece. The young men were out walking with the young maidens, the old folks were sitting on the front steps,—not the ones that led to the religiously shuttered best drawing-room, but the side-front-steps,—and the husbands and wives were tying back pear trees or gathering cherries. A scent of hay reached me, and in the stillness we could hear the cattle bells as the cows came home across the lava-sprinkled fields. California swung down the wooden pavements, audibly criticising the housewives' hollyhocks and the more perfect ways of pear-grafting, and, as the young men and maidens passed, giving quaint stories of his youth. I felt that I knew all the people aforetime, I was so interested in them and their life. A woman hung over a gate talking to another woman, and as I passed I heard her say, 'skirts,' and again, 'skirts,' and 'I'll send you over the pattern'; and I knew they were talking dress. We stumbled upon a young couple saying good-bye in the twilight, and 'When shall I see you again?' quoth he; and I understood that to the doubting heart the tiny little town we paraded in twenty minutes might be as large as all London and as impassable as an armed camp. I gave them both my blessing, because 'When shall I see you again?' is a question that lies very near to hearts of all the world. The last garden gate shut with a click that travelled far down the street, and the lights of the comfortable families began to shine in the confidingly uncurtained windows.

'Say, Johnny Bull, doesn't all this make you feel lonesome?' said California. 'Have you got any folks at home? So've I—a wife and five children—and I'm only on a holiday.'

'And I'm only on a holiday,' I said, and we went back to the Spittoon-wood Hotel. Alas! for the peace and purity of the little town that I had babbled about. At the back of a shop, and discreetly curtained, was a room where the young men who had been talking to the young maidens could play poker and drink and swear, and on the shop were dime novels of bloodshed to corrupt the mind of the little boy, and prurient servant-girl-slush yarns to poison the mind of the girl.

California only laughed grimly. He said that all these little one-house towns were pretty much the same all over the States.

That night I dreamed I was back in India with no place to sleep in ; tramping up and down the Station Mall and asking everybody, 'When shall I see you again ?'

No. XXVII

SHOWS HOW I CAUGHT SALMON IN THE CLACKAMAS

The race is neither to the swift nor the battle to the strong; but time and chance cometh to all.

I HAVE lived! The American Continent may now sink under the sea, for I have taken the best that it yields, and the best was neither dollars, love, nor real estate. Hear now, gentlemen of the Punjab Fishing Club, who whip the reaches of the Tavi, and you who painfully import trout to Ootacamund, and I will tell you how 'old man California' and I went fishing, and you shall envy. We returned from The Dalles to Portland by the way we had come, the steamer stopping *en route* to pick up a night's catch of one of the salmon wheels on the river, and to deliver it at a cannery downstream. When the proprietor of the wheel announced that his take was two thousand two hundred and thirty pounds' weight of fish, 'and not a heavy catch, neither,' I thought he lied. But he sent the boxes aboard, and I counted the salmon by the hundred—huge fifty-pounders, hardly dead, scores of twenty- and thirty-pounders, and a host of smaller fish.

The steamer halted at a rude wooden warehouse built on piles in a lonely reach of the river, and sent in the fish. I followed them up a scale-strewn, fishy incline that led to the cannery. The crazy building was quivering with the machinery on its floors, and a glittering bank of tin-scraps twenty feet high showed where the waste was thrown after the cans had been punched. Only Chinamen were employed on the work, and they looked like blood-besmeared yellow devils, as they crossed the rifts of sunlight that lay upon the floor. When our consignment arrived, the rough wooden boxes broke of themselves as they were dumped down under a jet of water, and the salmon burst out in a stream of quicksilver. A Chinaman jerked up a twenty-pounder, beheaded and de-tailed it with two swift strokes of a knife, flicked out its internal arrangements with a third, and cast it into a blood-dyed tank. The headless fish leaped from under his hands as though they were facing a rapid. Other Chinamen pulled them from the vat and thrust them under a thing like a chaff-cutter, which, descending, hewed them into unseemly red gobbets fit for the can. More Chinamen with yellow, crooked fingers, jammed the stuff into the cans, which slid down some marvellous machine forthwith, soldering their own tops as they passed. Each can was hastily tested for flaws, and then sunk, with a hundred companions, into a vat of boiling water, there to be half cooked for a few minutes. The cans bulged slightly after the operation, and were therefore slidden along by the trolleyful to men with needles and soldering irons, who vented them, and soldered the aperture. Except for the label, the 'finest Columbia salmon' was ready for the market. I was impressed, not so much with the speed of the manufacture, as the character of the factory. Inside, on a floor ninety by forty, the most civilised and murderous of machinery. Outside, three footsteps, the thick-growing pines and the immense solitude of the hills. Our steamer only stayed twenty minutes at that place, but I counted two hundred and forty finished cans, made from the catch of the previous night, ere I left the slippery, blood-stained, scale-spangled, oily floors, and the offal-smeared Chinamen.

We reached Portland, California and I, crying for salmon, and the real-estate man, to whom we had been intrusted by 'Portland' the insurance man, met us in the street saying that fifteen miles away, across country, we should come upon a place called Clackamas where we might perchance find what we desired. And California, his coat-tails flying in the wind, ran to a livery stable and chartered a waggon and team forthwith. I could push the waggon about with one hand, so light was its structure. The team was purely American—that is to say, almost human in its intelligence and docility. Some one said that the roads were not good on the way to Clackamas and warned us against smashing the springs. 'Portland,' who had watched the preparations, finally reckoned 'he'd come along too,' and under heavenly skies we three companions of a day set forth; California carefully lashing our rods into the carriage, and the bystanders overwhelming us with directions as to the sawmills we were to pass, the ferries we were to cross, and the sign-posts we were to seek signs from. Half a mile from this city of fifty thousand souls we struck (and this must be taken literally) a plank-road that would have been a disgrace to an Irish village.

Then six miles of macadamised road showed us that the team could move. A railway ran between us and the banks of the Willamette, and another above us through the mountains. All the land was dotted with small townships, and the roads were full of farmers in their town waggons, bunches of tow-haired, boggle-eyed urchins sitting in the hay behind. The men generally looked like loafers, but their women were all well dressed. Brown hussar-braiding on a tailor-made jacket does not, however, consort with hay-waggons. Then we struck into the woods along what California called a '*camina reale*,'—a good road,—and Portland a 'fair track.' It wound in and out among fire-blackened stumps, under pine trees, along the corners of log-fences, through hollows which must be hopeless marsh in the winter, and up absurd gradients. But nowhere throughout its length did I see any evidence of road-making. There was a track,—you couldn't well get off it,—and it was all you could do to stay on it. The dust lay a foot thick in the blind ruts, and under the dust we found bits of planking and bundles of brushwood that sent the waggon bounding into the air. Sometimes we crashed through bracken; anon where the blackberries grew rankest we found a lonely little cemetery, the wooden rails all awry, and the pitiful stumpy headstones nodding drunkenly at the soft green mulleins. Then with oaths and the sound of rent underwood a yoke of mighty bulls would swing down a 'skid' road, hauling a forty-foot log along a rudely made slide. A valley full of wheat and cherry trees succeeded, and halting at a house we bought ten pound weight of luscious black cherries for something less than a rupee and got a drink of icy-cold water for nothing, while the untended team browsed sagaciously by the roadside. Once we found a wayside camp of horse-dealers lounging by a pool, ready for a sale or a swap, and once two sun-tanned youngsters shot down a hill on Indian ponies, their full creels banging from the high-pommelled saddles. They had been fishing, and were our brethren therefore. We shouted aloud in chorus to scare a wild-cat; we squabbled over the reasons that had led a snake to cross a road; we heaved bits of bark at a venturesome chipmunk, who was really the little grey squirrel of India and had come to call on me; we lost our way and got the waggon so beautifully fixed on a steep road that we had to tie the two hind-wheels to get it down. Above all, California told tales of Nevada and Arizona, of lonely nights spent out prospecting, of the slaughter of deer and the chase of men; of woman, lovely woman, who is a firebrand in a Western city, and leads to the popping of pistols; and of the sudden changes and chances of Fortune, who delights in making the miner or the lumberman a quadruplicate millionaire, and in 'busting' the railroad king. That was a day to be remembered, and it had only begun when we drew rein at a tiny farmhouse on the banks of the Clackamas and sought horse-feed and lodging ere we hastened to the river that broke over a weir not a quarter of a mile away.

Imagine a stream seventy yards broad divided by a pebbly island, running over seductive riffles, and swirling into deep, quiet pools where the good salmon goes to smoke his pipe after meals. Set such a stream amid fields of breast-high crops surrounded by hills of pines, throw in where you please quiet water, log-fenced meadows, and a hundred-foot bluff just to keep the scenery from growing too monotonous, and you will get some faint notion of the Clackamas.

Portland had no rod. He held the gaff and the whisky. California sniffed upstream and downstream across the racing water, chose his ground, and let the gaudy spoon drop in the tail of a riffle. I was getting my rod together when I heard the joyous shriek of the reel and the yells of California, and three feet of living silver leaped into the air far across the water. The forces were engaged. The salmon tore upstream, the tense line cutting the water like a tide-rip behind him, and the light bamboo bowed to breaking. What happened after I cannot tell. California swore and prayed, and Portland shouted advice, and I did all three for what appeared to be half a day, but was in reality a little over a quarter of an hour, and sullenly our fish came home with spurts of temper, dashes head on, and sarabands in the air; but home to the bank came he, and the remorseless reel gathered up the thread of his life inch by inch. We landed him in a little bay, and the spring-weight checked at eleven and a half pounds. Eleven and one-half pounds of fighting salmon! We danced a war dance on the pebbles, and California caught me round the waist in a hug that went near to breaking my ribs while he shouted: 'Partner! Partner! This *is* glory! Now you catch your fish! Twenty-four years I've waited for this!'

I went into that icy-cold river and made my cast just above a weir, and all but foul-hooked a blue and black water-snake with a coral mouth who coiled herself on a stone and hissed maledictions. The next cast—ah, the pride of it, the regal splendour of it! the thrill that ran down from finger-tip to toe! The water boiled. He broke for the spoon and got it! There remained enough sense in me to give him all he wanted when he jumped not once but twenty times before the upstream flight that ran my line out to the last half-dozen turns, and I saw the nickled reel-bar glitter under the thinning green coils. My thumb was burned deep when I strove to stopper the line, but I did not feel it till later, for my soul was out in the dancing water praying for him to turn ere he took my tackle away. The prayer was heard. As I bowed back, the butt of the rod on my left hip-bone and the top-joint dipping like unto a weeping willow, he turned, and I accepted each inch of slack that I could by any means get in as a favour from on High. There be several sorts of success in this world that taste well in the moment of enjoyment, but I question whether the stealthy theft of line from an able-bodied salmon who knows exactly what you are doing and why you are doing it, is not sweeter than any other victory within human scope. Like California's fish, he ran at me head-on and leaped against the line, but the Lord gave me two hundred and fifty pairs of fingers in that hour. The banks and the pine trees danced dizzily round me, but I only reeled—reeled as for life—reeled for hours, and at the end of the reeling continued to give him the butt while he sulked in a pool. California was farther up the reach, and with the corner of my eye I could see him casting with long casts and much skill. Then he struck, and my fish broke for the weir in the same instant, and down the reach we came, California and I; reel answering reel even as the Morning Stars sung together.

The first wild enthusiasm of capture had died away. We were both at work now in deadly earnest to prevent the lines fouling, to stall off a downstream rush for deep water just above the weir, and at the same time to get the fish into the shallow bay downstream that gave the best practicable landing. Portland bade us both be of good heart, and volunteered to take the rod from my hands. I would rather have died among the pebbles than surrender my right to play and land my first salmon, weight unknown, on an eight-ounce rod. I heard California, at my ear it seemed, gasping: 'He's a fighter from Fightersville sure!' as his fish made a fresh break across the stream. I saw Portland fall off a log fence, break the overhanging bank, and clatter down to the pebbles, all sand and landing-net, and I dropped on a log to rest for a moment. As I drew breath the weary hands slackened their hold, and I forgot to give him the butt. A wild scutter in the water, a plunge and a break for the head-waters of the Clackamas was my reward, and the hot toil of reeling-in with one eye under the water and the other on the top joint of the rod, was renewed. Worst of all, I was blocking California's path to the little landing-bay aforesaid, and he had to halt and tire his prize where he was. 'The Father of all Salmon!' he shouted. 'For the love of Heaven, get your *trout* to bank, Johnny Bull!' But I could no more. Even the insult failed to move me. The rest of the game was with the salmon. He suffered himself to be drawn, skipping with pretended delight at getting to the haven where I would fain have him. Yet no sooner did he feel shoal water under his ponderous belly than he backed like a torpedo-boat, and the snarl of the reel told me that my labour was in vain. A dozen times at least this happened ere the line hinted he had given up that battle and would be towed in. He was towed. The landing-net was useless for one of his size, and I would not have him gaffed. I stepped into the shallows and heaved him out with a respectful hand under the gill, for which kindness he battered me about the legs with his tail, and I felt the strength of him and was proud. California had taken my place in the shallows, his fish hard held. I was up the bank lying full length on the sweet-scented grass, and gasping in company with my first salmon caught, played and landed on an eight-ounce rod. My hands were cut and bleeding. I was dripping with sweat, spangled like harlequin with scales, wet from the waist down, nose-peeled by the sun, but utterly, supremely, and consummately happy. He, the beauty, the darling, the daisy, my Salmon Bahadur, weighed twelve pounds ; and I had been seven-and-thirty minutes bringing him to bank! He had been lightly hooked on the angle of the right jaw, and the hook had not wearied him. That hour I sat among princes and crowned heads —greater than them all. Below the bank we heard California scuffling with his salmon, and swearing Spanish oaths. Portland and I assisted at the capture, and the fish dragged the spring-balance out by the roots. It was only constructed to weigh up to fifteen pounds. We stretched the three fish on the grass,—the eleven and a half, the twelve, and fifteen pounder,—and we swore an oath that all who came after should merely be weighed and put back again.

How shall I tell the glories of that day so that you may be interested? Again and again did California and I prance down that reach to the little bay, each with a salmon in tow, and land him in the shallows. Then Portland took my rod, and caught some ten-pounders, and my spoon was carried away by an unknown leviathan. Each fish, for the merits of the three that had died so gamely, was hastily hooked on the balance and flung back, Portland recording the weight in a pocket-book, for he was a real-estate man. Each fish fought for all he was worth, and none more savagely than the smallest—a game little six-pounder. At the end of six hours we added up the list. Total: 16 fish, aggregate weight 142 lbs. The score in detail runs something like this—it is only interesting to those concerned: 15, 11½, 12, 10, 9¾, 8, and so forth; as I have said, nothing under six pounds, and three ten-pounders.

Very solemnly and thankfully we put up our rods—it was glory enough for all time—and returned weeping in each other's arms—weeping tears of pure joy—to that simple bare-legged family in the packing-case house by the waterside. The old farmer recollected days and nights of fierce warfare with the Indians—'way back in the Fifties,' when every ripple of the Columbia River and her tributaries hid covert danger. God had dowered him with a queer crooked gift of expression, and a fierce anxiety for the welfare of his two little sons—tanned and reserved children who attended school daily, and spoke good English in a strange tongue. His wife was an austere woman who had once been kindly and perhaps handsome. Many years of toil had taken the elasticity out of step and voice. She looked for nothing better than everlasting work—the chafing detail of housework, and then a grave somewhere up the hill among the blackberries and the pines. But in her grim way she sympathised with her eldest daughter, a small and silent maiden of eighteen, who had thoughts very far from the meals she tended or the pans she scoured. We stumbled into the ousehold at a crisis; and there was a deal of ownright humanity in that same. A bad, icked dressmaker had promised the maiden a ·ess in time for a to-morrow's railway journey, id, though the barefooted Georgie, who stood in ery wholesome awe of his sister, had scoured the oods on a pony in search, that dress never rived. So with sorrow in her heart, and a undred Sister Anne glances up the road, she aited upon the strangers, and, I doubt not, irsed them for the wants that stood between her id her need for tears. It was a genuine little agedy. The mother in a heavy, passionless voice ebuked her impatience, yet sat bowed over a heap f sewing for the daughter's benefit. These things beheld in the long marigold-scented twilight and hispering night, loafing round the little house ith California, who unfolded himself like a lotus) the moon; or in the little boarded bunk that 'as our bedroom, swapping tales with Portland id the old man. Most of the yarns began in iis way: 'Red Larry was a bull-puncher back of .one County, Montanna,' or 'There was a man ding the trail met a jack-rabbit sitting in a cactus,' r ''Bout the time of the San Diego land boom, a 'oman from Monterey,' etc. You can try to iece out for yourselves what sort of stories they 'ere.

And next day California tucked me under his 'ing and told me we were going to see a city mitten by a boom, and catch trout. So we took train and killed a cow—she wouldn't get out of he way, and the locomotive 'chanced' her and slew—and crossing into Washington Territory won the town of Tacoma, which stands at the head of Puget Sound upon the road to Alaska and Vancouver.

California was right. Tacoma was literally staggering under a boom of the boomiest. I do not quite remember what her natural resources were supposed to be, though every second man shrieked a selection in my ear. They included coal and iron, carrots, potatoes, lumber, shipping, and a crop of thin newspapers all telling Portland that her days were numbered. California and I struck the place at twilight. The rude boarded pavements of the main streets rumbled under the heels of hundreds of furious men all actively engaged in hunting drinks and eligible corner-lots. They sought the drinks first. The street itself alternated five-story business blocks of the later and more abominable forms of architecture with board shanties. Overhead the drunken telegraph, telephone, and electric-light wires tangled on the tottering posts whose butts were half-whittled through by the knife of the loafer. Down the muddy, grimy, unmetalled thoroughfare ran a horse-car line—the metals three inches above road level. Beyond this street rose many hills, and the town was thrown like a broken set of dominoes over all. A steam tramway—it left the track the only time I used it—was nosing about the hills, but the most prominent features of the landscape were the foundations in brick and stone of a gigantic opera house and the blackened stumps of the pines. California sized up the town with one comprehensive glance. 'Big boom,' said he ; and a few instants later : 'About time to step off, *I* think,' meaning thereby that the boom had risen to its limit, and it would be expedient not to meddle with it. We passed down ungraded streets that ended abruptly in a fifteen-foot drop and a nest of brambles ; along pavements that beginning in pine-plank ended in the living tree ; by hotels with Turkish mosque trinketry on their shameless tops, and the pine-stumps at their very doors ; by a female seminary, tall, gaunt and red, which a native of the town bade us marvel at, and we marvelled ; by houses built in imitation of the ones on Nob Hill, San Francisco,—after the Dutch fashion ; by other houses plenteously befouled with jig-saw work, and others flaring with the castlemented, battlemented bosh of the wooden Gothic school.

'You can tell just about when those fellers had their houses built,' quoth California. 'That one yonder wanted to be *I*talian, and his architect built him what he wanted. The new houses with the low straddle roofs and windows pitched in sideways and red brick walls are Dutch. That's the latest idea. I can read the history of the town.' I had no occasion so to read. The natives were only too glad and too proud to tell me. The hotel walls bore a flaming panorama of Tacoma in which by the eye of faith I saw a faint resemblance to the real town. The hotel stationery advertised that Tacoma bore on its face all the advantages of the highest civilisation, and the newspapers sang the same tune in a louder key. The real-estate agents were selling house-lots on unmade streets miles away for thousands of dollars. On the streets—the rude, crude streets, where the unshaded electric light was fighting with the gentle northern twilight—men were babbling of money, town lots, and again money—how Alf or Ed had done such and such a thing that had brought him so much money; and round the corner in a creaking boarded hall the red-jerseyed Salvationists were calling upon mankind to renounce all and follow their noisy God. The men dropped in by twos and threes, listened silently for a while, and as silently went their way, the cymbals clashing after them in vain. I think it was the raw, new smell of fresh sawdust everywhere pervading the air that threw upon me a desolating homesickness. It brought back in a moment all remembrances of that terrible first night at school when the establishment has been newly whitewashed, and a soft smell of escaping gas mingles with the odour of trunks and wet overcoats. I was a little boy, and the school was very new. A vagabond among collarless vagabonds, I loafed up the street, looking into the fronts of little shops where they sold slop shirts at fancy prices, which shops I saw later described in the papers as 'great.' California had gone off to investigate on his own account, and presently returned, laughing noiselessly. 'They are all mad here,' he said, 'all mad. A man nearly pulled a gun on me because I didn't agree with him that Tacoma was going to whip San Francisco on the strength of carrots and potatoes. I asked him to tell me what the town produced, and I couldn't get anything out of him except those two darned vegetables. Say, what do you think?'

I responded firmly, 'I'm going into British territory a little while—to draw breath.'

'I'm going up the Sound, too, for a while,' said he, 'but I'm coming back—coming back to our salmon on the Clackamas. A man has been pressing me to buy a real estate here. Young feller, don't you buy real estate here.'

California disappeared with a kindly wave of his overcoat into worlds other than mine,—good luck go with him for he was a true sportsman!—and I took a steamer up Puget Sound for Vancouver, which is the terminus of the Canadian Pacific Railway. That was a queer voyage. The water, landlocked among a thousand islands, lay still as oil under our bows, and the wake of the screw broke up the unquivering reflections of pines and cliffs a mile away. 'Twas as though we were trampling on glass. No one, not even the Government, knows the number of islands in the Sound. Even now you can get one almost for the asking; can build a house, raise sheep, catch salmon, and become a king on a small scale—your subjects the Indians of the reservation, who glide among the islets in their canoes and scratch their hides monkey-wise by the beach. A Sound Indian is unlovely and only by accident picturesque. His wife drives the canoe, but he himself is so thorough a mariner that he can spring up in his cockle-craft and whack his wife over the head with a paddle without tipping the whole affair into the water. This I have seen him do unprovoked. I fancy it must have been to show off before the whites.

Have I told you anything about Seattle—the town that was burned out a few weeks ago when the insurance men at San Francisco took their losses with a grin? In the ghostly twilight, just as the forest fires were beginning to glare from the unthrifty islands, we struck it—struck it heavily, for the wharves had all been burned down, and we tied up where we could, crashing into the rotten foundations of a boathouse as a pig roots in high grass. The town, like Tacoma, was built upon a hill. In the heart of the business quarters there was a horrible black smudge, as though a Hand had come down and rubbed the place smooth. I know now what being wiped out means. The smudge seemed to be about a mile long, and its blackness was relieved by tents in which men were doing business with the wreck of the stock they had saved. There were shouts and counter-shouts from the steamer to the temporary wharf, which was laden with shingles for roofing, chairs, trunks, provision-boxes, and all the lath and string arrangements out of which a western town is made. This is the way the shouts ran:—

'Oh, George! What's the best with you?'

'Nawthin'. Got the old safe out. She's burned to a crisp. Books all gone.'

''Save anythin'?'

'Bar'l o' crackers and my wife's bunnit. Goin' to start store on them though.'

'Bully for you. Where's that Emporium? I'll drop in.'

'Corner what used to be Fourth and Main—little brown tent close to militia picquet. Sa-ay! We're under martial law, an' all the saloons are shut down!'

'Best for you, George. Some men gets crazy with a fire, and liquor makes 'em crazier.'

''Spect any creator-condemned son of a female dog who has lost all his fixin's in a conflagration is going to put ice on his head an' run for Congress, do you? How'd you like us act?'

The Job's comforter on the steamer retired into himself.

'Oh George' dived into the bar for a drink.

P.S.—Among many curiosities I have unearthed one. It was a Face on the steamer—a face above a pointed straw-coloured beard, a face with thin lips and eloquent eyes. We conversed, and presently I got at the ideas of the Face. It was, though it lived for nine months of the year in the wilds of Alaska and British Columbia, an authority on the canon law of the Church of England—a zealous and bitter upholder of the supremacy of the aforesaid Church. Into my amazed ears, as the steamer plodded through the reflections of the stars, it poured the battle-cry of the Church Militant here on earth, and put forward as a foul injustice that in the prisons of British Columbia the Protestant chaplain did not always belong to the Church. The Face had no official connection with the august body, and by force of his life very seldom attended service.

'But,' said he proudly, 'I should think it direct disobedience to the orders of my Church if I attended any other places of worship than those prescribed. I was once for three months in a place where there was only a Wesleyan Methodist chapel, and I never set foot in it once, Sir. Never once. 'Twould have been heresy. Rank heresy.'

And as I leaned over the rail methought that all the little stars in the water were shaking with austere merriment! But it may have been only the ripple of the steamer, after all.

No. XXVIII

TAKES ME FROM VANCOUVER TO THE YELLOWSTONE NATIONAL PARK

> But who shall chronicle the ways
> Of common folk, the nights and days
> Spent with rough goatherds on the snows,
> And travellers come whence no man knows?

THIS day I know how a deserter feels. Here in Victoria, a hundred and forty miles out of America, the mail brings me news from our Home—the land of regrets. I was enjoying myself by the side of a trout-stream, and I feel inclined to apologise for every rejoicing breath I drew in the diamond clear air. The sickness, they said, is heavy with you; from Rewari to the south good men are dying. Two names come in by the mail of two strong men dead—men that I dined and jested with only a little time ago, and it seems unfair that I should be here, cut off from the chain-gang and the shot-drill of our weary life. After all, there is no life like that we lead over yonder. Americans are Americans, and there are millions of them; English are English; but we of India are Us all the world over, knowing the mysteries of each other's lives and sorrowing for the death of a brother. How can I sit down and write to you of the mere joy of being alive? The news has killed the pleasure of the day for me, and I am ashamed of myself. There are seventy brook trout lying in a creel, fresh drawn from Harrison Hot Springs, and they do not console me. They are like the stolen apples that clinch the fact of a bad boy's playing truant. I would sell them all, with my heritage in the woods and air and the delight of meeting new and strange people, just to be back again in the old galling harness, the heat and the dust, the gatherings in the evenings by the flooded tennis-courts, the ghastly dull dinners at the Club when the very last woman has been packed off to the Hills and the four or five surviving men ask the doctor the symptoms of incubating smallpox. I should be troubled in body, but at peace in the soul. O excellent and toil-worn public of mine—men of the brotherhood, griffins new joined from the February troopers, and gentlemen waiting for your off-reckonings—take care of yourselves and keep well! It hurts so when any die. There are so few of Us, and we know one another too intimately.

. . . . .

Vancouver three years ago was swept off by fire in sixteen minutes, and only one house was left standing. To-day it has a population of fourteen thousand people, and builds its houses out of brick with dressed granite fronts. But a great sleepiness lies on Vancouver as compared with an American town: men don't fly up and down the streets telling lies, and the spittoons in the delightfully comfortable hotel are unused; the baths are free and their doors are unlocked. You do not have to dig up the hotel clerk when you want to bathe, which shows the inferiority of Vancouver. An American bade me notice the absence of bustle, and was alarmed when in a loud and audible voice I thanked God for it. 'Give me granite—hewn granite and peace,' quoth I, 'and keep your deal boards and bustle for yourselves.'

The Canadian Pacific terminus is not a very gorgeous place as yet, but you can be shot directly from the window of the train into the liner that will take you in fourteen days from Vancouver to Yokohama. The *Parthia*, of some five thousand tons, was at her berth when I came, and the sight of the ex-Cunard on what seemed to be a little lake was curious. Except for certain currents which are not much mentioned, but which make the entrance rather unpleasant for sailing-boats, Vancouver possesses an almost perfect harbour. The town is built all round and about the harbour, and young as it is, its streets are better than those of western America. Moreover, the old flag waves over some of the buildings, and this is cheering to the soul. The place is full of Englishmen who speak the English tongue correctly and with clearness, avoiding more blasphemy than is necessary, and taking a respectable length of time to getting outside their drinks. These advantages and others that I have heard about, such as the construction of elaborate workshops and the like by the Canadian Pacific in the near future, moved me to invest in real estate. He that sold it me was a delightful English Boy who, having tried for the Army and failed, had somehow meandered into a real-estate office, where he was doing well. I couldn't have bought it from an American. He would have overstated the case and proved me the possessor of the original Eden. All the Boy said was: 'I give you my word it isn't on a cliff or under water, and before long the town ought to move out that way. I'd advise you to take it.' And I took it as easily as a man buys a piece of tobacco. *Me voici*, owner of some four hundred well-developed pines, a few thousand tons of granite scattered in blocks at the roots of the pines, and a sprinkling of earth. That's a town-lot in Vancouver. You or your agent hold to it till property rises, then sell out and buy more land further out of town and repeat the process. I do not quite see how this sort of thing helps the growth of a town, but the English Boy says that it is the 'essence of speculation,' so it must be all right. But I wish there were fewer pines and rather less granite on my ground. Moved by curiosity and the lust of trout, I went seventy miles up the Canadian Pacific in one of the cross-Continent cars, which are cleaner and less stuffy than the Pullman. A man who goes all the way across Canada is liable to be disappointed—not in the scenery, but in the progress of the country. So a batch of wandering politicians from England told me. They even went so far as to say that Eastern Canada was a failure and unprofitable.

The place didn't move, they complained, and whole counties—they said provinces—lay under the rule of the Roman Catholic priests, who took care that the people should not be overcumbered with the good things of this world to the detriment of their souls. My interest was in the line—the real and accomplished railway which is to throw actual fighting troops into the East some day when our hold of the Suez Canal is temporarily loosened.

All that Vancouver wants is a fat earthwork fort upon a hill,—there are plenty of hills to choose from,—a selection of big guns, a couple of regiments of infantry, and later on a big arsenal. The raw self-consciousness of America would be sure to make her think these arrangements intended for her benefit, but she could be enlightened. It is not seemly to leave unprotected the head-end of a big railway; for though Victoria and Esquimalt, our naval stations on Vancouver Island, are very near, so also is a place called Vladivostok, and though Vancouver Narrows are strait, they allow room enough for a man-of-war. The people—I did not speak to more than two hundred of them—do not know about Russia or military arrangements. They are trying to open trade with Japan in lumber, and are raising fruit, wheat, and sometimes minerals. All of them agree that we do not yet know the resources of British Columbia, and all joyfully bade me note the climate, which was distinctly warm. 'We never have killing cold here. It's the most perfect climate in the world.' Then there are three perfect climates, for I have tasted 'em—California, Washington Territory, and

British Columbia. I cannot say which is the loveliest.

When I left by steamer and struck across the Sound to our naval station at Victoria, Vancouver Island, I found in that quiet English town of beautiful streets quite a colony of old men doing nothing but talking, fishing, and loafing at the Club. That means that the retired go to Victoria. On a thousand a year pension a man would be a millionaire in these parts, and for four hundred he could live well. It was at Victoria they told me the tale of the fire in Vancouver. How the inhabitants of New Westminster, twelve miles from Vancouver, saw a glare in the sky at six in the evening, but thought it was a forest fire; how later bits of burnt paper flew about their streets, and they guessed that evil had happened; how an hour later a man rode into the city crying that there was no Vancouver left. All had been wiped out by the flames in sixteen minutes. How, two hours later, the Mayor of New Westminster having voted nine thousand dollars from the Municipal funds, relief-waggons with food and blankets were pouring into where Vancouver stood. How fourteen people were supposed to have died in the fire, but how even now when they laid new foundations the workmen unearthed charred skeletons, many more than fourteen. 'That night,' said the teller, 'all Vancouver was houseless. The wooden town had gone in a breath. Next day they began to build in brick, and you have seen what they have achieved.'

The sight afar off of three British men-of-war

and a torpedo-boat consoled me as I returned from Victoria to Tacoma and discovered *en route* that I was surfeited with scenery. There is a great deal in the remark of a discontented traveller: 'When you have seen a fine forest, a bluff, a river, and a lake you have seen all the scenery of western America. Sometimes the pine is three hundred feet high, and sometimes the rock is, and sometimes the lake is a hundred miles long. But it's all the same, don't you know. I'm getting sick of it.' I dare not say getting sick. I'm only tired. If Providence could distribute all this beauty in little bits where people most wanted it,—among you in India,—it would be well. But it is *en masse*, overwhelming, with nobody but the tobacco-chewing captain of a river steamboat to look at it. Men said if I went to Alaska I should see islands even more wooded, snow-peaks loftier, and rivers more lovely than those around me. That decided me not to go to Alaska. I went east—east to Montana, after another horrible night in Tacoma among the men who spat. Why does the Westerner spit? It can't amuse him, and it doesn't interest his neighbour.

But I am beginning to mistrust. Everything good as well as everything bad is supposed to come from the East. Is there a shooting-scrape between prominent citizens? Oh, you'll find nothing of that kind in the East. Is there a more than usually revolting lynching? They don't do that in the East. I shall find out when I get there whether this unnatural perfection be real.

Eastward then to Montana I took my way for

the Yellowstone National Park, called in the guide-books 'Wonderland.' But the real Wonderland began in the train. We were a merry crew. One gentleman announced his intention of paying no fare and grappled the conductor, who neatly cross-buttocked him through a double plate-glass window. His head was cut open in four or five places. A doctor on the train hastily stitched up the biggest gash, and he was dropped at a wayside station, spurting blood at every hair—a scarlet-headed and ghastly sight. The conductor guessed that he would die, and volunteered the information that there was no profit in monkeying with the North Pacific Railway.

Night was falling as we cleared the forests and sailed out upon a wilderness of sage brush. The desolation of Montgomery, the wilderness of Sind, the hummock-studded desert of Bikaneer, are joyous and homelike compared to the impoverished misery of the sage. It is blue, it is stunted, it is dusty. It wraps the rolling hills as a mildewed shroud wraps the body of a long-dead man. It makes you weep for sheer loneliness, and there is no getting away from it. When Childe Roland came to the dark Tower he traversed the sage brush.

Yet there is one thing worse than sage unadulterated, and that is a prairie city. We stopped at Pasco Junction, and a man told me that it was the Queen City of the Prairie. I wish Americans didn't tell such useless lies. I counted fourteen or fifteen frame-houses, and a portion of a road that showed like a bruise on the untouched surface of the blue sage, running away and away up to the setting sun. The sailor sleeps with a half-inch plank between himself and death. He is at home beside the handful of people who curl themselves up o' nights with nothing but a frail scantling, almost as thin as a blanket, to shut out the unmeasurable loneliness of the sage.

When the train stopped on the road, as it did once or twice, the solid silence of the sage got up and shouted at us. It was like a nightmare, and one not in the least improved by having to sleep in an emigrant-car; the regularly ordained sleepers being full. There was a row in our car toward morning, a man having managed to get querulously drunk in the night. Up rose a Cornishman with a red head full of strategy, and strapped the obstreperous one, smiling largely as he did so, and a delicate little woman in a far bunk watched the fray and called the drunken man a 'damned hog,' which he certainly was, though she needn't have put it quite so coarsely. Emigrant cars are clean, but the accommodation is as hard as a plank bed.

Later we laid our bones down to crossing the Rockies. An American train can climb up the side of a house if need be, but it is not pleasant to sit in it. We clomb till we struck violent cold and an Indian reservation, and the noble savage came to look at us. He was a Flathead and unlovely. Most Americans are charmingly frank about the Indian. 'Let us get rid of him as soon as possible,' they say. 'We have no use for him.' Some of the men I meet have a notion that we in India are exterminating the native in the same fashion, and I have been asked to fix a date for the final extinguishment of the Aryan. I answer that it will be a long business. Very many Americans have an offensive habit of referring to natives as 'heathen.' Mahometans and Hindus are heathen alike in their eyes, and they vary the epithet with 'pagan' and 'idolater.' But this is beside the matter, which is the Stampede Tunnel—our actual point of crossing the Rockies. Thank Heaven, I need never take that tunnel again! It is about two miles long, and in effect is nothing more than the gallery of a mine shored with timber and lighted with electric lamps. Black darkness would be preferable, for the lamps just reveal the rough cutting of the rocks, and that is very rough indeed. The train crawls through, brakes down, and you can hear the water and little bits of stone falling on the roof of the car. Then you pray, pray fervently, and the air gets stiller and stiller, and you dare not take your unwilling eyes off the timber shoring, lest a prop should fall, for lack of your moral support. Before the tunnel was built you crossed in the open air by a switchback line. A watchman goes through the tunnel after each train, but that is no protection. He just guesses that another train will pull through, and the engine-driver guesses the same thing. Some day between the two of them there will be a cave in the tunnel. Then the enterprising reporter will talk about the shrieks and groans of the buried and the heroic efforts of the Press in securing first information, and—that will be all. Human life is of small account out here.

I was listening to yarns in the smoking-compartment of the Pullman, all the way to Helena, and with very few exceptions, each had for its point, violent, brutal, and ruffianly murder—murder by fraud and the craft of the savage—murder unavenged by the law, or at the most by an outbreak of fresh lawlessness. At the end of each tale I was assured that the old days had passed away, and that these were anecdotes of five years' standing. One man in particular distinguished himself by holding up to admiration the exploits of some cowboys of his acquaintance, and their skill in the use of the revolver. Each tale of horror wound up with 'and that's the sort of man he was,' as who should say: 'Go and do likewise.' Remember that the shootings, the cuttings, and the stabbings were not the outcome of any species of legitimate warfare; the heroes were not forced to fight for their lives. Far from it. The brawls were bred by liquor in which they assisted—in saloons and gambling-hells they were wont to 'pull their guns' on a man, and in the vast majority of cases without provocation. The tales sickened me, but taught one thing. A man who carries a pistol may be put down as a coward—a person to be shut out from every decent mess and club, and gathering of civilised folk. There is neither chivalry nor romance in the weapon, for all that American authors have seen fit to write. I would I could make you understand the full measure of contempt with which certain aspects of Western life inspired me. Let us try a comparison. Sometimes it happens that a young, a very young, man, whose first dress-coat is yet glossy, gets slightly flushed at a dinner-party among his seniors. After the ladies are gone, he begins to talk. He talks, you will remember, as a 'man of the world' and a person of varied experiences, an authority on all things human and divine. The grey heads of the elders bow assentingly to his wildest statement; some one tries to turn the conversation when what the youngster conceives to be wit has offended a sensibility; and another deftly slides the decanters beyond him as they circle round the table. You know the feeling of discomfort—pity mingled with aversion—over the boy who is making an exhibition of himself. The same emotion came back to me, when an old man who ought to have known better appealed from time to time for admiration of his pitiful sentiments. It was right in his mind to insult, to maim, and to kill; right to evade the law where it was strong and to trample over it where it was weak; right to swindle in politics, to lie in affairs of State, and commit perjury in matters of municipal administration. The car was full of little children, utterly regardless of their parents, fretful, peevish, spoilt beyond anything I have ever seen in Anglo-India. They in time would grow up into men such as sat in the smoker, and had no regard for the law; men who would conduct papers siding 'with defiance of any and every law.' But it's of no consequence, as Mr. Toots says.

During the descent of the Rockies we journeyed for a season on a trestle only two hundred and eighty-six feet high. It was made of iron, but up till two years ago a wooden structure bore up the train, and was used long after it had been condemned by the civil engineers. Some day the iron one will come down, just as Stampede Tunnel will, and the results will be even more startling.

Late in the night we ran over a skunk—ran over it in the dark. Everything that has been said about the skunk is true. It is an Awesome Stink.

No. XXIX

SHOWS HOW YANKEE JIM INTRODUCED ME TO DIANA OF THE CROSSWAYS ON THE BANKS OF THE YELLOWSTONE, AND HOW A GERMAN JEW SAID I WAS NO TRUE CITIZEN. ENDS WITH THE CELEBRATION OF THE 4TH OF JULY AND A FEW LESSONS THEREFROM.

LIVINGSTONE is a town of two thousand people, and the junction for the little side-line that takes you to the Yellowstone National Park. It lies in a fold of the prairie, and behind it is the Yellowstone River and the gate of the mountains through which the river flows. There is one street in the town, where the cowboy's pony and the little foal of the brood-mare in the buggy rest contentedly in the blinding sunshine while the cowboy gets himself shaved at the only other barber's shop, and swaps lies at the bar. I exhausted the town, including the saloons, in ten minutes, and got away on the rolling grass downs where I threw myself to rest. Directly under the hill I was on, swept a drove of horses in charge of two mounted men. That was a picture I shall not soon forget. A light haze of dust went up from the hoof-trodden green, scarcely veiling the unfettered deviltries of three hundred horses who very much wanted to stop and graze. 'Yow! Yow! Yow!' yapped the mounted men in chorus like coyotes. The column moved forward at a trot, divided as it met a hillock and scattered into fan shape all among the suburbs of Livingstone. I heard the 'snick' of a stock-whip, half a dozen 'Yow, yows,' and the mob had come together again, and, with neighing and whickering and squealing and a great deal of kicking on the part of the youngsters, rolled like a wave of brown water toward the uplands.

I was within twenty feet of the leader, a grey stallion—lord of many brood-mares all deeply concerned for the welfare of their fuzzy foals. A cream-coloured beast—I knew him at once for the bad character of the troop—broke back, taking with him some frivolous fillies. I heard the snick of the whips somewhere in the dust, and the fillies came back at a canter, very shocked and indignant. On the heels of the last rode both the stockmen—picturesque ruffians who wanted to know 'what in hell' I was doing there, waved their hats, and sped down the slope after their charges. When the noise of the troop had died there came a wonderful silence on all the prairie—that silence, they say, which enters into the heart of the old-time hunter and trapper and marks him off from the rest of his race. The town disappeared in the darkness, and a very young moon showed herself over a bald-headed, snow-flecked peak. Then the Yellowstone, hidden by the water-willows, lifted up its voice and sang a little song to the mountains, and an old horse that had crept up in the dusk breathed inquiringly on the back of my neck. When I reached the hotel I found all manner of preparation under way for the 4th of July, and a drunken man with a Winchester rifle over his shoulder patrolling the sidewalk. I do not think he wanted any one. He carried the gun as other folk carry walking-sticks. None the less I avoided the direct line of fire and listened to the blasphemies of miners and stockmen till far into the night. In every bar-room lay a copy of the local paper, and every copy impressed it upon the inhabitants of Livingstone that they were the best, finest, bravest, richest, and most progressive town of the most progressive nation under Heaven ; even as the Tacoma and Portland papers had belauded their readers. And yet, all my purblind eyes could see was a grubby little hamlet full of men without clean collars and perfectly unable to get through one sentence unadorned by three oaths. They raise horses and minerals round and about Livingstone, but they behave as though they raised cherubims with diamonds in their wings.

From Livingstone the National Park train follows the Yellowstone River through the gate of the mountains and over arid volcanic country. A stranger in the cars saw me look at the ideal trout-stream below the windows and murmured softly : 'Lie off at Yankee Jim's if you want good fishing.' They halted the train at the head of a narrow valley, and I leaped literally into the arms of Yankee Jim, sole owner of a log hut, an indefinite amount of hay-ground, and constructor of twenty-seven miles of waggon-road over which he held toll-right. There was the hut—the river fifty yards away, and the polished line of metals that disappeared round a bluff. That was all. The railway added the finishing touch to the already complete loneliness of the place. Yankee Jim was a picturesque old man with a talent for yarns that Ananias might have envied. It seemed to me, presumptuous in my ignorance, that I might hold my own with the old-timer if I judiciously painted up a few lies gathered in the course of my wanderings. Yankee Jim saw every one of my tales and went fifty better on the spot. He dealt in bears and Indians—never less than twenty of each; had known the Yellowstone country for years, and bore upon his body marks of Indian arrows; and his eyes had seen a squaw of the Crow Indians burned alive at the stake. He said she screamed considerable. In one point did he speak the truth—as regarded the merits of that particular reach of the Yellowstone. He said it was alive with trout. It was. I fished it from noon till twilight, and the fish bit at the brown hook as though never a fat trout-fly had fallen on the water. From pebbly reaches, quivering in the heat-haze where the foot caught on stumps cut four-square by the chisel-tooth of the beaver; past the fringe of the water-willow crowded with the breeding trout-fly and alive with toads and water-snakes; over the drifted timber to the grateful shadow of big trees that darkened the holes where the fattest fish lay, I worked for seven hours. The mountain flanks on either side of the valley gave back the heat as the desert gives it, and the dry sand by the railway track, where I found a rattle-snake, was hot-iron to the touch. But the trout did not care for the heat. They breasted the boiling river for my fly and they got it. I simply dare not give my bag. At the fortieth trout I gave up counting, and I had reached the fortieth in less than two hours. They were small fish,—not one over two pounds, —but they fought like small tigers, and I lost three flies before I could understand their methods of escape. Ye gods! That was fishing, though it peeled the skin from my nose in strips.

At twilight Yankee Jim bore me off, protesting, to supper in the hut. The fish had prepared me for any surprise, wherefore when Yankee Jim introduced me to a young woman of five-and-twenty, with eyes like the deep-fringed eyes of the gazelle, and 'on the neck the small head buoyant, like a bell-flower in its bed,' I said nothing. It was all in the day's events. She was California-raised, the wife of a man who owned a stock-farm 'up the river a little ways,' and, with her husband, tenant of Yankee Jim's shanty. I know she wore list slippers and did not wear stays; but I know also that she was beautiful by any standard of beauty, and that the trout she cooked were fit for a king's supper. And after supper strange men loafed up in the dim delicious twilight, with the little news of the day—how a heifer had 'gone strayed' from Nicholson's; how the widow at Grant's Fork wouldn't part with a little hayland nohow, though 'she an' her big brothers can't manage more than ha-af their land now. She's so darned proud.' Diana of the Crossways entertained them in queenly wise, and her husband and Yankee Jim bade them sit right down and make themselves at home. Then did Yankee Jim uncurl his choicest lies on Indian warfare aforetime; then did the whisky-flask circle round the little crowd; then did Diana's husband 'low that he was quite handy with the lariat, but had seen men rope a steer by any foot or horn indicated; then did Diana unburden herself about her neighbours. The nearest house was three miles away, 'but the women aren't nice, neighbourly folk. They talk so. They haven't got anything else to do seemingly. If a woman goes to a dance and has a good time, they talk, and if she wears a silk dress, they want to know how jest ranchin' folks—folk on a ranche—come by such things; and they make mischief down all the lands here from Gardiner City way back up to Livingstone. They're mostly Montanna raised, and they haven't been nowheres. Ah, how they talk!' Were things like this, demanded Diana, in the big world outside, whence I had come? Yes, I said, things were very much the same all over the world, and I thought of a far-away station in India where new dresses and the having of good times at dances raised cackle more grammatical perhaps, but no less venomous than the gossip of the 'Montanna-raised' folk on the ranches of the Yellowstone.

Next morn I fished again and listened to Diana telling the story of her life. I forget what she told me, but I am distinctly aware that she had royal eyes and a mouth that the daughter of a hundred earls might have envied—so small and so delicately cut it was. 'An' you come back an' see us again,' said the simple-minded folk. 'Come back an' we'll show you how to catch six-pound trout at the head of the cañon.'

To-day I am in the Yellowstone Park, and I wish I were dead. The train halted at Cinnabar station, and we were decanted, a howling crowd of us, into stages, variously horsed, for the eight-mile drive to the first spectacle of the Park—a place called the Mammoth Hot Springs. 'What means this eager, anxious throng?' I asked the driver. 'You've struck one of Rayment's excursion parties—that's all—a crowd of creator-condemned fools mostly. Aren't you one of 'em?' 'No,' I said. 'May I sit up here with you, great chief and man with a golden tongue? I do not know Mister Rayment. I belong to T. Cook and Son.' The other person, from the quality of the material he handles, must be the son of a sea-cook. He collects masses of Down-Easters from the New England States and elsewhere and hurls them across the continent and into the Yellowstone Park on tour. A brake-load of Cook's Continental tourists trapezing through Paris (I've seen 'em) are angels of light compared to the Rayment trippers. It is not the ghastly vulgarity, the oozing, rampant Bessemer-steel self-sufficiency and ignorance of the men that revolts me, so much as the display of these same qualities in the women-folk. I saw a new type in the coach, and all my dreams of a better and more perfect East died away. 'Are these—um—persons here any sort of persons in their own places?' I asked a shepherd who appeared to be herding them.

'Why, certainly. They include very many prominent and representative citizens from seven States of the Union, and most of them are wealthy. Yes, *sir*. Representative and prominent.'

We ran across bare hills on an unmetalled road under a burning sun in front of a volley of playful repartee from the prominent citizens inside. It was the 4th of July. The horses had American flags in their headstalls, some of the women wore flags and coloured handkerchiefs in their belts, and a young German on the box-seat with me was bewailing the loss of a box of crackers. He said he had been sent to the Continent to get his schooling and so had lost his American accent; but no Continental schooling writes German Jew all over a man's face and nose. He was a rabid American citizen—one of a very difficult class to deal with. As a general rule, praise unsparingly, and without discrimination. That keeps most men quiet: but some, if you fail to keep up a continuous stream of praise, proceed to revile the old country—Germans and Irish who are more American than the Americans are the chief offenders. This young American began to attack the English army. He had seen some of it on parade and he pitied the men in bearskins as 'slaves.' The citizen, by the way, has a contempt for his own army which exceeds anything you meet among the most illiberal classes in England. I admitted that our army was very poor, had done nothing, and had been nowhere. This exasperated him, for he expected an argument, and he trampled on the British Lion generally. Failing to move me, he vowed that I had no patriotism like his own. I said I had not, and further ventured that very few Englishmen had; which, when you come to think of it, is quite true. By the time he had proved conclusively that before the Prince of Wales came to the throne we should be a blethering republic, we struck a road that overhung a river, and my interest in 'politics' was lost in admiration of the driver's skill as he sent his four big horses along that winding road. There was no room for any sort of accident—a shy or a swerve would have dropped us sixty feet into the roaring Gardiner River. Some of the persons in the coach remarked that the scenery was 'elegant.' Wherefore, even at the risk of my own life, I did urgently desire an accident and the massacre of some of the more prominent citizens. What 'elegance' lies in a thousand-foot pile of honey-coloured rock, riven into peak and battlement, the highest peak defiantly crowned by an eagle's nest, the eaglet peering into the gulf and screaming for his food, I could not for the life of me understand. But they speak a strange tongue.

En route we passed other carriages full of trippers, who had done their appointed five days in the Park, and yelped at us fraternally as they disappeared in clouds of red dust. When we struck the Mammoth Hot Spring Hotel—a huge yellow barn—a sign-board informed us that the altitude was six thousand two hundred feet. The Park is just a howling wilderness of three thousand square miles, full of all imaginable freaks of a fiery nature. An hotel company, assisted by the Secretary of State for the Interior, appears to control it; there are hotels at all the points of interest, guide-books, stalls for the sale of minerals, and so forth, after the model of Swiss summer places.

The tourists—may their master die an evil death at the hand of a mad locomotive!—poured into that place with a joyful whoop, and, scarce washing the dust from themselves, began to celebrate the 4th of July. They called it 'patriotic exercises'; elected a clergyman of their own faith as president, and, sitting on the landing of the first floor, began to make speeches and read the Declaration of Independence. The clergyman rose up and told them they were the greatest, freest, sublimest, most chivalrous, and richest people on the face of the earth, and they all said Amen. Another clergyman asserted in the words of the Declaration that all men were created equal, and equally entitled to Life, Liberty, and the pursuit of Happiness. I should like to know whether the wild and woolly West recognises this first right as freely as the grantors intended. The clergyman then bade the world note that the tourists included representatives of seven of the New England States; whereat I felt deeply sorry for the New England States in their latter days. He opined that this running to and fro upon the earth, under the auspices of the excellent Rayment, would draw America more closely together, especially when the Westerners remembered the perils that they of the East had surmounted by rail and river. At duly appointed intervals the congregation sang 'My country, 'tis of thee' to the tune of 'God Save the Queen' (here they did not stand up) and the 'Star-Spangled

Banner' (here they did), winding up the exercise with some doggerel of their own composition to the tune of 'John Brown's Body,' movingly setting forth the perils before alluded to. They then adjourned to the verandahs and watched fire-crackers of the feeblest, exploding one by one, for several hours.

What amazed me was the calm with which these folks gathered together and commenced to belaud their noble selves, their country, and their 'institootions' and everything else that was theirs. The language was, to these bewildered ears, wild advertisement, gas, bunkum, blow, anything you please beyond the bounds of common sense. An archangel, selling town-lots on the Glassy Sea, would have blushed to the tips of his wings to describe his property in similar terms. Then they gathered round the pastor and told him his little sermon was 'perfectly glorious,' really grand, sublime, and so forth, and he bridled ecclesiastically. At the end a perfectly unknown man attacked me and asked me what I thought of American patriotism. I said there was nothing like it in the Old Country. By the way, always tell an American this. It soothes him.

Then said he: 'Are you going to get out your letters,—your letters of naturalisation?'

'Why?' I asked.

'I presoom you do business in this country, and make money out of it,—and it seems to me that it would be your dooty.'

'Sir,' said I sweetly, 'there is a forgotten little island across the seas called England. It is not much bigger than the Yellowstone Park. In that island a man of your country could work, marry, make his fortune or twenty fortunes, and die. Throughout his career not one soul would ask him whether he were a British subject or a child of the Devil. Do you understand?'

I think he did, because he said something about 'Britishers' which wasn't complimentary.

No. XXX

SHOWS HOW I ENTERED MAZANDERAN OF THE PERSIANS AND SAW DEVILS OF EVERY COLOUR, AND SOME TROOPERS. HELL AND THE OLD LADY FROM CHICAGO. THE CAPTAIN AND THE LIEUTENANT.

> That desolate land and lone
> Where the Big Horn and Yellowstone
> Roar down their mountain path.

TWICE have I written this letter from end to end. Twice have I torn it up, fearing lest those across the water should say that I had gone mad on a sudden. Now we will begin for the third time quite solemnly and soberly. I have been through the Yellowstone National Park in a buggy, in the company of an adventurous old lady from Chicago and her husband, who disapproved of scenery as being 'ongodly.' I fancy it scared them.

We began, as you know, with the Mammoth Hot Springs. They are only a gigantic edition of those pink and white terraces not long ago destroyed by earthquake in New Zealand. At one end of the little valley in which the hotel stands, the lime-laden springs that break from the pine-covered hillsides have formed a frozen cataract of white, lemon, and palest pink formation, through and over and in which water of the warmest bubbles and drips and trickles from pale-green lagoon to exquisitely fretted basin. The ground rings hollow as a kerosene-tin, and some day the Mammoth Hotel, guests and all, will sink into the caverns below and be turned into a stalactite. When I set foot on the first of the terraces, a tourist-trampled ramp of scabby grey stuff, I met a stream of iron-red hot water which ducked into a hole like a rabbit. Followed a gentle chuckle of laughter, and then a deep, exhausted sigh from nowhere in particular. Fifty feet above my head a jet of stream rose up and died out in the blue. It was worse than the boiling mountain at Myanoshita. The dirty white deposit gave place to lime whiter than snow; and I found a basin which some learned hotel-keeper has christened Cleopatra's pitcher, or Mark Antony's whisky-jug, or something equally poetical. It was made of frosted silver; it was filled with water as clear as the sky. I do not know the depth of that wonder. The eye looked down beyond grottoes and caves of beryl into an abyss that communicated directly with the central fires of earth. And the pool was in pain, so that it could not refrain from talking about it; muttering and chattering and moaning. From the lips of the lime-ledges, forty feet under water, spurts of silver bubbles would fly up and break the peace of the crystal atop. Then the whole pool would shake and grow dim, and there were noises. I removed myself only to find other pools all equally unhappy, rifts in the ground, full of running, red-hot water, slippery sheets of deposit overlaid with greenish-grey hot water, and here and there pit-holes dry as a rifled tomb in India, dusty and waterless. Elsewhere the infernal waters had first boiled dead and then embalmed the pines and underwood, or the forest trees had taken heart and smothered up a blind formation with greenery, so that it was only by scraping the earth you could tell what fires had raged beneath. Yet the pines will win the battle in years to come, because Nature, who first forges all her work in her great smithies, has nearly finished this job, and is ready to temper it in the soft brown earth. The fires are dying down; the hotel is built where terraces have overflowed into flat wastes of deposit; the pines have taken possession of the high ground whence the terraces first started. Only the actual curve of the cataract stands clear, and it is guarded by soldiers who patrol it with loaded six-shooters, in order that the tourist may not bring up fence-rails and sink them in a pool, or chip the fretted tracery of the formations with a geological hammer, or, walking where the crust is too thin, foolishly cook himself.

I manœuvred round those soldiers. They were cavalry in a very slovenly uniform, dark-blue blouse, and light-blue trousers unstrapped, cut spoon-shape over the boot; cartridge belt, revolver, peaked cap, and worsted gloves—black buttons! By the mercy of Allah I opened conversation with a spectacled Scot. He had served the Queen in the Marines and a Line regiment, and the 'go-fever' being in his bones, had drifted to

America, there to serve Uncle Sam. We sat on the edge of an extinct little pool, that under happier circumstances would have grown into a geyser, and began to discuss things generally. To us appeared yet another soldier. No need to ask his nationality or to be told that the troop called him 'The Henglishman.' A Cockney was he, who had seen something of warfare in Egypt, and had taken his discharge from a Fusilier regiment not unknown to you.

'And how do things go?'

'Very much as you please,' said they. 'There's not half the discipline here that there is in the Queen's service—not half—nor the work either, but what there is, is rough work. Why, there's a sergeant now with a black eye that one of our men gave him. They won't say anything about that, of course. Our punishments? Fines mostly, and then if you carry on too much you go to the cooler—that's the clink. Yes, Sir. Horses? Oh, they're devils, these Montanna horses. Bronchos mostly. We don't slick 'em up for parade—not much. And the amount of schooling that you put into one English troop-horse would be enough for a whole squadron of these creatures. You'll meet more troopers further up the Park. Go and look at their horses and their turnouts. I fancy it'll startle you. I'm wearing a made tie and a breastpin under my blouse? Of course I am! I can wear anything I darn please. We aren't particular here. I shouldn't dare come on parade—no, nor yet fatigue duty—in this condition in the Old Country; but it don't matter here. But don't you forget, Sir, that it's taught me how to trust to myself, and my shooting irons. I don't want fifty orders to move me across the Park, and catch a poacher. Yes, they poach here. Men come in with an outfit and ponies, smuggle in a gun or two, and shoot the bison. If you interfere, they shoot at you. Then you confiscate all their outfit and their ponies. We have a pound full of them now down below. There's our Captain over yonder. Speak to him if you want to know anything special. This service isn't a patch on the Old Country's service ; but you look, if it was worked up it would be just a Hell of a service. But these citizens despise us, and they put us on to road-mending, and such like. 'Nough to ruin any army.'

To the Captain I addressed myself after my friends had gone. They told me that a good many American officers dressed by the French army. The Captain certainly might have been mistaken for a French officer of light cavalry, and he had more than the courtesy of a Frenchman. Yes, he had read a good deal about our Indian border warfare, and had been much struck with the likeness it bore to Red Indian warfare. I had better, when I reached the next cavalry post, scattered between two big geyser basins, introduce myself to a Captain and Lieutenant. They could show me things. He himself was devoting all his time to conserving the terraces, and surreptitiously running hot water into dried-up basins that fresh pools might form. 'I get very interested in that sort of thing. It's not duty, but it's what I'm put here for.' And then he began to talk of his troop as I have heard his brethren in India talk. Such a troop! Built up carefully, and watched lovingly; 'not a man that I'd wish to exchange, and, what's more, I believe not a man that would wish to leave on his own account. We're different, I believe, from the English. Your officers value the horses; we set store on the men. We train them more than we do the horses.'

Of the American trooper I will tell you more hereafter. He is not a gentleman to be trifled with.

Next dawning, entering a buggy of fragile construction, with the old people from Chicago, I embarked on my perilous career. We ran straight up a mountain till we could see, sixty miles away, the white houses of Cook City on another mountain, and the whiplash-like trail leading thereto. The live air made me drunk. If Tom, the driver, had proposed to send the mares in a bee-line to the city, I should have assented, and so would the old lady, who chewed gum and talked about her symptoms. The tub-ended rock-dog, which is but the translated prairie-dog, broke across the road under our horses' feet, the rabbit and the chipmunk danced with fright; we heard the roar of the river, and the road went round a corner. On one side piled rock and shale, that enjoined silence for fear of a general slide-down; on the other a sheer drop, and a fool of a noisy river below. Then, apparently in the middle of the road, lest any should find driving too easy, a post of rock. Nothing beyond that save the flank of a cliff. Then my stomach departed from me, as it does when you swing, for we left the dirt, which was at least some guarantee of safety, and sailed out round the curve, and up a steep incline, on a plank-road built out from the cliff. The planks were nailed at the outer edge, and did not shift or creak very much—but enough, quite enough. That was the Golden Gate. I got my stomach back again when we trotted out on to a vast upland adorned with a lake and hills. Have you ever seen an untouched land—the face of virgin Nature? It is rather a curious sight, because the hills are choked with timber that has never known an axe, and the storm has rent a way through this timber, so that a hundred thousand trees lie matted together in swathes; and, since each tree lies where it falls, you may behold trunk and branch returning to the earth whence they sprang—exactly as the body of man returns—each limb making its own little grave, the grass climbing above the bark, till at last there remains only the outline of a tree upon the rank undergrowth.

Then we drove under a cliff of obsidian, which is black glass, some two hundred feet high; and the road at its foot was made of black glass that crackled. This was no great matter, because half an hour before Tom had pulled up in the woods that we might sufficiently admire a mountain who stood all by himself, shaking with laughter or rage.

The glass cliff overlooks a lake where the beavers built a dam about a mile and a half long in a zig-zag line, as their necessities prompted. Then came the Government and strictly preserved them, and, as you shall learn later on, they be damn impudent beasts. The old lady had hardly explained the natural history of beavers before we climbed some hills—it really didn't matter in that climate, because we could have scaled the stars—and (this mattered very much indeed) shot down a desperate, dusty slope, brakes shrieking on the wheels, the mares clicking among unseen rocks, the dust dense as a fog, and a wall of trees on either side. 'How do the heavy four-horse coaches take it, Tom?' I asked, remembering that some twenty-three souls had gone that way half an hour before. 'Take it at the run!' said Tom, spitting out the dust. Of course there was a sharp curve, and a bridge at the bottom, but luckily nothing met us, and we came to a wooden shanty called an hotel, in time for a crazy tiffin served by very gorgeous handmaids with very pink cheeks. When health fails in other and more exciting pursuits, a season as 'help' in one of the Yellowstone hotels will restore the frailest constitution.

Then by companies after tiffin we walked chattering to the uplands of Hell. They call it the Norris Geyser Basin on Earth. It was as though the tide of desolation had gone out, but would presently return, across innumerable acres of dazzling white geyser formation. There were no terraces here, but all other horrors. Not ten yards from the road a blast of steam shot up roaring every few seconds, a mud volcano spat filth to Heaven, streams of hot water rumbled under foot, plunged through the dead pines in steaming cataracts and died on a waste of white where green-grey, black-yellow, and pink pools roared, shouted, bubbled, or hissed as their wicked fancies prompted. By the look of the eye the place should have been frozen over. By the feel of the feet it was warm. I ventured out among the pools, carefully following tracks, but one unwary foot began to sink, a squirt of water followed, and having no desire to descend quick into Tophet I returned to the shore where the mud and the sulphur and the nameless fat ooze-vegetation of Lethe lay. But the very road rang as though built over a gulf; and besides, how was I to tell when the raving blast of steam would find its vent insufficient and blow the whole affair into Nirvana? There was a potent stench of stale eggs everywhere, and crystals of sulphur crumbled under the foot, and the glare of the sun on the white stuff was blinding. Sitting under a bank, to me appeared a young trooper—ex-Cape Mounted Rifles, this man: the real American seems to object to his army—mounted on a horse half-maddened by the noise and steam and smell. He carried only the six-shooter and cartridge-belt. On service the Springfield carbine (which is clumsy) and a cartridge-belt slung diagonally complete equipment. The sword is no earthly use for Border warfare and, except at state parades, is never worn. The saddle is the M'Clellan tree over a four-folded blanket. Sweat-leathers you must pay for yourself. And the beauty of the tree is that it necessitates first very careful girthing and a thorough knowledge of tricks with the blanket to suit the varying conditions of the horse—a broncho will bloat in a night if he can get at a bellyful—and, secondly, even more careful riding to prevent galling.

Crupper and breast-band do not seem to be used, —but they are casual about their accoutrements, —and the bit is the single, jaw-breaking curb which American war-pictures show us. That young man was very handsome, and the grey service hat—most like the under half of a seedy terai—shaded his strong face admirably as his horse backed and shivered and sidled and plunged all over the road, and he lectured from his saddle, one foot out of the heavy-hooded stirrup, one hand on the sweating neck. 'He's not used to the Park, this brute, and he's a confirmed bolter on parade; but we understand each other.' *Whoosh!* went the steam-blast down the road with a dry roar. Round spun the troop horse prepared to bolt, and, his momentum being suddenly checked, reared till I thought he would fall back on his rider. 'Oh no; we've settled that little matter when I was breaking him,' said Centaur. 'He used to try to fall back on me. Isn't he a devil? I think you'd laugh to see the way our regiments are horsed. Sometimes a big Montana beast like mine has a thirteen-two broncho pony for neighbour, and it's annoying if you're used to better things. And oh, how you have to ride your mount! It's necessary; but I can tell you at the end of a long day's march, when you'd give all the world to ride like a sack, it isn't sweet to get extra drill for slouching. When we're turned out, we're turned out for *anything*—not a fifteen-mile trot, but for the use and behoof of all the Northern States. I've been in Arizona. A trooper there who had been in India told me that Arizona was like Afghanistan. There's nothing under Heaven there except horned toads and rattlesnakes—and Indians. Our trouble is that we only deal with Indians and they don't teach us much, and of course the citizens look down on us and all that. As a matter of fact, I suppose we're really only mounted infantry, but remember we're the best mounted infantry in the world.' And the horse danced a fandango in proof.

'My faith!' said I, looking at the dusty blouse, grey hat, soiled leather accoutrements, and whalebone poise of the wearer. 'If they are all like you, you are.'

'Thanks, whoever you may be. Of course if we were turned into a lawn-tennis court and told to resist, say, your heavy cavalry, we'd be ridden off the face of the earth if we couldn't get away. We have neither the weight nor the drill for a charge. My horse, for instance, by English standards, is half-broken, and like all the others, he bolts when we're in line. But cavalry charge against cavalry charge doesn't happen often, and if it did, well—all our men know that up to a hundred yards they are absolutely safe behind this old thing.' He patted his revolver pouch. 'Absolutely safe from any shooting of yours. What man do you think would dare to use a pistol at even thirty yards, if his life depended on it? Not one of *your* men. They can't shoot. We can. You'll hear about that down the Park—further up.'

Then he added, courteously: 'Just now it seems that the English supply all the men to the American Army. That's what makes them so good perhaps.' And with mutual expressions of good-will we parted—he to an outlying patrol fifteen miles away, I to my buggy and the old lady, who, regarding the horrors of the fire-holes, could only say, 'Good Lord!' at thirty-second intervals. Her husband talked about 'dreffel waste of steam-power,' and we went on in the clear, crisp afternoon, speculating as to the formation of geysers.

'What I say,' shrieked the old lady *apropos* of matters theological, 'and what I say more, after having seen all that, is that the Lord has ordained a Hell for such as disbelieve His gracious works.'

Nota bene.—Tom had profanely cursed the near mare for stumbling. He looked straight in front of him and said no word, but the left corner of his left eye flickered in my direction.

'And if,' continued the old lady, 'if we find a thing so dreffel as all that steam and sulphur allowed on the face of the earth, mustn't we believe that there is something ten thousand times more terrible below prepared un*toe* our destruction?'

Some people have a wonderful knack of extracting comfort from things. I am ashamed to say I agreed ostentatiously with the old lady. She developed the personal view of the matter.

'*Now* I shall be able to say something to Anna Fincher about her way of living. Shan't I, Blake?' This to her husband.

'Yes,' said he, speaking slowly after a heavy tiffin. 'But the girl's a good girl'; and they fell to arguing as to whether the luckless Anna Fincher really stood in need of lectures edged with Hell fire (she went to dances, I believe), while I got out and walked in the dust alongside of Tom.

'I drive blame cur'ous kinder folk through this place,' said he. 'Blame cur'ous. 'Seems a pity that they should ha' come so far just to liken Norris Basin to Hell. 'Guess Chicago would ha' served 'em, speaking in comparison, jest as good.'

We curved the hill and entered a forest of spruce, the path serpentining between the tree-boles, the wheels running silent on immemorial mould. There was nothing alive in the forest save ourselves. Only a river was speaking angrily somewhere to the right. For miles we drove till Tom bade us alight and look at certain falls. Wherefore we stepped out of that forest and nearly fell down a cliff which guarded a tumbled river and returned demanding fresh miracles. If the water had run uphill, we should perhaps have taken more notice of it; but 'twas only a waterfall, and I really forget whether the water was warm or cold. There is a stream here called Firehole River. It is fed by the overflow from the various geysers and basins,—a warm and deadly river wherein no fish breed. I think we crossed it a few dozen times in the course of a day.

Then the sun began to sink, and there was a taste of frost about, and we went swiftly from the forest into the open, dashed across a branch of the Firehole River and found a wood shanty, even rougher than the last, at which, after a forty-mile drive, we were to dine and sleep. Half a mile from this place stood, on the banks of the

Firehole River, a 'beaver-lodge,' and there were rumours of bears and other cheerful monsters in the woods on the hill at the back of the building.

In the cool, crisp quiet of the evening I sought that river, and found a pile of newly gnawed sticks and twigs. The beaver works with the cold-chisel, and a few clean strokes suffice to level a four-inch bole. Across the water on the far bank glimmered, with the ghastly white of peeled dead timber, the beaver-lodge—a mass of dishevelled branches. The inhabitants had dammed the stream lower down and spread it into a nice little lake. The question was would they come out for their walk before it got too dark to see. They came—blessings on their blunt muzzles, they came—as shadows come, drifting down the stream, stirring neither foot nor tail. There were three of them. One went down to investigate the state of the dam; the other two began to look for supper. There is only one thing more startling than the noiselessness of a tiger in the jungle, and that is the noiselessness of a beaver in the water. The straining ear could catch no sound whatever till they began to eat the thick green river-scudge that they call beaver-grass. I, bowed among the logs, held my breath and stared with all my eyes. They were not ten yards from me, and they would have eaten their dinner in peace so long as I had kept absolutely still. They were dear and desirable beasts, and I was just preparing to creep a step nearer when that wicked old lady from Chicago clattered down the bank, an umbrella in her hand, shrieking:

'Beavers, beavers! young man, whurr are those beavers? Good Lord! what was that now?'

The solitary watcher might have heard a pistol shot ring through the air. I wish it had killed the old lady, but it was only the beaver giving warning of danger with the slap of his tail on the water. It was exactly like the 'phink' of a pistol fired with damp powder. Then there were no more beavers—not a whisker-end. The lodge, however, was there, and a beast lower than any beaver began to throw stones at it because the old lady from Chicago said: 'P'raps, if you rattle them up they'll come out. I do so want to see a beaver.'

Yet it cheers me to think I have seen the beaver in his wilds. Never will I go to the Zoo. That even, after supper—'twere flattery to call it dinner—a Captain and a Subaltern of the cavalry post appeared at the hotel. These were the officers of whom the Mammoth Springs Captain had spoken. The Lieutenant had read everything that he could lay hands on about the Indian army, especially our cavalry arrangements, and was very full of a scheme for raising the riding Red Indians—it is not every noble savage that will make a trooper—into frontier levies—a sort of Khyber guard. 'Only,' as he said ruefully, 'there is no frontier these days, and all our Indian wars are nearly over. Those beautiful beasts will die out, and nobody will ever know what splendid cavalry they can make.'

The Captain told stories of Border warfare—of ambush, firing on the rear-guard, heat that split the skull better than any tomahawk, cold that wrinkled the very liver, night-stampedes of baggage-mules, raiding of cattle, and hopeless stern-chases into inhospitable hills, when the cavalry knew that they were not only being outpaced but outspied. Then he spoke of one fair charge when a tribe gave battle in the open and the troopers rode in swordless, firing right and left with their revolvers and—it was excessively uncomfy for that tribe. And I spoke of what men had told me of huntings in Burma, of hill-climbing in the Black Mountain affair, and so forth.

'Exactly!' said the Captain. 'Nobody knows and nobody cares. What does it matter to the Down-Easter who Wrap-up-his-Tail was?'

'And what does the fat Briton know or care about Boh Hla-Oo?' said I. Then both together: 'Depend upon it, my dear Sir, the army in both Anglo-Saxon countries is a mischievously under-estimated institution, and it's a pleasure to meet a man who,' etc., etc. And we nodded triangularly in all good-will, and swore eternal friendship. The Lieutenant made a statement which rather amazed me. He said that, on account of the scarcity of business, many American officers were to be found getting practical instruction from little troubles among the South American Republics. When the need broke out they would return 'There is so little for us to do, and the Republic has a trick of making us hedge and ditch for our pay. A little road-making on service is not a bad thing, but continuous navvying is enough to knock the heart out of any army.'

I agreed, and we sat up till two in the morning swapping the lies of East and West. As that glorious chief Man-afraid-of-Pink-Rats once said to the Agent on the Reservation: '’Melican officer good man. Heap good man. Drink me. Drink he. Drink me. Drink he. Drink *he.* Me blind. *Heap* good man!'

No. XXXI

ENDS WITH THE CAÑON OF THE YELLOWSTONE. THE MAIDEN FROM NEW HAMPSHIRE—LARRY—'WRAP-UP-HIS-TAIL'—TOM—THE OLD LADY FROM CHICAGO—AND A FEW NATURAL PHENOMENA—INCLUDING ONE BRITON.

What man would read and read the selfsame faces
And like the marbles which the windmill grinds,
Rub smooth forever with the same smooth minds,
This year retracing last year's every year's dull traces,
When there are woods and unmanstified places?
Lowell.

ONCE upon a time there was a carter who brought his team and a friend into the Yellowstone Park without due thought. Presently they came upon a few of the natural beauties of the place, and that carter turned his team into his friend's team howling: 'Get back o' this, Jim. All Hell's alight under our noses.' And they call the place Hell's Half-acre to this day. We, too, the old lady from Chicago, her husband, Tom, and the good little mares, came to Hell's Half-acre, which is about sixty acres, and when Tom said: 'Would you like to drive over it?' we said · 'Certainly no, and if you do, we shall report you to the authorities.' There was a plain, blistered and peeled and abominable, and it was given over to the sportings and spoutings of devils who threw mud and steam and dirt at each other with whoops and halloos and bellowing curses. The place smelt of the refuse of the Pit, and that odour mixed with the clean, wholesome aroma of the pines in our nostrils throughout the day. Be it known that the Park is laid out, like Ollendorf, in exercises of progressive difficulty. Hell's Half-acre was a prelude to ten or twelve miles of geyser formation. We passed hot streams boiling in the forest; saw whiffs of steam beyond these, and yet other whiffs breaking through the misty green hills in the far distance; we trampled on sulphur, and sniffed things much worse than any sulphur which is known to the upper world; and so came upon a park-like place where Tom suggested we should get out and play with the geysers.

Imagine mighty green fields splattered with lime beds · all the flowers of the summer growing up to the very edge of the lime. That was the first glimpse of the geyser basins. The buggy had pulled up close to a rough, broken, blistered cone of stuff between ten and twenty feet high. There was trouble in that place—moaning, splashing, gurgling, and the clank of machinery. A spurt of boiling water jumped into the air and a wash of water followed. I removed swiftly. The old lady from Chicago shrieked. 'What a wicked waste!' said her husband. I think they call it the Riverside Geyser. Its spout was torn and ragged like the mouth of a gun when a shell has burst there. It grumbled madly for a moment or two and then was still. I crept over the steaming lime—it was the burning marl on which Satan lay—and looked fearfully down its mouth. You should never look a gift geyser in the mouth. I beheld a horrible, slippery, slimy funnel with water rising and falling ten feet at a time. Then the water rose to lip-level with a rush and an infernal bubbling troubled this Devil's Bethesda before the sullen heave of the crest of a wave lapped over the edge and made me run. Mark the nature of the human soul! I had begun with awe, not to say terror. I stepped back from the flanks of the Riverside Geyser saying: 'Pooh! Is that all it can do?' Yet for aught I knew the whole thing might have blown up at a minute's notice; she, he, or it, being an arrangement of uncertain temper.

We drifted on up that miraculous valley. On either side of us were hills from a thousand to fifteen feet high and wooded from heel to crest. As far as the eye could range forward were columns of steam in the air, misshapen lumps of lime, most like preadamite monsters, still pools of turquoise blue, stretches of blue cornflowers, a river that coiled on itself twenty times, boulders of strange colours, and ridges of glaring, staring white.

The old lady from Chicago poked with her parasol at the pools as though they had been alive. On one particularly innocent-looking little puddle she turned her back for a moment, and there rose behind her a twenty-foot column of water and steam. Then she shrieked and protested that 'she never thought it would ha' done it,' and the old man chewed his tobacco steadily, and mourned for steam-power wasted. I embraced the whitened stump of a middle-sized pine that had grown all too close to a hot pool's lip, and the whole thing turned over under my hand as a tree would do in a nightmare. From right and left came the trumpetings of elephants at play. I stepped into a pool of old dried blood rimmed with the nodding cornflowers; the blood changed to ink even as I trod; and ink and blood were washed away in a spurt of boiling sulphurous water spat out from the lee of a bank of flowers. This sounds mad, doesn't it?

A moon-faced trooper of German extraction—never was Park so carefully patrolled—came up to inform us that as yet we had not seen any of the real geysers, that they were all a mile or so up the valley, tastefully scattered round the hotel in which we would rest for the night. America is a free country, but the citizens look down on the soldier. *I* had to entertain that trooper. The old lady from Chicago would have none of him; so we loafed along together, now across half-rotten pine logs sunk in swampy ground, anon over the ringing geyser formation, then knee-deep through long grass.

'And why did you 'list?' said I.

The moonfaced one's face began to work. I thought he would have a fit, but he told me a story instead—such a nice tale of a naughty little girl who wrote love-letters to two men at once. She was a simple village wife, but a wicked 'Family Novelette' countess couldn't have accomplished her ends better. She drove one man nearly wild with her pretty little treachery; and the other man abandoned her and came West to forget. Moonface was that man. We rounded a low spur of hill, and came out upon a field of aching snowy lime, rolled in sheets, twisted into knots, riven with rents and diamonds and stars, stretching for more than half a mile in every direction. In this place of despair lay most of the big geysers who know when there is trouble in Krakatoa, who tell the pines when there is a cyclone on the Atlantic seaboard, and who — are exhibited to visitors under pretty and fanciful names. The first mound that I encountered belonged to a goblin splashing in his tub. I heard him kick, pull a shower-bath on his shoulders, gasp, crack his joints, and rub himself down with a towel; then he let the water out of the bath, as a thoughtful man should, and it all sank down out of sight till another goblin arrived. Yet they called this place the Lioness and the Cubs. It lies not very far from the Lion, which is a sullen, roaring beast, and they say that when it is very active the other geysers presently follow suit. After the Krakatoa eruption all the geysers went mad together, spouting, spurting, and bellowing till men feared that they would rip up the whole field. Mysterious sympathies exist among them, and when the Giantess speaks (of her more anon) they all hold their peace.

I was watching a solitary spring, when, far across the fields, stood up a plume of spun glass, iridescent and superb, against the sky. 'That,' said the trooper, 'is Old Faithful. He goes off every sixty-five minutes to the minute, plays for five minutes, and sends up a column of water a hundred and fifty feet high. By the time you have looked at all the other geysers he will be ready to play.'

So we looked and we wondered at the Beehive, whose mouth is built up exactly like a hive; at the Turban (which is not in the least like a turban); and at many, many other geysers, hot holes, and springs. Some of them rumbled, some hissed, some went off spasmodically, and others lay still in sheets of sapphire and beryl.

Would you believe that even these terrible creatures have to be guarded by the troopers to prevent the irreverent American from chipping the cones to pieces, or worse still, making the geysers sick? If you take of soft-soap a small barrelful and drop it down a geyser's mouth, that geyser will presently be forced to lay all before you and for days afterwards will be of an irritated and inconsistent stomach. When they told me the tale I was filled with sympathy. Now I wish that I had stolen soap and tried the experiment on some lonely little beast of a geyser in the woods. It sounds so probable—and so human!

Yet he would be a bold man who would administer emetics to the Giantess. She is flat-lipped, having no mouth, she looks like a pool, fifty feet long and thirty wide, and there is no ornamentation about her. At irregular intervals she speaks, and sends up a column of water over two hundred feet high to begin with; then she is angry for a day and a half—sometimes for two days. Owing to her peculiarity of going mad in the night not many people have seen the Giantess at her finest; but the clamour of her unrest, men say, shakes the wooden hotel, and echoes like thunder among the hills. When I saw her trouble was brewing. The pool bubbled seriously, and at five-minute intervals, sank a foot or two, then rose, washed over the rim, and huge steam bubbles broke on the top. Just before an eruption the water entirely disappears from view. Whenever you see the water die down in a geyser-mouth get away as fast as you can. I saw a tiny little geyser suck in its breath in this way, and instinct made me retire while it hooted after me.

Leaving the Giantess to swear, and spit, and thresh about, we went over to Old Faithful, who by reason of his faithfulness has benches close to him whence you may comfortably watch. At the appointed hour we heard the water flying up and down the mouth with the sob of waves in a cave. Then came the preliminary gouts, then a roar and a rush, and that glittering column of diamonds rose, quivered, stood still for a minute. Then it broke, and the rest was a confused snarl of water not thirty feet high. All the young ladies—not more than twenty—in the tourist band remarked that it was 'elegant,' and betook themselves to writing their names in the bottoms of shallow pools. Nature fixes the insult indelibly, and the after-years will learn that 'Hattie,' 'Sadie,' 'Mamie,' 'Sophie,' and so forth, have taken out their hair-pins and scrawled in the face of Old Faithful.

The congregation returned to the hotel to put down their impressions in diaries and note-books which they wrote up ostentatiously in the verandahs. It was a sweltering hot day, albeit we stood somewhat higher than the summit of Jakko, and I left that raw pine-creaking caravanserai for the cool shade of a clump of pines between whose trunks glimmered tents. A batch of troopers came down the road, and flung themselves across country into their rough lines. Verily the 'Melican cavalry-man *can* ride, though he keeps his accoutrements pig, and his horse cow-fashion.

I was free of that camp in five minutes—free to play with the heavy lumpy carbines, to have the saddles stripped, and punch the horses knowingly in the ribs. One of the men had been in the fight with 'Wrap-up-his-Tail' before alluded to, and he told me how that great chief, his horse's tail tied up in red calico, swaggered in front of the United States cavalry, challenging all to single combat. But he was slain, and a few of his tribe with him. 'There's no use in an Indian, anyway,' concluded my friend.

A couple of cowboys—real cowboys, not the Buffalo Bill article—jingled through the camp amid a shower of mild chaff. They were on their way to Cook City, I fancy, and I know that they never washed. But they were picturesque ruffians with long spurs, hooded stirrups, slouch hats, fur weather-cloths over their knees, and pistol-butts easy to hand.

'The cowboy's goin' under before long,' said my friend. 'Soon as the country's settled up he'll have to go. But he's mighty useful now. What should we do without the cowboy?'

'As how?' said I, and the camp laughed.

'He has the money. We have the know-how. He comes in in winter to play poker at the military posts. *We* play poker—a few. When he's lost his money we make him drunk and let him go. Sometimes we get the wrong man.' And he told a tale of an innocent cowboy who turned up, cleaned out, at a post, and played poker for thirty-six hours. But it was the post that was cleaned out when that long-haired Caucasian Ah Sin removed himself, heavy with everybody's pay, and declining the proffered liquor. 'Naow,' said the historian, 'I don't play with no cowboy unless he's a little bit drunk first.'

Ere I departed I gathered from more than one man that significant fact that *up to one hundred yards* he felt absolutely secure behind his revolver.

'In England, I understand,' quoth a limber youth from the South, 'in England a man aren't allowed to play with no firearms. He's got to be taught all that when he enlists. I didn't want much teaching how to shoot straight 'fore I served Uncle Sam. And that's just where it is. But you was talking about your horse guards now?'

I explained briefly some peculiarities of equipment connected with our crackest crack cavalry. I grieve to say the camp roared.

'Take 'em over swampy ground. Let 'em run around a bit an' work the starch out of 'em, an' then, Almighty, if we wouldn't plug 'em at ease I'd eat their horses!'

'But suppose they engaged in the open?' said I.

'Engage the Hades. Not if there was a tree-trunk within twenty miles they *couldn't* engage in the open!'

Gentlemen, the officers, have you ever seriously considered the existence on earth of a cavalry who by preference would fight in timber? The evident sincerity of the proposition made me think hard as I moved over to the hotel and joined a party exploration, which, diving into the woods, unearthed a pit pool of burningest water fringed with jet black sand—all the ground near by being pure white. But miracles pall when they arrive at the rate of twenty a day. A flaming dragon-fly flew over the pool, reeled and dropped on the water, dying without a quiver of his gorgeous wings, and the pool said nothing whatever, but sent its thin steam wreaths up to the burning sky. I prefer pools that talk.

There was a maiden—a very trim maiden—who had just stepped out of one of Mr. James's novels. She owned a delightful mother and an equally delightful father, a heavy-eyed, slow-voiced man of finance. The parents thought that their daughter wanted change. She lived in New Hampshire. Accordingly, she had dragged them up to Alaska, to the Yosemite Valley, and was now returning leisurely *via* the Yellowstone just in time for the tail-end of the summer season at Saratoga. We had met once or twice before in the Park, and I had been amazed and amused at her critical commendation of the wonders that she saw. From that very resolute little mouth I received a lecture on American literature, the nature and inwardness of Washington society, the precise value of Cable's works as compared with 'Uncle Remus' Harris, and a few other things that had nothing whatever to do with geysers, but were altogether delightful. Now an English maiden who had stumbled on a dust-grimed, lime-washed, sun-peeled, collarless wanderer come from and going to goodness knows where, would, her mother inciting her and her father brandishing his umbrella, have regarded him as a dissolute adventurer. Not so those delightful people from New Hampshire. They were good enough to treat me—it sounds almost incredible—as a human being, possibly respectable, probably not in immediate need of financial assistance. Papa talked pleasantly and to the point. The little maiden strove valiantly with the accent of her birth and that of her reading, and mamma smiled benignly in the background.

Balance this with a story of a young English idiot I met knocking about inside his high collars, attended by a valet. He condescended to tell me that 'you can't be too careful who you talk to in these parts,' and stalked on, fearing, I suppose, every minute for his social chastity. Now that man was a barbarian (I took occasion to tell him so), for he comported himself after the manner of the head-hunters of Assam, who are at perpetual feud one with another.

You will understand that these foolish tales are introduced in order to cover the fact that this pen cannot describe the glories of the Upper Geyser basin. The evening I spent under the lee of the Castle Geyser sitting on a log with some troopers and watching a baronial keep forty feet high spouting hot water. If the Castle went off first, they said the Giantess would be quiet, and *vice versa*; and then they told tales till the moon got up and a party of campers in the woods gave us all something to eat.

Next morning Tom drove us on, promising new wonders. He pulled up after a few miles at a clump of brushwood where an army was drowning. I could hear the sick gasps and thumps of the men going under, but when I broke through the brushwood the hosts had fled, and there were only pools of pink, black, and white lime, thick as turbid honey. They shot up a pat of mud every minute or two, choking in the effort. It was an uncanny sight. Do you wonder that in the old days the Indians were careful to avoid the Yellowstone? Geysers are permissible, but mud is terrifying. The old lady from Chicago took a piece of it, and in half an hour it died into lime-dust and blew away between her fingers. All *maya*,—illusion,—you see! Then we clinked over sulphur in crystals; there was a waterfall of boiling water; and a road across a level park hotly contested by the beavers. Every winter they build their dam and flood the low-lying land; every summer that dam is torn up by the Government, and for half a mile you must plough axle-deep in water, the willows brushing into the buggy, and little waterways branching off right and left. The road is the main stream—just like the Bolan line in flood. If you turn up a byway, there is no more of you, and the beavers work your buggy into next year's dam.

Then came soft, turfy forest that deadened the wheels, and two troopers—on detachment duty—came noiselessly behind us. One was the Wrap-up-his-Tail man, and we talked merrily while the half-broken horses bucked about among the trees till we came to a mighty hill all strewn with moss agates, and everybody had to get out and pant in that thin air. But how intoxicating it was! The old lady from Chicago clucked like an emancipated hen as she scuttled about the road cramming pieces of rock into her reticule. She sent me fifty yards down the hill to pick up a piece of broken bottle which she insisted was moss agate. 'I've some o' that at home an' they shine. You go get it, young feller.'

As we climbed the long path the road grew viler and viler till it became without disguise the bed of a torrent; and just when things were at their rockiest we emerged into a little sapphire lake—but never sapphire was so blue—called Mary's Lake; and that between eight and nine thousand feet above the sea. Then came grass downs, all on a vehement slope, so that the buggy following the new-made road ran on to the two off-wheels mostly, till we dipped head-first into a ford, climbed up a cliff, raced along a down, dipped again and pulled up dishevelled at 'Larry's' for lunch and an hour's rest. Only 'Larry' could have managed that school-feast tent on the lonely hillside. Need I say that he was an Irishman? His supplies were at their lowest ebb, but Larry enveloped us all in the golden glamour of his speech ere we had descended, and the tent with the rude trestle-table became a palace, the rough fare, delicacies of Delmonico, and we, the abashed recipients of Larry's imperial bounty. It was only later that I discovered I had paid eight shillings for tinned beef, biscuits, and beer, but on the other hand Larry had said: 'Will I go out an' kill a buffalo?' And I felt that for me and for me alone would he have done it. Everybody else felt that way. Good luck go with Larry!

'An' now you'll all go an' wash your pocket-handkerchiefs in that beautiful hot spring round the corner,' said he. 'There's soap an' a wash-board ready, an' 'tis not every day that ye can get hot water for nothing.' He waved us large-handedly to the open downs while he put the tent to rights. There was no sense of fatigue on the body or distance in the air. Hill and dale rode on the eyeball. I could have clutched the far-off snowy peaks by putting out my hand. Never was such maddening air. Why we should have washed pocket-handkerchiefs Larry alone knows. It appeared to be a sort of religious rite. In a little valley overhung with gay painted rocks ran a stream of velvet brown and pink. It was hot—hotter than the hand could bear—and it coloured the boulders in its course.

There was the maiden from New Hampshire, the old lady from Chicago, papa, mamma, the woman who chewed gum, and all the rest of them, gravely bending over a washboard and soap. Mysterious virtues lay in that queer stream. It turned the linen white as driven snow in five minutes, and then we lay on the grass and laughed with sheer bliss of being alive. This have I known once in Japan, once on the banks of the Columbia, what time the salmon came in and 'California' howled, and once again in the Yellowstone by the light of the eyes of the maiden from New Hampshire. Four little pools lay at my elbow: one was of black water (tepid), one clear water (cold), one clear water (hot), one red water (boiling); my newly washed handkerchief covered them all. We marvelled as children marvel.

'This evening we shall do the grand cañon of the Yellowstone?' said the maiden.

'Together?' said I; and she said yes.

The sun was sinking when we heard the roar of falling waters and came to a broad river along whose banks we ran. And then—oh, then! I might at a pinch describe the infernal regions, but not the other place. Be it known to you that the Yellowstone River has occasion to run through a gorge about eight miles long. To get to the bottom of the gorge it makes two leaps, one of about one hundred and twenty and the other of three hundred feet. I investigated the upper or lesser fall, which is close to the hotel. Up to that time nothing particular happens to the Yellowstone, its banks being only rocky, rather steep, and plentifully adorned with pines. At the falls it comes round a corner, green, solid, ribbed with a little foam and not more than thirty yards wide. Then it goes over still green and rather more solid than before. After a minute or two you, sitting upon a rock directly above the drop, begin to understand that something has occurred; that the river has jumped a huge distance between solid cliff walls and what looks like the gentle froth of ripples lapping the sides of the gorge below is really the outcome of great waves. And the river yells aloud; but the cliffs do not allow the yells to escape.

That inspection began with curiosity and finished in terror, for it seemed that the whole world was sliding in chrysolite from under my feet. I followed with the others round the corner to arrive at the brink of the cañon: we had to climb up a nearly perpendicular ascent to begin with, for the ground rises more than the river drops. Stately pine woods fringe either lip of the gorge, which is—the Gorge of the Yellowstone.

All I can say is that, without warning or preparation, I looked into a gulf seventeen hundred feet deep, with eagles and fish-hawks circling far below. And the sides of that gulf were one wild welter of colour—crimson, emerald, cobalt, ochre, amber, honey splashed with port-wine, snow-white, vermilion, lemon, and silver-grey, in wide washes. The sides did not fall sheer, but were graven by time and water and air into monstrous heads of kings, dead chiefs, men and women of the old time. So far below that no sound of its strife could reach us, the Yellowstone River ran—a finger-wide strip of jade-green. The sunlight took those wondrous walls and gave fresh hues to those that nature had already laid there. Once I saw the dawn break over a lake in Rajputana and the sun set over the Oodey Sagar amid a circle of Holman Hunt hills. This time I was watching both performances going on below me—upside down, you understand—and the colours were real! The cañon was burning like Troy town; but it would burn for ever, and, thank goodness, neither pen nor brush could ever portray its splendours adequately. The Academy would reject the picture for a chromolithograph. The public would scoff at the letterpress for *Daily Telegraphese*. 'I will leave this thing alone,' said I; ''tis my peculiar property. Nobody else shall share it with me.' Evening crept through the pines that shadowed us, but the full glory of the day flamed in that cañon as we went out very cautiously to a jutting piece of rock—blood-red or pink it was—that overhung the deepest deeps of all. Now I know what it is to sit enthroned amid the clouds of sunset. Giddiness took away all sensation of touch or form; but the sense of blinding colour remained. When I reached the mainland again I had sworn that I had been floating. The maid from New Hampshire said no word for a very long time. She then quoted poetry, which was perhaps the best thing she could have done.

'And to think that this show-place has been going on all these days an' none of we ever saw it,' said the old lady from Chicago, with an acid glance at her husband.

'No, only the Injuns,' said he, unmoved; and the maiden and I laughed long. Inspiration is fleeting, beauty is vain, and the power of the mind for wonder limited. Though the shining hosts themselves had risen choiring from the bottom of the gorge they would not have prevented her papa and one baser than himself from rolling stones down those stupendous rainbow-washed slides. Seventeen hundred feet of steepest pitch and rather more than seventeen hundred colours for log or boulder to whirl through! So we heaved things and saw them gather way and bound from white rock to red or yellow, dragging behind them torrents of colour, till the noise of their descent ceased and they bounded a hundred yards clear at the last into the Yellowstone.

'I've been down there,' said Tom that evening. 'It's easy to get down if you're careful—just sit and slide; but getting up is worse. An' I found, down below there, two rocks just marked with a pictur of the cañon. I wouldn't sell those rocks not for fifteen dollars.'

And papa and I crawled down to the Yellowstone—just above the first little fall—to wet a line for good luck. The round moon came up and turned the cliffs and pines into silver; a two-pound trout came up also, and we slew him among the rocks, nearly tumbling into that wild river.

. . . . .

Then out and away to Livingstone once more. The maiden from New Hampshire disappeared;

papa and mamma with her disappeared. Disappeared, too, the old lady from Chicago and all the rest, while I thought of all that I had *not* seen—the forest of petrified trees with amethyst crystals in their black hearts; the great Yellowstone Lake where you catch your trout alive in one spring and drop him into another to boil him; and most of all of that mysterious Hoodoo region where all the devils not employed in the geysers live and kill the wandering bear and elk, so that the scared hunter finds in Death Gulch piled carcasses of the dead whom no man has smitten. Hoodoo-land with the overhead noises, the bird and beast and devil-rocks, the mazes and the bottomless pits,—all these things I missed. On the return road Yankee Jim and Diana of the Crossways gave me kindly greeting as the train paused an instant before their door, and at Livingstone whom should I see but Tom the driver?

'I've done with the Yellowstone and decided to clear out East somewheres,' said he. 'Your talkin' about movin' round so gay an' careless made me kinder restless; I'm movin' out.'

Lord forgi'e us for our responsibility one to another!

'And your partner?' said I.

'Here's him,' said Tom, introducing a gawky youth with a bundle; and I saw those two young men turn their faces to the East.

No. XXXII

OF THE AMERICAN ARMY AND THE CITY OF THE SAINTS. THE TEMPLE, THE BOOK OF MORMON, AND THE GIRL FROM DORSET AN ORIENTAL CONSIDERATION OF POLYGAMY.

A fool also is full of words: a man cannot tell what shall be; and what shall be after him who can tell?

It has just occurred to me with great force that delightful as these letters are to myself their length and breadth and depth may be just the least little bit in the world wearisome to you over there. I will compress myself rigorously, though I should very much like to deliver a dissertation on the American Army and the possibilities of its extension.

The American Army is a beautiful little army. Some day, when all the Indians are happily dead or drunk, it ought to make the finest scientific and survey corps that the world has ever seen. It does excellent work now, but there is this defect in its nature: it is officered, as you know, from West Point, but the mischief of it is that West Point seems to be created for the purpose of spreading a general knowledge of military matters among the people. A boy goes up to that institution, gets his pass, and returns to civil life, so they tell me, with a dangerous knowledge that he is a sucking Moltke, and may apply his learning when occasion offers. Given trouble, that man will be a nuisance, because he is a hideously versatile American to begin with, as cocksure of himself as a man can be, and with all the racial disregard for human life to back him through his demi-semi-professional generalship. In a country where, as the records of the daily papers show, men engaged in a conflict with police or jails are all too ready to adopt a military formation, and get heavily shot in a sort of cheap, half-instructed warfare instead of being decently scared by the appearance of the military, this sort of arrangement does not seem wise. The bond between the States is of amazing tenuity. So long as they do not absolutely march into the District of Columbia, sit on the Washington statues, and invent a flag of their own, they can legislate, lynch, hunt negroes through swamps, divorce, railroad, and rampage as much as ever they choose. They do not need knowledge of their own military strength to back their genial lawlessness. That Regular Army, which is a dear little army, should be kept to itself, blooded on detachment duty, turned into the paths of science, and now and again assembled at feasts of Freemasons and so forth. It's too tiny to be a political power. The immortal wreck of the Grand Army of the Republic is a political power of the largest and most unblushing description. It ought not to help to lay the foundations of an amateur military power that is blind and irresponsible. . . .

Be thankful that the balance of this lecture is suppressed, and with it the account of a 'shiveree' which I attended in Livingstone City: and the story of the editor and the sub-editor (the latter was a pet cougar, or mountain lion, who used, they said, skilfully to sub-edit disputants in the office) of the Livingstone daily paper.

Omitting a thousand matters of first importance, let me pick up the thread of things on a narrow-gauge line that took me down to Salt Lake. The run between Delhi and Ahmedabad on a May day would have been bliss compared to this torture. There was nothing but glare and desert and alkali dust. There was no smoking-accommodation. I sat in the lavatory with the conductor and a prospector who told stories about Indian atrocities in the voice of a dreaming child—oath following oath as smoothly as clotted cream laps the mouth of the jug. I don't think he knew he was saying anything out of the way, but nine or ten of those oaths were new to me, and one even made the conductor raise his eyebrows.

'And when a man's alone mostly, leadin' his horse across the hills, he gets to talk aloud to himself as it was,' said the weather-worn retailer of tortures. A vision rose before me of this man trampling the Bannack City trail under the stars—swearing, always swearing.

Bundles of rags that were pointed out as Red Indians boarded the train from time to time. Their race privileges allow them free transit on the platforms of the cars. They mustn't come inside of course, and equally of course the train never thinks of pulling up for them. I saw a squaw take us flying and leave us in the same manner when we were spinning round a curve. Like the Punjabi, the Red Indian gets out by preference on the trackless plain and walks stolidly to the horizon. He never says where he is going. . . .

Salt Lake. I am concerned for the sake of Mr. Phil Robinson, his soul. You will remember that he wrote a book called *Sinners and Saints* in which he proved very prettily that the Mormon was almost altogether an estimable person. Ever since my arrival at Salt Lake I have been wondering what made him write that book. On mature reflection, and after a long walk round the city, I am inclined to think it was the sun, which is very powerful hereabouts.

By great good luck the evil-minded train, already delayed twelve hours by a burnt bridge, brought me to the city on a Saturday by way of that valley which the Mormons aver their efforts had caused to blossom like the rose. Some hours previously I had entered a new world where, in conversation, every one was either a Mormon or a Gentile. It is not seemly for a free and independent citizen to dub himself a Gentile, but the Mayor of Ogden—which is the Gentile city of the valley—told me that there must be some distinction between the two flocks. Long before the fruit orchards of Logan or the shining levels of the Salt Lake had been reached that Mayor —himself a Gentile, and one renowned for his dealings with the Mormons—told me that the great question of the existence of the power within the power was being gradually solved by the ballot and by education. 'We have,' quoth he, 'hills round and about here stuffed full of silver and gold and lead, and all Hell atop of the Mormon church can't keep the Gentile from flocking in when that's the case. At Ogden, thirty miles from Salt Lake, this year the Gentile vote swamped the Mormon at the Municipal elections, and next year we trust that we shall be able to repeat our success in Salt Lake itself. In that city the Gentiles are only one-third of the total population, but the mass of 'em are grown men, capable of voting. Whereas the Mormons are cluttered up with children. I guess as soon as we have purely Gentile officers in the township, and the control of the policy of the city, the Mormons will have to back down considerable. They're bound to go before long. My own notion is that it's the older men who keep alive the opposition to the Gentile and all his works. The younger ones, spite of all the elders tell 'em, *will* mix with the Gentile, and read Gentile books, and you bet your sweet life there's a holy influence working toward conversion in the kiss of an average Gentile—specially when the girl knows that he won't think it necessary for her salvation to load the house up with other women-folk. I guess the younger generation are giving sore trouble to the elders. What's that you say about polygamy? It's a penal offence now under a Bill passed not long ago. The

Mormon has to elect one wife and keep to her. If he's caught visiting any of the others—do you see that cool and restful brown stone building way over there against the hillside? That's the penitentiary. He is sent there to consider his sins, and he pays a fine, too. But most of the police in Salt Lake are Mormons, and I don't suppose they are too hard on their friends. I presoom there's a good deal of polygamy practised on the sly. But the chief trouble is to get the Mormon to see that the Gentile isn't the doubly-damned beast that the elders represent. Only get the Gentiles well into the State, and the whole concern is bound to go to pieces in a very little time.'

And the wish being father to the thought, 'Why, certainly,' said I, and began to take in the valley of Deseret, the home of the latter-day saints, and the abode perhaps of as much misery as has ever been compressed into forty years. The good folk at home will not understand, but you will, what follows. You know how in Bengal to this day the child-wife is taught to curse her possible co-wife, ere yet she has gone to her husband's house? And the Bengali woman has been accustomed to polygamy for a few hundred years. You know, too, the awful jealousy between mother wife and barren behind the purdah—the jealousy that culminates sometimes in the poisoning of the well-beloved son? Now and again, an Englishwoman employs a high-caste Mussulman nurse, and in the offices of that hire women are apt to forget the differences of colour, and to speak unreservedly as twin daughters under Eve's curse. The nurse tells very strange and awful things. She has, and this the Mormons count a privilege, been born into polygamy; but she loathes and detests it from the bottom of her jealous soul. And to the lot of the Bengali co-wife—'the cursed of the cursed—the daughter of the dung-hill—the scald-head and the barren-mute' (you know the rest of that sweet commination-service)—one creed, of all the White creeds to-day, deliberately introduces the white woman taken from centuries of training, which have taught her that it is right to control the undivided heart of one man. To quench her most natural rebellion, that amazing creed and fantastic jumble of Mahometanism, the Mosaical law, and imperfectly comprehended fragments of Freemasonry, calls to its aid all the powers of a hell conceived and elaborated by coarse-minded hedgers and ditchers. A sweet view, isn't it?

All the beauty of the valley could not make me forget it. But the valley is very fair. Bench after bench of land, flat as a table against the flanks of the ringing hills, marks where the Salt Lake rested for a while as it sunk from an inland sea to a lake fifty miles long and thirty broad. Before long the benches will be covered with houses. At present these are hidden among the green trees on the dead flat of the valley. You have read a hundred times how the streets of Salt Lake City are very broad, furnished with rows of shade trees and gutters of fresh water. This is true, but I struck the town in a season of great drouth—that same drouth which is playing havoc with the herds of Montana. The trees were limp, and the rills of sparkling water that one reads about were represented by dusty, paved courses. Main Street appears to be inhabited by the commercial Gentile, who has made of it a busy, bustling thoroughfare, and, in the eye of the sun, swigs the ungodly lager and smokes the improper cigar all day long. For which I like him. At the head of Main Street stand the lions of the place; the Temple and the Tabernacle, the Tithing House, and the houses of Brigham Young, whose portrait is on sale in most of the booksellers' shops. Incidentally it may be mentioned that the late Amir of Utah does not unremotely resemble His Highness the Amir of Afghanistan, whom these fortunate eyes have seen. And I have no desire to fall into the hands of the Amir. The first thing to be seen was, of course, the Temple, the outward exponent of a creed. Armed with a copy of the Book of Mormon, for better comprehension, I went to form rash opinions. Some day the Temple will be finished. It was begun only thirty years ago, and up to date rather more than three million dollars and a half have been expended in its granite bulk. The walls are ten feet thick; the edifice itself is about a hundred feet high; and its towers will be nearly two hundred. And that is all there is of it, unless you choose to inspect more closely; always reading the Book of Mormon as you walk. Then the wondrous puerility, of what I suppose we must call the design, becomes apparent. These men, directly inspired from on High, heaped stone on stone and pillar on pillar, without achieving either dignity, relief, or interest. There is, over the main door, some pitiful scratching in stone representing the all-seeing eye, the Masonic grip, the sun, moon, and stars, and, perhaps, other skittles. The flatness and meanness of the thing almost makes you weep when you look at the magnificent granite in blocks strewn abroad, and think of the art that three million dollars might have called in to the aid of the church. It is as though a child had said: 'Let us draw a great, big, fine house—finer than any house that ever was,'—and in that desire had laboriously smudged along with a ruler and pencil, piling meaningless straight lines on compass-drawn curves, with his tongue following every movement of the inept hand. Then sat I down on a wheelbarrow and read the Book of Mormon, and behold the spirit of the book was the spirit of the stone before me. The estimable Joseph and Hyrum Smith struggling to create a new Bible, when they knew nothing of the history of Old and New Testament, and the inspired architect muddling with his bricks—they were brothers. But the book was more interesting than the building. It is written, and all the world has read, how to Joseph Smith an angel came down from Heaven with a pair of celestial gig-lamps, whereby he was marvellously enabled to interpret certain plates of gold scribbled over with dots and scratches, and discovered by him in the ground. Which plates Joseph Smith did translate—only he spelt the mysterious characters 'caractors'—and out of the dots and scratches produced a volume of six hundred closely printed pages, containing the books of Nephi, first and second, Jacob, Enos, Jarom, Omni, Mormon, Mosiah, the Record of Zeniff, the book of Alma Helaman, the third of Nephi, the book of Ether (the whole thing is a powerful anæsthetic, by the way), and the final book of Mononi. Three men, of whom one I believe is now living, bear solemn witness that the angel with the spectacles appeared unto them; eight other men swear solemnly that they have seen the golden plates of the revelation; and upon this testimony the book of Mormon stands. The Mormon Bible begins at the days of Zedekiah, King of Judah, and ends in a wild and weltering quagmire of tribal fights, bits of revelation, and wholesale cribs from the Bible. Very sincerely did I sympathise with the inspired brothers as I waded through their joint production. As a humble fellow-worker in the field of fiction, I knew what it was to get good names for one's characters. But Joseph and Hyrum were harder bestead than ever I have been; and bolder men to boot. They created Teancum and Coriantumy Pahoran, Kishkumen, and Gadianton, and other priceless names which the memory does not hold; but of geography they wisely steered clear, and were astutely vague as to the localities of places, because you see they were by no means certain what lay in the next county to their own. They marched and countermarched bloodthirsty armies across their pages; and added new and amazing chapters to the records of the New Testament, and reorganised the heavens and the earth as it is always lawful to do in print. But they could not achieve style, and it was foolish of them to let into their weird mosaic pieces of the genuine Bible whenever the labouring pen dropped from its toilsome parody to a sentence or two of vile, bad English or downright 'penny dreadfulism.' 'And Moses said unto the people of Israel· "Great Scott! what air you doing?"' There is no sentence in the Book of Mormon word for word like the foregoing; but the general tone is not widely different.

There are the makings of a very fine creed about Mormonism. To begin with, the Church is rather more absolute than that of Rome. Drop the polygamy plank in the platform, but on the other hand deal lightly with certain forms of excess. Keep the quality of the recruits down to a low mental level and see that the best of the agricultural science available is in the hands of the Elders, and you have there a first-class engine for pioneer work. The tawdry mysticism and the borrowings from Freemasonry serve the low-caste Swede and the Dane, the Welshman and the Cornish cottar, just as well as a highly organised Heaven.

I went about the streets and peeped into people's front windows, and the decorations upon the tables were after the manner of the year 1850. Main Street was full of country folk from the outside come in to trade with the Zion Mercantile

Co-operative Institute. The Church, I fancy, looks after the finances of this thing, and it consequently pays good dividends. The faces of the women were not lovely. Indeed, but for the certainty that ugly persons are just as irrational in the matter of undivided love as the beautiful, it seemed that polygamy was a blessed institution for the women, and that only the spiritual power could drive the hulking, board-faced men into it. The women wore hideous garments, and the men seemed to be tied up with string. They would market all that afternoon, and on Sunday go to the praying-place. I tried to talk to a few of them, but they spoke strange tongues and stared and behaved like cows. Yet one woman, and not an altogether ugly one, confided to me that she hated the idea of Salt Lake City being turned into a show-place for the amusement of the Gentile.

'If we 'ave our own institutions, that ain't no reason why people should come 'ere and stare at us, his it?'

The dropped 'h' betrayed her.

'And when did you leave England?' I said.

'Summer of '84. I am from Dorset,' she said. 'The Mormon agents was very good to us, and we was very poor. Now we're better off—my father an' mother an' me.'

'Then you like the State?'

She misunderstood at first. 'Oh, I ain't livin' in the state of polygamy. Not me yet. I ain't married. I like where I am. I've got things o' my own—and some land.'

'But I suppose you will—'

'Not me. I ain't like them Swedes an' Danes. I ain't got nothin' to say for or against polygamy. It's the Elders' business, an' between you an' me I don't think it's going on much longer. You'll 'ear them in the 'ouse to-morrer talkin' as if it was spreadin' all over America. The Swedes they think it *his*. I know it hisn't.'

'But you've got your land all right.'

'Oh, yes, we've got our land an' we never say aught against polygamy o' course — father an' mother an' me.'

It strikes me that there is a fraud somewhere. You've never heard of the rice-Christians, have you?'

I should have liked to have spoken to the maiden at length, but she dived into the Zion Co-op. and a man captured me, saying that it was my bounden duty to see the sights of Salt Lake. These comprised the egg-shaped Tabernacle, the Beehive, and town houses of Brigham Young; the same great ruffian's tomb with assorted samples of his wives sleeping round him (just as the eleven faithful ones sleep round the ashes of Runjit Singh outside Fort Lahore), and one or two other curiosities. But all these things have been described by abler pens than mine. The animal-houses where Brigham used to pack his wives are grubby villas; the Tabernacle is a shingled fraud, and the Tithing House where all the revenue returns seem to be made, much resembles a stable. The Mormons have a paper currency of their own — ecclesiastical bank-notes which are exchanged for local produce. But the little boys of the place prefer the bullion of the Gentiles. It is not pleasant to be taken round a township with your guide stopping before every third house to say: 'That's where Elder So-and-so kept Amelia Bathershins, his fifth wife—no, his third. Amelia she was took on after Keziah, but Keziah was the Elder's pet, an' he didn't dare to let Amelia come across Keziah for fear of her spilin' Keziah's beauty.' The Mussulmans are quite right. The minute that all the domestic details of polygamy are discussed in the mouths of the people, that institution is ready to fall. I shook off my guide when he had told me his very last doubtful tale, and went on alone. An ordered peace and a perfection of quiet luxury is the note of the city of Salt Lake. The houses stand in generous and well-groomed grass-plots, none very much worse or better than their neighbours. Creepers grow over the house fronts, and there is a very pleasant music of wind among the trees in the vast empty streets bringing a smell of hay and the flowers of summer.

On a tableland overlooking all the city stands the United States garrison of infantry and artillery. The State of Utah can do nearly anything it pleases until that much-to-be-desired hour when the Gentile vote shall quietly swamp out Mormonism; but the garrison is kept there in case of accidents. The big, shark-mouthed, pig-eared, heavy-boned farmers sometimes take to their creed with wildest fanaticism, and in past years have made life excessively unpleasant for the

Gentile when he was few in the land. But to-day, so far from killing openly or secretly, or burning Gentile farms, it is all the Mormon dares do to feebly try to boycott the interloper. His journals preach defiance to the United States Government, and in the Tabernacle of a Sunday the preachers follow suit. When I went down there the place was full of people who would have been much better for a washing. A man rose up and told them that they were the chosen of God, the elect of Israel, that they were to obey their priest, and that there was a good time coming. I fancy that they had heard all this before so many times it produced no impression whatever; even as the sublimest mysteries of another Faith lose salt through constant iteration. They breathed heavily through their noses and stared straight in front of them—impassive as flat-fish.

And that evening I went up to the garrison post—one of the most coveted of all the army commands—and overlooked the City of the Saints as it lay in the circle of its forbidding hills. You can speculate a good deal about the mass of human misery, the loves frustrated, the gentle hearts broken, and the strong souls twisted from the law of life to a fiercer following of the law of death, that the hills have seen. How must it have been in the old days when the footsore emigrants broke through into the circle and knew that they were cut off from hope of return or sight of friends—were handed over to the power of the friends that called themselves priests of the Most High? 'But for the grace of God there goes Richard

Baxter,' as the eminent divine once said. It seemed good that fate did not order me to be a brick in the up-building of the Mormon Church, that has so aptly established herself by the borders of a lake bitter, salt, and hopeless.

No. XXXIII

HOW I MET CERTAIN PEOPLE OF IMPORTANCE BETWEEN SALT LAKE AND OMAHA

Much have I seen,
Cities and men.

LET there be no misunderstanding about the matter. I love this People, and if any contemptuous criticism has to be done, I will do it myself. My heart has gone out to them beyond all other peoples; and for the life of me I cannot tell why. They are bleeding-raw at the edges, almost more conceited than the English, vulgar with a massive vulgarity which is as though the Pyramids were coated with Christmas-cake sugar-works. Cocksure they are, lawless and as casual as they are cocksure; but I love them, and I realised it when I met an Englishman who laughed at them. He proved conclusively that they were all wrong, from their tariff to their go-as-you-please Civil Service, and beneath the consideration of a true Briton.

'I admit everything,' said I. 'Their Government's provisional; their law's the notion of the moment; their railways are made of hairpins and match-sticks, and most of their good luck lives in their woods and mines and rivers and not in their brains; but for all that, they be the biggest, finest, and best people on the surface of the globe! Just you wait a hundred years and see how they'll behave when they've had the screw put on them and have forgotten a few of the patriarchal teachings of the late Mister George Washington. Wait till the Anglo-American-German-Jew—the Man of the Future—is properly equipped. He'll have just the least little kink in his hair now and again; he'll carry the English lungs above the Teuton feet that can walk for ever; and he will wave long, thin, bony Yankee hands with the big blue veins on the wrist, from one end of the earth to the other. He'll be the finest writer, poet, and dramatist, 'specially dramatist, that the world as it recollects itself has ever seen. By virtue of his Jew blood—just a little, little drop—he'll be a musician and a painter too. At present there is too much balcony and too little Romeo in the life-plays of his fellow-citizens. Later on, when the proportion is adjusted and he sees the possibilities of his land, he will produce things that will make the effete East stare. He will also be a complex and highly composite administrator. There is nothing known to man that he will not be, and his country will sway the world with one foot as a man tilts a see-saw plank!'

'But this is worse than the Eagle at its worst. Do you seriously believe all that?' said the Englishman.

'If I believe anything seriously, all this I most firmly believe. You wait and see. Sixty million people, chiefly of English instincts, who are trained from youth to believe that nothing is impossible, don't slink through the centuries like Russian peasantry. They are bound to leave their mark somewhere, and don't you forget it.'

But isn't it sad to think that with all Eternity behind and before us we cannot, even though we would pay for it with sorrow, filch from the Immensities one hundred poor years of life, wherein to watch the two Great Experiments? A hundred years hence India and America will be worth observing. At present the one is burned out and the other is only just stoking up. When I left my opponent there was much need for faith, because I fell into the hands of a perfectly delightful man whom I had met casually in the street, sitting in a chair on the pavement, smoking a huge cigar. He was a commercial traveller, and his beat lay through Southern Mexico, and he told me tales, of forgotten cities, stone gods up to their sacred eyes in forest growth, Mexican priests, rebellions, and dictatorships, that made my hair curl. It was he who dragged me forth to bathe in Salt Lake, which is some fifteen miles away from the city, and reachable by many trains which are but open tram-cars. The track, like all American tracks, was terrifying in its roughness; and the end of the journey disclosed the nakedness of the accommodation. There were piers and band houses and refreshment stalls built over the solid grey levels of the lake, but they only accentuated the utter barrenness of the place. Americans don't mix with their scenery as yet.

And 'Have faith,' said the commercial traveller s he walked into water heavy as quicksilver. Walk!' I walked, and I walked till my legs lew up and I had to walk as one struggling with high wind, but still I rode head and shoulders bove the water. It was a horrible feeling, this nability to sink. Swimming was not much use. You couldn't get a grip of the water, so I e'en sat ne down and drifted like a luxurious anemone mong the hundreds that were bathing in that place. You could wallow for three-quarters of an hour in that warm, sticky brine and fear no evil onsequences; but when you came out you were oated with white salt from top to toe. And if you accidentally swallowed a mouthful of the water, you died. This is true, because I swallowed half a nouthful and was half-dead in consequence.

The commercial traveller on our return journey across the level flats that fringe the lake's edge nade me note some of the customs of his people The great open railway car held about a hundred men and maidens, 'coming up with a song from the sea.' They sang and they shouted and they exchanged witticisms of the most poignant, and comported themselves like their brothers and sisters over the seas—the 'Arries and the Arriets of the older world. And there sat behind me two modest maidens in white, alone and unattended. To these the privileged youth of he car—a youth of a marvellous range of voice—proffered undying affection. They laughed, but nade no reply in words. The suit was renewed, and with extravagant imagery; the nearest seats applauding. When we arrived at the city the maidens turned and went their way up a dark tree-shaded street, and the boys elsewhere. Whereat, recollecting what the London rough was like, I marvelled that they did not pursue. 'It's all right,' said the commercial traveller. 'If they had followed—well, I guess some one would ha' shot 'em.' The very next day on those very peaceful cars returning from the Lake some one was shot—dead. He was what they call a 'sport,' which is American for a finished 'leg,' and he had an argument with a police officer, and the latter slew him. I saw his funeral go down the main street. There were nearly thirty carriages, filled with doubtful men, and women not in the least doubtful, and the local papers said that deceased had his merits, but it didn't much matter, because if the Sheriff hadn't dropped him he would assuredly have dropped the Sheriff. Somehow this jarred on my sensitive feelings, and I went away, though the commercial traveller would fain have entertained me in his own house, he knowing not my name. Twice through the long hot nights we talked, tilting up our chairs on the sidewalk, of the future of America.

You should hear the Saga of the States reeled off by a young and enthusiastic citizen who had just carved out for himself a home, filled it with a pretty little wife, and is preparing to embark on commerce on his own account. I was tempted to believe that pistol-shots were regrettable accidents and lawlessness only the top-scum on the great sea of humanity. I am tempted to believe that still, hough baked and dusty Utah is very many miles ehind me.

Then chance threw me into the arms of another nd very different commercial traveller, as we ulled out of Utah on our way to Omaha *via* the Rockies. He travelled in biscuits, of which more non, and Fate had smitten him very heavily, aving at one stroke knocked all the beauty and oy out of his poor life. So he journeyed with a ase of samples as one dazed, and his eyes took no leasure in anything that he saw. In his despair e had withdrawn himself to his religion,—he was Baptist,—and spoke of its consolation with the rtless freedom that an American generally exhibits hen he is talking about his most sacred private ffairs. There was a desert beyond Utah, hot nd barren as Mian Mir in May. The sun baked he car-roof, and the dust caked the windows, and rough the dust and the glare the man with the iscuits bore witness to his creed, which seems to nclude one of the greatest miracles in the world— ne immediate unforeseen, self-conscious redemp-on of the soul by means very similar to those hich turned Paul to the straight path.

'You must experi*ence* religion,' he repeated, his outh twitching and his eyes black-ringed with is recent loss. 'You must experi*ence* religion. ou can't tell when you're goin' to get, or haow; ut it will come—it will come, Sir, like a lightning roke, an' you will wrestle with yourself before ou receive full conviction and assurance.'

'How long does that take?' I asked reverently.

'It may take hours. It may take days. I knew

a man in San Jo who lay under conviction for a month an' then he got the sperrit—as you *must* git it.'

'And then?'

'And then you are saved. You feel that, an' you can endure anything,' he sighed. 'Yes, anything. I don't care what it is, though I allow that some things are harder than others.'

'Then you have to wait for the miracle to be worked by powers outside yourself. And if the miracle doesn't work?'

'But it *must*. I tell you it must. It comes to all who profess with faith.'

I learned a good deal about that creed as the train fled on; and I wondered as I learned. It was a strange thing to watch that poor human soul, broken and bowed by its loss, nerving itself against each new pang of pain with the iterated assurance that it was safe against the pains of Hell.

The heat was stifling. We quitted the desert and launched into the rolling green plains of Colorado. Dozing uneasily with every removable rag removed, I was roused by a blast of intense cold, and the drumming of a hundred drums. The train had stopped. Far as the eye could range the land was white under two feet of hail—each hailstone as big as the top of a sherry-glass. I saw a young colt by the side of the track standing with his poor little fluffy back to the pitiless pelting. He was pounded to death. An old horse met his doom on the run. He galloped wildly towards the train, but his hind legs dropped into a hole half water and half ice. He beat the ground with his fore-feet for a minute and then rolling over on his side submitted quietly to be killed.

When the storm ceased, we picked our way cautiously and crippledly over a track that might give way at any moment. The Western driver urges his train much as does the Subaltern the bounding pony, and 'twould seem with an equal sense of responsibility. If a foot does go wrong, why there you are, don't you know, and if it is all right, why all right it is, don't you know. But I would sooner be on the pony than the train.

This seems a good place wherein to preach on American versatility. When Mr. Howells writes a novel, when a reckless hero dams a flood by heaving a dynamite-shattered mountain into it, or when a notoriety-hunting preacher marries a couple in a balloon, you shall hear the great American press rise on its hind-legs and walk round mouthing over the versatility of the American citizen. And he is versatile—horribly so. The unlimited exercise of the right of private judgment (which, by the way, is a weapon not one man in ten is competent to handle), his blatant cocksureness, and the dry-air-bred restlessness that makes him crawl all over the furniture when he is talking to you, conspire to make him versatile. But what he calls versatility the impartial bystander of Anglo-Indian extraction is apt to deem mere casualness, and dangerous casualness at that. No man can grasp the inwardness of an employ by the light of pure reason—even though that reason be Republican. He must serve an apprenticeship to one craft and learn that craft all the days of his life if he wishes to excel therein. Otherwise he merely 'puts the thing through somehow'; and occasionally he doesn't. But wherein lies the beauty of this form of mental suppleness? Old man California, whom I shall love and respect always, told me one or two anecdotes about American versatility and its consequences that came back to my mind with direful force as the train progressed. We didn't upset, but I don't think that that was the fault of the driver or the men who made the track. Take up—you can easily find them—the accounts of ten consecutive railway catastrophes—not little accidents, but first-class fatalities, when the long cars turn over, take fire, and roast the luckless occupants alive. To seven out of the ten you shall find appended the cheerful statement: 'The accident is supposed to have been due to the rails spreading.' That means the metals were spiked down to the ties with such versatility that the spikes or the tracks drew under the constant vibration of the traffic, and the metals opened out. No one is hanged for these little affairs.

We began to climb hills, and then we stopped—at night in darkness, while men threw sand under the wheels and crowbarred the track and then 'guessed' that we might proceed. Not being in the least anxious to face my Maker half asleep and rubbing my eyes, I went forward to a common car, and was rewarded by two hours' conversation with the stranded, broken-down, husband-abandoned actress of a fourth-rate, stranded, broken-down, manager-bereft company. She was muzzy with beer, reduced to her last dollar, fearful that there would be no one to meet her at Omaha, and wept at intervals because she had given the conductor a five-dollar bill to change, and he hadn't come back. He was an Irishman, so I knew he couldn't steal; and I addressed myself to the task of consolation. I was rewarded, after a decent interval, by the history of a life so wild, so mixed, so desperately improbable, and yet so simply probable, and above all so quick—not fast—in its kaleidoscopic changes that the *Pioneer* would reject any summary of it. And so you will never know how she, the beery woman with the tangled blonde hair, was once a girl on a farm in far-off New Jersey. How he, a travelling actor, had wooed and won her,—'but Paw he was always set against Alf,'—and how he and she embarked all their little capital on the word of a faithless manager who disbanded his company a hundred miles from nowhere, and how she and Alf and a third person who had not yet made any noise in the world, had to walk the railway-track and beg from the farm-houses; how that third person arrived and went away again with a wail, and how Alf took to the whisky, and other things still more calculated to make a wife unhappy; and how after barn-stormings, insults, shooting-scrapes, and pitiful collapses of poor companies, she had once won an encore. It was not a cheerful tale to listen to. There was a real actress in the Pullman,—such an one as travels sumptuously with a maid and dressing-case,—and my draggle-tail thought of appealing to her for help, but broke down after several attempts to walk into the car jauntily as befitted a sister in the profession. Then the conductor reappeared, — the five-dollar bill honestly changed,—and she wept by reason of beer and gratitude together, and then fell asleep waveringly, alone in the car, and became almost beautiful and quite kissable ; while the Man with the Sorrow stood at the door between actress and actress and preached grim sermons on the certain end of each if they did not mend their ways and find regeneration through the miracle of the Baptist creed. Yes, we were a queer company going up to the Rockies together. I was the luckiest, because when a break-down occurred, and we were delayed for twelve hours, I ate all the Baptist's sample-biscuits. They were various in composition, but nourishing. Always travel with a 'drummer.'

No. XXXIV

ACROSS THE GREAT DIVIDE; AND HOW THE MAN GRING SHOWED ME THE GARMENTS OF THE ELLEWOMEN.

After much dallying and more climbing we came to a pass like all the Bolan Passes in the world, and the Black Cañon of the Gunnison called they it. We had been climbing for very many hours, and attained a modest elevation of some seven or eight thousand feet above the sea, when we entered a gorge, remote from the sun, where the rocks were two thousand feet sheer, and where a rock-splintered river roared and howled ten feet below a track which seemed to have been built on the simple principle of dropping miscellaneous dirt into the river and pinning a few rails a-top. There was a glory and a wonder and a mystery about that mad ride which I felt keenly (you will find it properly dressed up in the guide-books), until I had to offer prayers for the safety of the train. There was no hope of seeing the track two hundred yards ahead. We seemed to be running into the bowels of the earth at the invitation of an irresponsible stream. Then the solid rock would open and disclose a curve of awful twistfulness. Then the driver put on all steam, and we would go round that curve on one wheel chiefly, the Gunnison River gnashing its teeth below. The cars overhung the edge of the water, and if a single one of the rails had chosen to spread, nothing in the wide world could have saved us from drowning. I knew we should damage something in the end—the sombre horrors of the gorge, the rush of the jade-green water below, and the cheerful tales told by the conductor made me certain of the catastrophe.

We had just cleared the Black Cañon and another gorge, and were sailing out into open country nine thousand feet above the level of the sea, when we came most suddenly round a corner upon a causeway across a waste water—half dam and half quarry-pool. The locomotive gave one wild 'Hoo! Hoo! Hoo!' but it was too late. He was a beautiful bull, and goodness only knows why he had chosen the track for a constitutional with his wife. She was flung to the left, but the cow-catcher caught him, and turning him round, heaved him shoulder-deep into the pool. The expression of blank, blind bewilderment on his bovine, jovine face was wonderful to behold. He was not angry. I don't think he was even scared, though he must have flown ten yards through the air. All he wanted to know was: 'Will somebody have the goodness to tell a respectable old gentleman what in the world, or out of it, has occurred?' And five minutes later the stream that had been snapping at our heels in the gorges split itself into a dozen silver threads on a breezy upland, and became an innocent trout beck, and we halted at a half-dead city, the name of which does not remain with me. It had originally been built on the crest of a wave of prosperity. Once ten thousand people had walked its street; but the boom had collapsed. The great brick houses and the factories were empty. The population lived in little timber shanties on the fringes of the deserted town. There were some railway workshops and things, and the hotel (whose pavement formed the platform of the station) contained one hundred and more rooms—empty. The place, in its half-inhabitedness, was more desolate than Amber or Chitor. But a man said: 'Trout—six pounds—two miles away,' and the Sorrowful Man and myself went in search of 'em. The town was ringed by a circle of hills all alive with little thunder-storms that broke across the soft green of the plain in wisps and washes of smoke and amber.

To our tiny party associated himself a lawyer from Chicago. We forgathered on the question of flies, but I didn't expect to meet Elijah Pogram in the flesh. He delivered orations on the future of England and America, and of the Great Federation that the years will bring forth when America and England will belt the globe with their linked hands. According to the notions of the British, he made an ass of himself, but for all his high-falutin he talked sense. I might knock through England on a four months' tour and not find a man capable of putting into words the passionate patriotism that possessed the little Chicago lawyer. And he was a man with points, for he offered me three days' shooting in Illinois, if I would step out of my path a little. I might travel for ten years up and down England ere I found a man who would give a complete stranger so much as a sandwich, and for twenty ere I squeezed as much enthusiasm out of a Britisher. He and I talked politics and trout-flies all one sultry day as we wandered up and down the shallows of the stream aforesaid. Little fish are sweet. I spent two hours whipping a ripple for a fish that I knew was there, and in the pasture-scented dusk caught a three-pounder on a ragged old brown hackle and landed him after ten minutes' excited argument. He was a beauty. If ever any man works the Western trout-streams, he would do well to bring out with him the dingiest flies he possesses. The natives laugh at the tiny English hooks, but they hold; and duns and drabs and sober greys seem to tickle the æsthetic tastes of the trout. For salmon (but don't say that I told you) use the spoon—gold on one side, silver on the other. It is as killing as is a similar article with fish of another calibre. The natives seem to use much too coarse tackle.

It was a search for a small boy who should know the river that revealed to me a new phase of life—slack, slovenly, and shiftless, but very interesting. There was a family in a packing-case hut on the outskirts of the town. They had seen the city when it was on the boom and made pretence of being the metropolis of the Rockies; and when the boom was over, they did not go. She was affable, but deeply coated with dirt; he was grim and grimy, and the little children were simply caked with filth of various descriptions. But they lived in a certain sort of squalid luxury, six or eight of them in two rooms; and they enjoyed the local society. It was their eight-year-old son whom I tried to take out with me, but he had been catching trout all his life and 'guessed he didn't feel like coming,' though I proffered him six shillings for what ought to have been a day's pleasuring. 'I'll stay with Maw,' he said, and from that attitude I could not move him. Maw didn't attempt to argue with him. 'If he says he won't come, he won't,' she said, as though he were one of the elemental forces of nature instead of a spankable brat; and 'Paw,' lounging by the stove, refused to interfere. Maw told me that she had been a school-teacher in her not-so-distant youth, but did not tell me what I was dying to know—how she arrived at this mucky tenement at the back of beyond, and why. Though preserving the prettinesses of her New England speech, she had come to regard washing as a luxury. Paw chewed tobacco and spat from time to time. Yet, when he opened his mouth for other purposes, he spoke like a well-educated man. There was a story there, but I couldn't get at it.

Next day the Man with the Sorrow and myself and a few others began the real ascent of the Rockies; up to that time our climbing didn't count. The train ran violently up a steep place and was taken to pieces. Five cars were hitched on to two locomotives, and two cars to one locomotive. This seemed to be a kind and thoughtful act, but I was idiot enough to go forward and watch the coupling-on of the two rear cars in which Cæsar and his fortunes were to travel. Some one had lost or eaten the regularly ordained coupling, and a man picked up from the tailboard of the engine a single iron link about as thick as a fetter-link watch-chain, and 'guessed it would do.' Get hauled up a Simla cliff by the hook of a lady's parasol if you wish to appreciate my sentiments when the cars moved uphill and the link drew tight. Miles away and two thousand feet above our heads rose the shoulder of a hill epauletted with the long line of a snow-tunnel. The first section of the cars crawled a quarter of a mile ahead of us, the track snaked and looped behind, and there was a black drop to the left. So we went up and up and up till the thin air grew thinner and the *chunk-chunk-chunk* of the labouring locomotive was answered by the oppressed beating of the exhausted heart. Through the chequered light and shade of the snow-tunnels (horrible caverns of rude timbering) we ground our way, halting now and again to allow a down-train to pass. One monster of forty mineral-cars slid past, scarce held by four locomotives, their brakes screaming and chortling in chorus; and in the end, after a glimpse at half America spread mapwise leagues below us, we halted at the head of the longest snow-tunnel of all, on the crest of the divide, between ten and eleven thousand feet above the level of the sea. The locomotive wished to draw breath, and the passengers to gather the flowers that nodded impertinently through the chinks of the boarding. A lady passenger's nose began to bleed, and other ladies threw themselves down on the seats and gasped with the gasping train, while a wind as keen as a knife-edge rioted down the grimy tunnel.

Then, despatching a pilot-engine to clear the way, we began the downward portion of the journey with every available brake on, and frequent shrieks, till after some hours we reached the level plain, and later the city of Denver, where the Man with the Sorrow went his way and left me to journey on to Omaha alone, after one hasty glance at Denver. The pulse of that town was too like the rushing mighty wind in the Rocky Mountain tunnel. It made me tired because complete strangers desired me to do something to mines which were in mountains, and to purchase building blocks upon inaccessible cliffs; and once, a woman urged that I should supply her with strong drinks. I had almost forgotten that such attacks were possible in any land, for the outward and visible signs of public morality in American towns are generally safe-guarded. For that I respect this people. Omaha, Nebraska, was but a halting-place on the road to Chicago, but it revealed to me horrors that I would not willingly have missed. The city to casual investigation seemed to be populated entirely by Germans, Poles, Slavs, Hungarians, Croats, Magyars, and all the scum of the Eastern European States, but it must have been laid out by Americans. No other people would cut the traffic of a main street with two streams of railway lines, each some eight or nine tracks wide, and cheerfully drive tram-cars across the metals. Every now and again they have horrible railway-crossing accidents at Omaha, but nobody seems to think of building an over-head-bridge. That would interfere with the vested interests of the undertakers.

Be blessed to hear some details of one of that class.

There was a shop the like of which I had never seen before: its windows were filled with dress-coats for men, and dresses for women. But the studs of the shirts were made of stamped cloth upon the shirt front, and there were no trousers to those coats—nothing but a sweep of cheap black cloth falling like an abbé's frock. In the doorway sat a young man reading Pollock's *Course of Time*, and by that I knew that he was an undertaker. His name was Gring, which is a beautiful name, and I talked to him on the mysteries of his Craft. He was an enthusiast and an artist. I told him how corpses were burnt in India. Said he: 'We're vastly superior. We hold—that is to say, embalm—our dead. So!' Whereupon he produced the horrible weapons of his trade, and most practically showed me how you 'held' a man back from that corruption which is his birthright. 'And I wish I could live a few generations just to see how my people keep. But I'm sure it's all right. Nothing can touch 'em after *I*'ve embalmed 'em.' Then he displayed one of those ghastly dress-suits, and when I laid a shuddering hand upon it, behold it crumpled to nothing, for the white linen was sewn on to the black cloth and—

there was no back to it! That was the horror The garment was a shell. 'We dress a man in that,' said Gring, laying it out tastily on the counter. 'As you see here, our caskets have a plate-glass window in front' (Oh me, but that window in the coffin was fitted with plush like a brougham window!), 'and you don't see anything below the level of the man's waistcoat. Consequently . . .' He unrolled the terrible cheap black cloth that falls down over the stark feet, and I jumped back. 'Of course a man can be dressed in his own clothes if he likes, but these are the regular things: and for women look at this!' He took up the body of a high-necked dinner-dress in subdued lilac, slashed and puffed and bedevilled with black, but, like the dress-suit, backless, and below the waist turning to shroud. 'That's for an old maid. But for young girls we give white with imitation pearls round the neck. That looks very pretty through the window of the casket—you see there's a cushion for the head—with flowers banked all round.' Can you imagine anything more awful than to take your last rest as much of a dead fraud as ever you were a living lie—to go into the darkness one half of you shaved, trimmed and dressed for an evening party, while the other half—the half that your friends cannot see—is enwrapped in a flapping black sheet?

I know a little about burial customs in various places in the world, and I tried hard to make Mr. Gring comprehend dimly the awful heathendom that he was responsible for—the grotesquerie—the giggling horror of it all. But he couldn't see it. Even when he showed me a little boy's last suit, he couldn't see it. He said it was quite right to embalm and trick out and hypocritically bedizen the poor innocent dead in their superior cushioned and pillowed caskets with the window in front.

Bury me cased in canvas like a fishing-rod, in the deep sea; burn me on a back-water of the Hughli with damp wood and no oil; pin me under a Pullman car and let the lighted stove do its worst; sizzle me with a fallen electric wire or whelm me in the sludge of a broken river dam; but may I never go down to the Pit grinning out of a plate-glass window, in a backless dress-coat, and the front half of a black stuff dressing-gown; not though I were 'held' against the ravage of the grave for ever and ever. Amen!

No. XXXV

HOW I STRUCK CHICAGO, AND HOW CHICAGO STRUCK ME. OF RELIGION, POLITICS, AND PIG-STICKING, AND THE INCARNATION OF THE CITY AMONG SHAMBLES.

> I know thy cunning and thy greed,
> Thy hard, high lust and wilful deed,
> And all thy glory loves to tell
> Of specious gifts material.

I HAVE struck a city,—a real city,—and they call it Chicago. The other places do not count. San Francisco was a pleasure-resort as well as a city, and Salt Lake was a phenomenon. This place is the first American city I have encountered. It holds rather more than a million people with bodies, and stands on the same sort of soil as Calcutta. Having seen it, I urgently desire never to see it again. It is inhabited by savages. Its water is the water of the Hughli, and its air is dirt. Also it says that it is the 'boss' town of America.

I do not believe that it has anything to do with this country. They told me to go to the Palmer House, which is a gilded and mirrored rabbit-warren, and there I found a huge hall of tessellated marble, crammed with people talking about money and spitting about everywhere. Other barbarians charged in and out of this inferno with letters and telegrams in their hands, and yet others shouted at each other. A man who had drunk quite as much as was good for him told me that this was 'the finest hotel in the finest city on God Almighty's earth.' By the way, when an American wishes to indicate the next county or State he says, 'God A'mighty's earth.' This prevents discussion and flatters his vanity.

Then I went out into the streets, which are long and flat and without end. And verily it is not a good thing to live in the East for any length of time. Your ideas grow to clash with those held by every right-thinking white man. I looked down interminable vistas flanked with nine, ten, and fifteen storied houses, and crowded with men and women, and the show impressed me with a great horror. Except in London—and I have forgotten what London is like—I had never seen so many white people together, and never such a collection of miserables. There was no colour in the street and no beauty—only a maze of wire-ropes overhead and dirty stone flagging underfoot. A cab-driver volunteered to show me the glory of the town for so much an hour, and with him I wandered far. He conceived that all this turmoil and squash was a thing to be reverently admired; that it was good to huddle men together in fifteen layers, one atop of the other, and to dig holes in the ground for offices. He said that Chicago was a live town, and that all the creatures hurrying by me were engaged in business. That is to say, they were trying to make some money, that they might not die through lack of food to put into their bellies. He took me to canals, black as ink, and filled with untold abominations, and bade me watch the stream of traffic across the bridges. He then took me into a saloon, and, while I drank, made me note that the floor was covered with coins sunk into cement. A Hottentot would not have been guilty of this sort of barbarism. The coins made an effect pretty enough, but the man who put them there had no thought to beauty, and therefore he was a savage. Then my cab-driver showed me business-blocks, gay with signs and studded with fantastic and absurd advertisements of goods, and looking down the long street so adorned it was as though each vender stood at his door howling: 'For the sake of money, employ or buy of *me* and me only!' Have you ever seen a crowd at our famine-relief distributions? You know then how men leap into the air, stretching out their arms above the crowd in the hope of being seen; while the women dolorously slap the stomachs of their children and whimper. I had sooner watch famine-relief than the white man engaged in what he calls legitimate competition. The one I understand. The other makes me ill. And the cabman said that these things were the proof of progress; and by that I knew he had been reading his newspaper, as every intelligent

American should. The papers tell their readers in language fitted to their comprehension that the snarling together of telegraph wires, the heaving up of houses, and the making of money is progress.

I spent ten hours in that huge wilderness, wandering through scores of miles of these terrible streets, and jostling some few hundred thousand of these terrible people who talked money through their noses. The cabman left me: but after a while I picked up another man who was full of figures, and into my ears he poured them as occasion required or the big blank factories suggested. Here they turned out so many hundred thousand dollars' worth of such and such an article; there so many million other things; this house was worth so many million dollars; that one so many million more or less. It was like listening to a child babbling of its hoard of shells. It was like watching a fool playing with buttons. But I was expected to do more than listen or watch. He demanded that I should admire; and the utmost that I could say was: 'Are these things so? Then I am very sorry for you.' That made him angry, and he said that insular envy made me unresponsive. So you see I could not make him understand.

About four and a half hours after Adam was turned out of the garden of Eden he felt hungry, and so, bidding Eve take care that her head was not broken by the descending fruit, shinned up a cocoanut palm. That hurt his legs, cut his breast, and made him breathe heavily, and Eve was tormented with fear lest her lord should miss his footing and so bring the tragedy of this world to an end ere the curtain had fairly risen. Had I met Adam then, I should have been sorry for him. To-day I find eleven hundred thousand of his sons just as far advanced as their father in the art of getting food, and immeasurably inferior to him in that they think that their palm-trees lead straight to the skies. Consequently I am sorry in rather more than a million different ways. In our East bread comes naturally even to the poorest by a little scratching or the gift of a friend not quite so poor. In less favoured countries one is apt to forget. Then I went to bed. And that was on a Saturday night.

Sunday brought me the queerest experience of all—a revelation of barbarism complete. I found a place that was officially described as a church. It was a circus really, but that the worshippers did not know. There were flowers all about the building, which was fitted up with plush and stained oak and much luxury, including twisted brass candlesticks of severest Gothic design. To these things, and a congregation of savages, entered suddenly a wonderful man completely in the confidence of their God, whom he treated colloquially and exploited very much as a newspaper reporter would exploit a foreign potentate. But, unlike the newspaper reporter, he never allowed his listeners to forget that he and not He was the centre of attraction. With a voice of silver and with imagery borrowed from the auction-room, he built up for his hearers a heaven on the lines of the Palmer House (but with all the gilding real gold and all the plate-glass diamond) and set in the centre of it a loud-voiced, argumentative, and very shrewd creation that he called God. One sentence at this point caught my delighted ear. It was *apropos* of some question of the Judgment Day and ran: 'No! I tell you God doesn't do business that way.' He was giving them a deity whom they could comprehend, in a gold and jewel heaven in which they could take a natural interest. He interlarded his performance with the slang of the streets, the counter, and the Exchange, and he said that religion ought to enter into daily life. Consequently I presume he introduced it *as* daily life—his own and the life of his friends.

Then I escaped before the blessing, desiring no benediction at such hands. But the persons who listened seemed to enjoy themselves, and I understood that I had met with a popular preacher. Later on when I had perused the sermons of a gentleman called Talmage and some others, I perceived that I had been listening to a very mild specimen. Yet that man, with his brutal gold and silver idols, his hands-in-pocket, cigar-in-mouth, and hat-on-the-back-of-the-head style of dealing with the sacred vessels would count himself spiritually quite competent to send a mission to convert the Indians. All that Sunday I listened to people who said that the mere fact of spiking down strips of iron to wood and getting a steam and iron thing to run along them was progress. That the telephone was progress, and the network of wires overhead was progress. They repeated their statements again and again. One of them took me to their city hall and board of trade works and pointed it out with pride. It was very ugly, but very big, and the streets in front of it were narrow and unclean. When I saw the faces of the men who did business in that building I felt that there had been a mistake in their billeting.

By the way, 'tis a consolation to feel that I am not writing to an English audience. Then should I have to fall into feigned ecstasies over the marvellous progress of Chicago since the days of the great fire, to allude casually to the raising of the entire city so many feet above the level of the lake which it faces, and generally to grovel before the golden calf. But you, who are desperately poor, and therefore by these standards of no account, know things, and will understand when I write that they have managed to get a million of men together on flat land, and that the bulk of these men appear to be lower than *mahajans* and not so companionable as a punjabi *jat* after harvest. But I don't think it was the blind hurry of the people, their argot, and their grand ignorance of things beyond their immediate interests that displeased me so much as a study of the daily papers of Chicago. Imprimis, there was some sort of dispute between New York and Chicago as to which town should give an exhibition of products to be hereafter holden, and through the medium of their more dignified journals the two cities were ya-hooing and hi-yi-ing at each other like opposition newsboys. They called it humour, but it sounded like something quite different. That was only the first trouble. The second lay in the tone of the productions. Leading articles which include gems such as: 'Back of such and such a place,' or 'We noticed, Tuesday, such an event,' or 'don't' for 'does not' are things to be accepted with thankfulness. All that made me want to cry was that, in these papers, were faithfully reproduced all the war-cries and 'back-talk' of the Palmer House bar, the slang of the barbers' shops, the mental elevation and integrity of the Pullman-car porter, the dignity of the Dime Museum, and the accuracy of the excited fishwife. I am sternly forbidden to believe that the paper educates the public. Then I am compelled to believe that the public educate the paper?

Just when the sense of unreality and oppression were strongest upon me, and when I most wanted help, a man sat at my side and began to talk what he called politics. I had chanced to pay about six shillings for a travelling-cap worth eighteen pence, and he made of the fact a text for a sermon. He said that this was a rich country and that the people liked to pay two hundred per cent on the value of a thing. They could afford it. He said that the Government imposed a protective duty of from ten to seventy per cent on foreign-made articles, and that the American manufacturer consequently could sell his goods for a healthy sum. Thus an imported hat would, with duty, cost two guineas. The American manufacturer would make a hat for seventeen shillings and sell it for one pound fifteen. In these things, he said, lay the greatness of America and the effeteness of England. Competition between factory and factory kept the prices down to decent limits, but I was never to forget that this people were a rich people, not like the pauper Continentals, and that they enjoyed paying duties. To my weak intellect this seemed rather like juggling with counters. Everything that I have yet purchased costs about twice as much as it would in England, and when native-made is of inferior quality. Moreover, since these lines were first thought of I have visited a gentleman who owned a factory which used to produce things. He owned the factory still. Not a man was in it, but he was drawing a handsome income from a syndicate of firms for keeping it closed in order that it might not produce things. This man said that if protection were abandoned, a tide of pauper labour would flood the country, and as I looked at his factory I thought how entirely better it was to have no labour of any kind whatever, rather than face so horrible a future. Meantime, do you remember that this peculiar country enjoys paying money for value not received. I am an alien, and for the life of me cannot see why six shillings should be paid for eighteen-penny caps, or eight shillings for half-crown cigar-cases. When the country fills up to a decently populated level a few million people who are not aliens will be smitten with the same sort of blindness.

But my friend's assertion somehow thoroughly suited the grotesque ferocity of Chicago. See now and judge! In the village of Isser Jang on the road to Montgomery there be four *changar* women who winnow corn—some seventy bushels a year. Beyond their hut lives Puran Dass, the money-lender, who on good security lends as much as five thousand rupees in a year. Jowala Singh, the *lohar*, mends the village ploughs—some thirty, broken at the share, in three hundred and sixty-five days; and Hukm Chund, who is letter-writer and head of the little club under the travellers' tree, generally keeps the village posted in such gossip as the barber and the midwife have not yet made public property. Chicago husks and winnows her wheat by the million bushels, a hundred banks lend hundreds of millions of dollars in the year, and scores of factories turn out plough gear and machinery by steam. Scores of daily papers do work which Hukm Chund and the barber and the midwife perform, with due regard for public opinion, in the village of Isser Jang. So far as manufactures go, the difference between Chicago on the lake and Isser Jang on the Montgomery road is one of degree only, and not of kind. As far as the understanding of the uses of life goes Isser Jang, for all its seasonal cholera, has the advantage over Chicago. Jowala Singh knows and takes care to avoid the three or four ghoul-haunted fields on the outskirts of the village; but he is not urged by millions of devils to run about all day in the sun and swear that his ploughshares are the best in the Punjab; nor does Puran Dass fly forth in a cart more than once or twice a year, and he knows, on a pinch, how to use the railway and the telegraph as well as any son of Israel in

Chicago. But this is absurd. The East is not the West, and these men must continue to deal with the machinery of life, and to call it progress. Their very preachers dare not rebuke them. They gloss over the hunting for money and the twice-sharpened bitterness of Adam's curse by saying that such things dower a man with a larger range of thoughts and higher aspirations. They do not say: 'Free yourself from your own slavery,' but rather, 'If you can possibly manage it, do not set quite so much store on the things of this world.' And they do not know what the things of this world are.

I went off to see cattle killed by way of clearing my head, which, as you will perceive, was getting muddled. They say every Englishman goes to the Chicago stock-yards. You shall find them about six miles from the city; and once having seen them will never forget the sight. As far as the eye can reach stretches a township of cattle-pens, cunningly divided into blocks so that the animals of any pen can be speedily driven out close to an inclined timber path which leads to an elevated covered way straddling high above the pens. These viaducts are two-storied. On the upper story tramp the doomed cattle, stolidly for the most part. On the lower, with a scuffling of sharp hooves and multitudinous yells, run the pigs. The same end is appointed for each. Thus you will see the gangs of cattle waiting their turn—as they wait sometimes for days; and they need not be distressed by the sight of their fellows running about in the fear of death. All they know is that a man on horseback causes their next-door neighbours to move by means of a whip Certain bars and fences are unshipped, and, behold, that crowd have gone up the mouth of a sloping tunnel and return no more. It is different with the pigs. They shriek back the news of the exodus to their friends, and a hundred pens skirl responsive. It was to the pigs I first addressed myself. Selecting a viaduct which was full of them, as I could hear though I could not see, I marked a sombre building whereto it ran, and went there, not unalarmed by stray cattle who had managed to escape from their proper quarters. A pleasant smell of brine warned me of what was coming. I entered the factory and found it full of pork in barrels, and on another story more pork unbarrelled, and in a huge room, the halves of swine for whose use great lumps of ice were being pitched in at the window. That room was the mortuary chamber where the pigs lie for a little while in state ere they begin their progress through such passages as kings may sometimes travel. Turning a corner and not noting an overhead arrangement of greased rail, wheel, and pulley, I ran into the arms of four eviscerated carcasses, all pure white and of a human aspect, being pushed by a man clad in vehement red. When I leaped aside, the floor was slippery under me. There was a flavour of farmyard in my nostrils and the shouting of a multitude in my ears. But there was no joy in that shouting. Twelve men stood in two lines — six a-side. Between them and overhead ran the railway of death that had nearly shunted me through the window. Each man carried a knife, the sleeves of his shirt were cut off at the elbows, and from bosom to heel he was blood-red. The atmosphere was stifling as a night in the Rains, by reason of the steam and the crowd. I climbed to the beginning of things and, perched upon a narrow beam, overlooked very nearly all the pigs ever bred in Wisconsin. They had just been shot out of the mouth of the viaduct and huddled together in a large pen. Thence they were flicked persuasively, a few at a time, into a smaller chamber, and there a man fixed tackle on their hinder legs so that they rose in the air suspended from the railway of death. Oh! it was then they shrieked and called on their mothers and made promises of amendment, till the tackle-man punted them in their backs, and they slid head down into a brick-floored passage, very like a big kitchen sink that was blood-red. There awaited them a red man with a knife which he passed jauntily through their throats, and the full-voiced shriek became a sputter, and then a fall as of heavy tropical rain. The red man who was backed against the passage wall stood clear of the wildly kicking hooves and passed his hand over his eyes, not from any feeling of compassion, but because the spurted blood was in his eyes, and he had barely time to stick the next arrival. Then that first stuck swine dropped, still kicking, into a great vat of boiling water, and spoke no more words, but wallowed in obedience to some unseen machinery, and presently came forth at the lower end of the vat and was heaved on the blades of a blunt paddle-wheel-thing which said, 'Hough! Hough! Hough!' and skelped all the hair off him except what little a couple of men with knives could remove. Then he was again hitched by the heels to that sad railway and passed down the line of the twelve men—each man with a knife—leaving with each man a certain amount of his individuality which was taken away in a wheelbarrow, and when he reached the last man he was very beautiful to behold, but immensely unstuffed and limp. Preponderance of individuality was ever a bar to foreign travel. That pig could have been in no case to visit you in India had he not parted with some of his most cherished notions.

The dissecting part impressed me not so much as the slaying. They were so excessively alive, these pigs. And then they were so excessively dead, and the man in the dripping, clammy, hot passage did not seem to care, and ere the blood of such an one had ceased to foam on the floor, such another, and four friends with him, had shrieked and died. But a pig is only the Unclean animal—forbidden by the Prophet.

I was destined to make rather a queer discovery when I went over to the cattle-slaughter. All the buildings here were on a much larger scale, and there was no sound of trouble, but I could smell the salt reek of blood before I set foot in the place. The cattle did not come directly through the viaduct as the pigs had done. They debouched into a yard by the hundred, and they were big red brutes carrying much flesh. In the centre of that yard stood a red Texan steer with a head-stall on his wicked head. No man controlled him. He was, so to speak, picking his teeth and whistling in an open byre of his own when the cattle arrived. As soon as the first one had fearfully quitted the viaduct, this red devil put his hands in his pockets and slouched across the yard, no man guiding him. Then he lowed something to the effect that he was the regularly appointed guide of the establishment and would show them round. They were country folk, but they knew how to behave; and so followed Judas some hundred strong, patiently, and with a look of bland wonder in their faces. I saw his broad back jogging in advance of them, up a lime-washed incline where I was forbidden to follow. Then a door shut, and in a minute back came Judas with the air of a virtuous plough-bullock and took up his place in his byre. Somebody laughed across the yard, but I heard no sound of cattle from the big brick building into which the mob had disappeared. Only Judas chewed the cud with a malignant satisfaction, and so I knew there was trouble, and ran round to the front of the factory and so entered and stood aghast.

Who takes count of the prejudices which we absorb through the skin by way of our surroundings? It was not the spectacle that impressed me. The first thought that almost spoke itself aloud was: 'They are killing kine'; and it was a shock. The pigs were nobody's concern, but cattle—the brothers of the Cow, the Sacred Cow—were quite otherwise. The next time an M.P. tells me that India either Sultanises or Brahminises a man, I shall believe about half what he says. It is unpleasant to watch the slaughter of cattle when one has laughed at the notion for a few years. I could not see actually what was done in the first instance, because the row of stalls in which they lay was separated from me by fifty impassable feet of butchers and slung carcasses. All I know is that men swung open the doors of a stall as occasion required, and there lay two steers already stunned, and breathing heavily. These two they pole-axed, and half raising them by tackle they cut their throats. Two men skinned each carcass, somebody cut off the head, and in half a minute more the overhead rail carried two sides of beef to their appointed place. There was clamour enough in the operating-room, but from the waiting cattle, invisible on the other side of the line of pens, never a sound. They went to their death, trusting Judas, without a word. They were slain at the rate of five a minute, and if the pig men were spattered with blood, the cow butchers were bathed in it. The blood ran in muttering gutters. There was no place for hand or foot that was not coated with thicknesses of dried blood, and the stench of it in the nostrils bred fear.

And then the same merciful Providence that has showered good things on my path throughout sent me an embodiment of the city of Chicago, so that I might remember it forever. Women come sometimes to see the slaughter, as they would come to see the slaughter of men. And there entered that vermilion hall a young woman of large mould, with brilliantly scarlet lips, and heavy eyebrows, and dark hair that came in a 'widow's peak' on the forehead. She was well and healthy and alive, and she was dressed in flaming red and black, and her feet (know you that the feet of American women are like unto the feet of fairies?) her feet, I say, were cased in red leather shoes. She stood in a patch of sunlight, the red blood under her shoes, the vivid carcasses stacked round her, a bullock bleeding its life away not six feet away from her, and the death-factory roaring all round her. She looked curiously, with hard, bold eyes, and was not ashamed.

Then said I: 'This is a special Sending. I have seen the City of Chicago.' And I went away to get peace and rest.

No. XXXVI

HOW I FOUND PEACE AT MUSQUASH ON THE MONONGAHELA

Prince, blown by many a western breeze
Our vessels greet you treasure-laden ;
We send them all—but best of these
A free and frank young Yankee maiden.

It is a mean thing and an unhandsome to 'do' a continent in five-hundred-mile jumps. But after those swine and bullocks at Chicago I felt that complete change of air would be good. The United States at present hinge in or about Chicago, as a double-leaved screen hinges. To be sure, the tiny New England States call a trip to Pennsylvania 'going west,' but the larger-minded citizen seems to reckon his longitude from Chicago. Twenty years hence the centre of population—that shaded square on the census map — will have shifted, men say, far west of Chicago. Twenty years later it will be on the Pacific slope. Twenty years after that America will begin to crowd up, and there will be some trouble. People will demand manufactured goods for their reduced-establishment households at the cheapest possible rates; and the cry that the land is rich enough to afford protection will cease with a great abruptness. At present it is the farmer who pays most dearly for the luxury of high prices. In the old days, when the land was fresh and there was plenty of it and it cropped like the Garden of Eden, he did not mind paying. Now there is not so much free land, and the old acres are needing stimulants, which cost money, and the farmer, who pays for everything, is beginning to ask questions. Also the great American Nation, which individually never shuts a door behind its noble self, very seldom attempts to put back anything that it has taken from Nature's shelves. It grabs all it can and moves on. But the moving-on is nearly finished and the grabbing must stop, and then the Federal Government will have to establish a Woods and Forests Department the like of which was never seen in the world before. And all the people who have been accustomed to hack, mangle, and burn timber as they please will object, with shots and protestations, to this infringement of their rights. The nigger will breed bounteously, and *he* will have to be reckoned with; and the manufacturer will have to be contented with smaller profits, and *he* will have to be reckoned with; and the railways will no longer rule the countries through which they run, and they will have to be reckoned with. And nobody will approve of it in the least.

Yes; it will be a spectacle for all the world to watch, this big, slashing colt of a nation, that has got off with a flying start on a freshly littered course, being pulled back to the ruck by that very mutton-fisted jockey Necessity. There will be excitement in America when a few score millions of 'sovereigns' discover that what they consider the outcome of their own Government is but the rapidly diminishing bounty of Nature; and that if they want to get on comfortably they must tackle every single problem from labour to finance humbly, without gasconade, and afresh. But at present they look 'that all the to-morrows shall be as to-day,' and if you argue with them they say that the Democratic Idea will keep things going. They believe in that Idea, and the less well-informed fortify themselves in their belief by curious assertions as to the despotism that exists in England. This is pure provincialism, of course; but it is very funny to listen to, especially when you compare the theory with the practice (pistol, chiefly) as proven in the newspapers. I have striven to find out where the central authority of the land lies. It isn't at Washington, because the Federal Government can't do anything to the States save run the mails and collect a Federal tax or two. It isn't in the States, because the townships can do as they like; and it isn't in the townships, because these are bossed by alien voters or rings of patriotic home-bred citizens. And it certainly is not in the citizens, because they are governed and coerced by a despotic power of public opinion as represented in their papers, preachers, or local society. I found one man who told me that if anything went wrong in this huge congress of kings,—if there was a split or an upheaval or a smash,—the people in detail would be subject to the Idea of the sovereign people in mass. This is a survival from the Civil War, when, you remember, the people in a majority did with guns and swords slay and wound the people in detail. All the same, the notion seems very much like the worship by the savage of the unloaded rifle as it leans against the wall.

But the men and women set Us an example in patriotism. They believe in their land and its future, and its honour, and its glory, and they are not ashamed to say so. From the largest to the least runs this same proud, passionate conviction to which I take off my hat and for which I love them. An average English householder seems to regard his country as an abstraction to supply him with policemen and fire-brigades. The Cockney cad cannot understand what the word means. The bloomin' toffs he knows, and the law, and the soldiers that supply him with a spectacle in the Parks; but he would laugh in your face at the notion of any duty being owed by himself to his land.[1] Pick an American of the second generation anywhere you please—from the cab-rank, the porters' room, or the plough-tail,—'specially the plough-tail,—and that man will make you understand in five minutes that he understands what manner of thing his Republic is. He might laugh at a law that didn't suit his convenience, draw your eye-teeth in a bargain, and applaud 'cuteness on the outer verge of swindling: but you should hear him stand up and sing:—

[1] Remember, this was written in 1889.

My country, 'tis of thee,
Sweet land of liberty,
Of thee I sing!

I have heard a few thousand of them engaged in that employment. I respect him. There is too much Romeo and too little balcony about our National Anthem. With the American article it is all balcony. There must be born a poet who shall give the English *the* song of their own, own country—which is to say, of about half the world. Remains then only to compose the greatest song of all—The Saga of the Anglo-Saxon all round the earth—a pæan that shall combine the terrible slow swing of the *Battle Hymn of the Republic* (which, if you know not, get chanted to you) with *Britannia Needs no Bulwarks*, the skirl of the *British Grenadiers* with that perfect quickstep, *Marching through Georgia*, and at the end the wail of the *Dead March*. For We, even We who share the earth between us as no gods have ever shared it, we also are mortal in the matter of our single selves. Will any one take the contract?

It was with these rambling notions that I arrived at the infinite peace of the tiny township of Musquash, on the Monongahela River. The clang and tumult of Chicago belonged to another world. Imagine a rolling, wooded, English landscape, under softest of blue skies, dotted at three-mile intervals with fat little, quiet little villages, or aggressive little manufacturing towns that the trees and the folds of the hills mercifully prevented from betraying their presence. The golden-rod blazed in the pastures against the green of the mulleins, and the cows picked their way home through the twisted paths between the blackberry bushes. All summer was on the orchards, and the apples—such apples as we dream of when we eat the woolly imitations of Kashmir—were ripe and toothsome. It was good to lie in a hammock with half-shut eyes, and, in the utter stillness, to hear the apples dropping from the trees, and the tinkle of the cowbells as the cows walked statelily down the main road of the village Everybody in that restful place seemed to have just as much as he wanted; a house with all comfortable appliances, a big or little verandah wherein to spend the day, a neatly shaved garden with a wild wealth of flowers, some cows, and an orchard. Everybody knew everybody else intimately, and what they did not know, the local daily paper—a daily for a village of twelve hundred people!—supplied. There was a court-house where justice was done, and a gaol where some most enviable prisoners lived, and there were four or five churches of four or five denominations. Also it was impossible to buy openly any liquor in that little paradise. But—and this is a very serious *but*—you could by procuring a medical certificate get strong drinks from the chemist. That is the drawback of prohibition. It makes a man who wants a drink a shirker and a contriver, which things are not good for the soul of a man, and presently, 'specially if he be young, causes him to believe that he may just as well be hanged for a sheep as for a lamb; and the end of that young man is not pretty. Nothing except a rattling fall will persuade an average colt that a fence is not meant to be jumped over; whereas if he be turned out into the open he learns to carry himself with discretion. One heard a good deal of this same dread of drink in Musquash, and even the maidens seemed to know too much about its effects upon certain unregenerate youths, who, if they had been once made thoroughly, effectually, and persistently drunk—with a tepid brandy and soda thrust before their goose-fleshed noses on the terrible Next Morning—would perhaps have seen the futility of their ways. It was a sin by village canons to imbibe lager, though—*experto crede*—you can get dropsy on that stuff long before you can get drunk. 'But what man knows his mind?' Besides, it is all their own affair.

The little community seemed to be as self-contained as an Indian village. Had the rest of the land sunk under the sea, Musquash would have gone on sending its sons to school in order to make them 'good citizens,' which is the constant prayer of the true American father, settling its own road-making, local cesses, town-lot arbitrations, and internal government by ballot and vote, with due respect to the voices of the headmen (which is the salvation of the ballot), until such time as all should take their places in the cemetery appointed for their faith. Here were Americans and no aliens—men ruling themselves by themselves and for themselves and their wives and their children—in peace, order, and decency.

But what went straightest to this heart, though they did not know it, was that they were Methody folk for the most part—ay, Methody as ever trod a Yorkshire Moor, or drove on a Sunday to some chapel of the Faith in the Dales. The old Methody talk was there, with the discipline whereby the souls of the Just are, sometimes to their intense vexation, made perfect on this earth in order that they may 'take out their letters and live and die in good standing.' If you don't know the talk, you won't know what that means. The discipline, or dis*cip*-line, is no thing to be trifled with, and its working among a congregation depends entirely upon the tact, humanity, and sympathy of the leader who works it. He, knowing what youth's desires are, can turn the soul in the direction of good, gently, instead of wrenching it savagely towards the right path only to see it break away quivering and scared. The arm of the Dis*cip*line is long. A maiden told me, as a new and strange fact and one that would interest a foreigner, of a friend of hers who had once been admonished by some elders somewhere —not in Musquash—for the heinous crime of dancing. She, the friend, did not in the least like it. She would not. Can't you imagine the delightful results of a formal wigging administered by a youngish and austere elder who was not accustomed to make allowances for the natural dancing instincts of the young of the human animal? The hot irons that are held forth to scare may also sear, as those who have ever lain under an unfortunate exposition of the old Faith can attest.

But it was all immensely interesting—the absolutely fresh, wholesome, sweet life that paid due reverence to the things of the next world, but took good care to get enough tennis in the cool of the evening; that concerned itself as honestly and thoroughly with the daily round, the trivial task (and that same task is anything but trivial when you are 'helped' by an American 'help') as with the salvation of the soul. I had the honour of meeting in the flesh, even as Miss Louisa Alcott drew them, Meg and Joe and Beth and Amy, whom you ought to know. There was no affectation of concealment in their lives who had nothing to conceal. There were many 'little women' in that place, because, even as is the case in England, the boys had gone out to seek their fortunes. Some were working in the thundering, clanging cities, others had removed to the infinite West, and others had disappeared in the languid, lazy South; and the maidens waited their return, which is the custom of maidens all over the world. Then the boys would come back in the soft sunlight, attired in careful raiment, their tongues cleansed of evil words and discourtesy. They had just come to call—bless their carefully groomed heads, so they had!—and the maidens in white dresses glimmered like ghosts on the stoop and received them according to their merits. Mamma had nothing to do with this, nor papa either, for he was down-town trying to drive reason into the head of a land surveyor; and all along the shaded, lazy, intimate street you heard the garden-gates click and clash, as the mood of the man varied, and bursts of pleasant laughter where three or four—be sure the white muslins were among them,—discussed a picnic past or a buggy-drive to come. Then the couples went their ways and talked together till the young men had to go at last on account of the trains, and all trooped joyously down to the station and thought no harm of it. And, indeed, why should they? From her fifteenth year the American maiden moves among 'the boys' as a sister among brothers. They are her servants to take her out riding,—which is driving,—to give her flowers and candy. The last two items are expensive, and this is good for the young man, as teaching him to value friendship that costs a little in cash and may necessitate economy on the cigar side. As to the maiden, she is taught to respect herself, that her fate is in her own hands, and that she is the more stringently bound by the very measure of the liberty so freely accorded to her. Wherefore, in her own language, 'she has a lovely time' with about two or three hundred boys who have sisters of their own, and a very accurate perception that if they were unworthy of their trust a syndicate of other boys would probably pass them into a world where there is neither marrying nor giving in marriage. And so time goes till the maiden knows the other side of the house,—knows that a man is not a demi-god nor a mysteriously veiled monster, but an average, egotistical, vain, gluttonous, but on the whole companionable, sort of person, to be soothed, fed and managed—knowledge that does not come to her sister in England till after a few years of matrimony. And then she makes her choice. The Golden Light touches eyes that are full of comprehension; but the light is golden none the less, for she makes just the same sweet, irrational choices that an English girl does. With this advantage: she knows a little more, has experience in entertaining, insight into the businesses, employ, and hobbies of men, gathered from countless talks with the boys, and talks with the other girls who find time at those mysterious conclaves to discuss what Tom, Ted, Stuke, or Jack have been doing. Thus it happens that she is a companion, in the fullest sense of the word, of the man she weds, zealous for the interest of the firm, to be consulted in time of stress and to be called upon for help and sympathy in time of danger. Pleasant it is that one heart should beat for you; but it is better when the head above that heart has been thinking hard on your behalf, and when the lips, that are also very pleasant to kiss, give wise counsel.

When the American maiden—I speak now for the rank and file of that noble army—is once married, why, it is finished. She has had her lovely time. It may have been five, seven, or ten years according to circumstances. She abdicates promptly with startling speed, and her place knows her no more except as with her husband. The Queen is dead, or looking after the house. This same household work seems to be the thing that ages the American woman. She is infamously 'helped' by the Irish trollop and the negress alike. It is not fair upon her, because she has to do three parts of the housework herself, and in dry, nerve-straining air the 'chores' are a burden. Be thankful, O my people, for Mauz Baksh, Kadir Baksh, and the *ayah* while they are with you. They are twice as handy as the unkempt slatterns of the furnished apartments to which you will return, Commissioners though you be; and five times as clever as the Amelia Araminta Rebellia Secessia Jackson (coloured) under whose ineptitude and insolence the young American housewife groans. But all this is far enough from peaceful, placid Musquash and its boundless cordiality, its simple, genuine hospitality, and its—what's the French word that just covers all?—*gra—gracieuseness*, isn't it? Oh, be good to an American wherever you meet him. Put him up for the club, and he will hold you listening till three in the morning; give him the best tent, and the gram-fed mutton. I have incurred a debt of salt that I can never repay, but do you return it piecemeal to any of that Nation, and the account will be on my head till our paths in the world cross again. He drinks iced water just as we do; but he doesn't quite like our cigars.

And how shall I finish the tale? Would it interest you to learn of the picnics in the hot, still woods that overhang the Monongahela, when those idiotic American buggies that can't turn round got stuck among the brambles and all but capsized; of boating in the blazing sun on the river that but a little time before had cast at the feet of the horrified village the corpses of the Johnstown tragedy? I saw one, only one, remnant of that terrible wreck. He had been a minister. House, church, congregation, wife, and children had been swept away from him in one night of terror. He had no employment; he could have employed himself at nothing; but God had been very good to him. He sat in the sun and smiled a little weakly. It was in his poor blurred mind that something had happened—he was not sure what it was, but undoubtedly something had occurred. One could only pray that the light would never return.

But there be many pictures on my mind. Of a huge manufacturing city of three hundred thousand souls lighted and warmed by natural gas, so that the great valley full of flaming furnaces sent up no smoke wreaths to the clear sky. Of Musquash itself lighted by the same mysterious agency, flares of gas eight feet long, roaring day and night at the corners of the grass-grown streets because it wasn't worth while to turn them out; of fleets of coal-flats being hauled down the river on an interminable journey to St. Louis; of factories nestling in woods where all the axe-handles and shovels in the world seemed to be manufactured daily; and last, of that quaint forgotten German community, the Brotherhood of Perpetual Separation, who founded themselves when the State was yet young and land cheap, and are now dying out because they will neither marry nor give in marriage and their recruits are very few. The advance in the value of land has almost smothered these poor old people in a golden affluence that they never desired. They live in a little village where the houses are built old Dutch fashion, with their front doors away from the road, and cobbled paths all about. The cloistered peace of Musquash is a metropolitan riot beside the hush of that village. And there is, too, a love-tale tucked away among the flowers. It has taken seventy years in the telling, for the brother and sister loved each other well, but they loved their duty to the Brotherhood more. So they have lived and still do live, seeing each other daily, and separated for all time. Any trouble that might have been is altogether wiped out of their faces, which are as calm as those of very little children. To the uninitiated those constant ones resemble extremely old people in garments of absurd cut But they love each other, and that seems to bring one back quite naturally to the girls and the boys in Musquash. The boys were nice boys—graduates of Yale of course ; you mustn't mention Harvard here—but none the less skilled in business, in stocks and shares, the boring for oil, and the sale of everything that can be sold by one sinner to another. Skilled, too, in baseball, big-shouldered, with straight eyes and square chins—but not above occasional diversion and mild orgies. They will make good citizens and possess the earth, and eventually wed one of the nice white muslin dresses. There are worse things in this world than being 'one of the boys' in Musquash.

No. XXXVII

AN INTERVIEW WITH MARK TWAIN

You are a contemptible lot, over yonder. Some of you are Commissioners, and some Lieutenant-Governors, and some have the V.C., and a few are privileged to walk about the Mall arm in arm with the Viceroy; but *I* have seen Mark Twain this golden morning, have shaken his hand, and smoked a cigar—no, two cigars—with him, and talked with him for more than two hours! Understand clearly that I do not despise you; indeed, I don't. I am only very sorry for you, from the Viceroy downward. To soothe your envy and to prove that I still regard you as my equals, I will tell you all about it.

They said in Buffalo that he was in Hartford, Conn.; and again they said 'perchance he is gone upon a journey to Portland'; and a big, fat drummer vowed that he knew the great man intimately, and that Mark was spending the summer in Europe—which information so upset me that I embarked upon the wrong train, and was incontinently turned out by the conductor three-quarters of a mile from the station, amid the wilderness of railway tracks. Have you ever, encumbered with great-coat and valise, tried to dodge diversely-minded locomotives when the sun was shining in your eyes? But I forgot that you have not seen Mark Twain, you people of no account!

Saved from the jaws of the cowcatcher, me wandering devious a stranger met.

'Elmira is the place. Elmira in the State of New York—this State, not two hundred miles away'; and he added, perfectly unnecessarily, 'Slide, Kelley, slide.'

I slid on the West Shore line, I slid till midnight, and they dumped me down at the door of a frowzy hotel in Elmira. Yes, they knew all about 'that man Clemens,' but reckoned he was not in town; had gone East somewhere. I had better possess my soul in patience till the morrow, and then dig up the 'man Clemens'' brother-in-law, who was interested in coal.

The idea of chasing half a dozen relatives in addition to Mark Twain up and down a city of thirty thousand inhabitants kept me awake. Morning revealed Elmira, whose streets were desolated by railway tracks, and whose suburbs were given up to the manufacture of door-sashes and window-frames. It was surrounded by pleasant, fat, little hills, rimmed with timber and topped with cultivation. The Chemung River flowed generally up and down the town, and had just finished flooding a few of the main streets.

The hotel-man and the telephone-man assured me that the much-desired brother-in-law was out of town, and no one seemed to know where 'the man Clemens' abode. Later on I discovered that he had not summered in that place for more than nineteen seasons, and so was comparatively a new arrival.

A friendly policeman volunteered the news that he had seen Twain or 'some one very like him' driving a buggy the day before. This gave me a delightful sense of nearness. Fancy living in a town where you could see the author of *Tom Sawyer*, or 'some one very like him,' jolting over the pavements in a buggy!

'He lives out yonder at East Hill,' said the policeman; 'three miles from here.'

Then the chase began—in a hired hack, up an awful hill, where sunflowers blossomed by the roadside, and crops waved, and *Harper's Magazine* cows stood in eligible and commanding attitudes knee-deep in clover, all ready to be transferred to photogravure. The great man must have been persecuted by outsiders aforetime, and fled up the hill for refuge.

Presently the driver stopped at a miserable, little white wood shanty, and demanded 'Mister Clemens.'

'I know he's a big bug and all that,' he explained, 'but you can never tell what sort of notions those sort of men take into their heads to live in, anyways.'

There rose up a young lady who was sketching thistle-tops and goldenrod, amid a plentiful supply of both, and set the pilgrimage on the right path.

'It's a pretty Gothic house on the left-hand side a little way farther on.'

'Gothic h——,' said the driver. 'Very few of the city hacks take this drive, 'specially if they know they are coming out here,' and he glared at me savagely.

It was a very pretty house, anything but Gothic, clothed with ivy, standing in a very big compound, and fronted by a verandah full of chairs and hammocks. The roof of the verandah was a trellis-work of creepers, and the sun peeping through moved on the shining boards below.

Decidedly this remote place was an ideal one for work, if a man could work among these soft airs and the murmur of the long-eared crops.

Appeared suddenly a lady used to dealing with rampageous outsiders. 'Mr. Clemens has just walked down-town. He is at his brother-in-law's house.'

Then he was within shouting distance, after all, and the chase had not been in vain. With speed I fled, and the driver, skidding the wheel and swearing audibly, arrived at the bottom of that hill without accidents. It was in the pause that followed between ringing the brother-in-law's bell and getting an answer that it occurred to me, for the first time, Mark Twain might possibly have other engagements than the entertainment of escaped lunatics from India, be they never so full of admiration. And in another man's house—anyhow, what had I come to do or say? Suppose the drawing-room should be full of people,—suppose a baby were sick, how was I to explain that I only wanted to shake hands with him?

Then things happened somewhat in this order.

A big, darkened drawing-room ; a huge chair ; a man with eyes, a mane of grizzled hair, a brown moustache covering a mouth as delicate as a woman's, a strong, square hand shaking mine, and the slowest, calmest, levellest voice in all the world saying :—

'Well, you think you owe me something, and you've come to tell me so. That's what I call squaring a debt handsomely.'

'Piff!' from a cob-pipe (I always said that a Missouri meerschaum was the best smoking in the world), and, behold! Mark Twain had curled himself up in the big armchair, and I was smoking reverently, as befits one in the presence of his superior.

The thing that struck me first was that he was an elderly man ; yet, after a minute's thought, I perceived that it was otherwise, and in five minutes, the eyes looking at me, I saw that the grey hair was an accident of the most trivial. He was quite young. I was shaking his hand. I was smoking his cigar, and I was hearing him talk—this man I had learned to love and admire fourteen thousand miles away.

Reading his books, I had striven to get an idea of his personality, and all my preconceived notions were wrong and beneath the reality. Blessed is the man who finds no disillusion when he is brought face to face with a revered writer. That was a moment to be remembered ; the landing of a twelve-pound salmon was nothing to it. I had hooked Mark Twain, and he was treating me as though under certain circumstances I might be an equal.

About this time I became aware that he was discussing the copyright question. Here, so far as I remember, is what he said. Attend to the words of the oracle through this unworthy medium transmitted. You will never be able to imagine the long, slow surge of the drawl, and the deadly gravity of the countenance, the quaint pucker of the body, one foot thrown over the arm of the chair, the yellow pipe clinched in one corner of the mouth, and the right hand casually caressing the square chin :—

'Copyright? Some men have morals, and some men have—other things. I presume a publisher is a man. He is not born. He is created—by circumstances. Some publishers have morals. Mine have. They pay me for the English productions of my books. When you hear men talking of Bret Harte's works and other works and my books being pirated, ask them to be sure of their facts. I think they'll find the books are paid for. It was ever thus.

'I remember an unprincipled and formidable publisher. Perhaps he's dead now. He used to take my short stories—I can't call it steal or pirate them. It was beyond these things altogether. He took my stories one at a time and made a book of it. If I wrote an essay on dentistry or theology or any little thing of that kind—just an essay that long (he indicated half an inch on his finger), any sort of essay—that publisher would amend and improve my essay.

'He would get another man to write some more to it or cut it about exactly as his needs required. Then he would publish a book called *Dentistry by*

Mark Twain, that little essay and some other things not mine added. Theology would make another book, and so on. I do not consider that fair. It's an insult. But he's dead now, I think. I didn't kill him.

'There is a great deal of nonsense talked about international copyright. The proper way to treat a copyright is to make it exactly like real estate in every way.

'It will settle itself under these conditions. If Congress were to bring in a law that a man's life was not to extend over a hundred and sixty years, somebody would laugh. That law wouldn't concern anybody. The man would be out of the jurisdiction of the court. A term of years in copyright comes to exactly the same thing. No law can make a book live or cause it to die before the appointed time.

'Tottletown, Cal., was a new town, with a population of three thousand—banks, fire-brigade, brick buildings, and all the modern improvements. It lived, it flourished, and it disappeared. To-day no man can put his foot on any remnant of Tottletown, Cal. It's dead. London continues to exist. Bill Smith, author of a book read for the next year or so, is real estate in Tottletown. William Shakespeare, whose works are extensively read, is real estate in London. Let Bill Smith, equally with Mr. Shakespeare now deceased, have as complete a control over his copyright as he would over his real estate. Let him gamble it away, drink it away, or—give it to the church. Let his heirs and assigns treat it in the same manner.

'Every now and again I go up to Washington, sitting on a board to drive that sort of view into Congress. Congress takes its arguments against international copyright delivered ready made, and —Congress isn't very strong. I put the real-estate view of the case before one of the Senators.

'He said: "Suppose a man has written a book that will live for ever?"

'I said: "Neither you nor I will ever live to see that man, but we'll assume it. What then?"

'He said: "I want to protect the world against that man's heirs and assigns, working under your theory."

'I said: "You think that all the world has no commercial sense. The book that will live for ever can't be artificially kept up at inflated prices. There will always be very expensive editions of it and cheap ones issuing side by side."

'Take the case of Sir Walter Scott's novels,' Mark Twain continued, turning to me. 'When the copyright notes protected them, I bought editions as expensive as I could afford, because I liked them. At the same time the same firm were selling editions that a cat might buy. They had their real estate, and not being fools, recognised that one portion of the plot could be worked as a gold mine, another as a vegetable garden, and another as a marble quarry. Do you see?'

What I saw with the greatest clearness was Mark Twain being forced to fight for the simple proposition that a man has as much right to the work of his brains (think of the heresy of it!) as to the labour of his hands. When the old lion roars, the young whelps growl. I growled assentingly, and the talk ran on from books in general to his own in particular.

Growing bold, and feeling that I had a few hundred thousand folk at my back, I demanded whether Tom Sawyer married Judge Thatcher's daughter and whether we were ever going to hear of Tom Sawyer as a man.

'I haven't decided,' quoth Mark Twain, getting up, filling his pipe, and walking up and down the room in his slippers. 'I have a notion of writing the sequel to *Tom Sawyer* in two ways. In one I would make him rise to great honour and go to Congress, and in the other I should hang him. Then the friends and enemies of the book could take their choice.'

Here I lost my reverence completely, and protested against any theory of the sort, because, to me at least, Tom Sawyer was real.

'Oh, he *is* real,' said Mark Twain. 'He's all the boy that I have known or recollect; but that would be a good way of ending the book'; then, turning round, 'because, when you come to think of it, neither religion, training, nor education avails anything against the force of circumstances that drive a man. Suppose we took the next four-and-twenty years of Tom Sawyer's life, and gave a little joggle to the circumstances that controlled him. He would, logically and according to the joggle, turn out a rip or an angel.'

'Do you believe that, then?'

'I think so. Isn't it what you call Kismet?'

'Yes; but don't give him two joggles and show the result, because he isn't your property any more. He belongs to us.'

He laughed—a large, wholesome laugh—and this began a dissertation on the rights of a man to do what he liked with his own creations, which being a matter of purely professional interest, I will mercifully omit.

Returning to the big chair, he, speaking of truth and the like in literature, said that an autobiography was the one work in which a man, against his own will and in spite of his utmost striving to the contrary, revealed himself in his true light to the world.

'A good deal of your life on the Mississippi is autobiographical, isn't it?' I asked.

'As near as it can be—when a man is writing to a book and about himself. But in genuine autobiography, I believe it is impossible for a man to tell the truth about himself or to avoid impressing the reader with the truth about himself.

'I made an experiment once. I got a friend of mine—a man painfully given to speak the truth on all occasions—a man who wouldn't dream of telling a lie—and I made him write his autobiography for his own amusement and mine. He did it. The manuscript would have made an octavo volume, but—good, honest man that he was—in every single detail of his life that I knew about he turned out, on paper, a formidable liar. He could not help himself.

'It is not in human nature to write the truth about itself. None the less the reader gets a general impression from an autobiography whether the man is a fraud or a good man. The reader can't give his reasons any more than a man can explain why a woman struck him as being lovely when he doesn't remember her hair, eyes, teeth, or figure. And the impression that the reader gets is a correct one.'

'Do you ever intend to write an autobiography?'

'If I do, it will be as other men have done—with the most earnest desire to make myself out to be the better man in every little business that has been to my discredit; and I shall fail, like the others, to make my readers believe anything except the truth.'

This naturally led to a discussion on conscience. Then said Mark Twain, and his words are mighty and to be remembered:—

'Your conscience is a nuisance. A conscience is like a child. If you pet it and play with it and let it have everything that it wants, it becomes spoiled and intrudes on all your amusements and most of your griefs. Treat your conscience as you would treat anything else. When it is rebellious, spank it—be severe with it, argue with it, prevent it from coming to play with you at all hours, and you will secure a good conscience; that is to say, a properly trained one. A spoiled one simply destroys all the pleasure in life. I think I have reduced mine to order. At least, I haven't heard from it for some time. Perhaps

I have killed it from over-severity. It's wrong to kill a child, but, in spite of all I have said, a conscience differs from a child in many ways. Perhaps it's best when it's dead.'

Here he told me a little—such things as a man may tell a stranger—of his early life and upbringing, and in what manner he had been influenced for good by the example of his parents. He spoke always through his eyes, a light under the heavy eyebrows ; anon crossing the room with a step as light as a girl's, to show me some book or other ; then resuming his walk up and down the room, puffing at the cob pipe. I would have given much for nerve enough to demand the gift of that pipe — value, five cents when new. I understood why certain savage tribes ardently desired the liver of brave men slain in combat. That pipe would have given me, perhaps, a hint of his keen insight into the souls of men. But he never laid it aside within stealing reach.

Once, indeed, he put his hand on my shoulder. It was an investiture of the Star of India, blue silk, trumpets, and diamond-studded jewel, all complete. If hereafter, in the changes and chances of this mortal life, I fall to cureless ruin, I will tell the superintendent of the workhouse that Mark Twain once put his hand on my shoulder ; and he shall give me a room to myself and a double allowance of paupers' tobacco.

'I never read novels myself,' said he, 'except when the popular persecution forces me to—when people plague me to know what I think of the last book that every one is reading.'

'And how did the latest persecution affect you?'

'Robert?' said he, interrogatively.

I nodded.

'I read it, of course, for the workmanship. That made me think I had neglected novels too long—that there might be a good many books as graceful in style somewhere on the shelves; so I began a course of novel reading. I have dropped it now; it did not amuse me. But as regards Robert, the effect on me was exactly as though a singer of street ballads were to hear excellent music from a church organ. I didn't stop to ask whether the music was legitimate or necessary. I listened, and I liked what I heard. I am speaking of the grace and beauty of the style.'

'You see,' he went on, 'every man has his private opinion about a book. But that is my private opinion. If I had lived in the beginning of things, I should have looked around the township to see what popular opinion thought of the murder of Abel before I openly condemned Cain. I should have had my private opinion, of course, but I shouldn't have expressed it until I had felt the way. You have my private opinion about that book. I don't know what my public ones are exactly. They won't upset the earth.'

He recurled himself into the chair and talked of other things.

'I spend nine months of the year at Hartford. I have long ago satisfied myself that there is no hope of doing much work during those nine months. People come in and call. They call at all hours, about everything in the world. One day I thought I would keep a list of interruptions. It began this way :—

'A man came and would see no one but Mr. Clemens. He was an agent for photogravure reproductions of Salon pictures. I very seldom use Salon pictures in my books.

'After that man another man, who refused to see any one but Mr. Clemens, came to make me write to Washington about something. I saw him. I saw a third man, then a fourth. By this time it was noon. I had grown tried of keeping the list. I wished to rest.

'But the fifth man was the only one of the crowd with a card of his own. He sent up his card. 'Ben Koontz, Hannibal, Mo.' I was raised in Hannibal. Ben was an old schoolmate of mine. Consequently I threw the house wide open and rushed with both hands out at a big, fat, heavy man, who was not the Ben I had ever known —nor anything like him

'"But *is* it you, Ben?" I said. "You've altered in the last thousand years."

'The fat man said : "Well, I'm not Koontz exactly, but I met him down in Missouri, and he told me to be sure and call on you, and he gave me his card, and"—here he acted the little scene for my benefit—"if you can wait a minute till I can get out the circulars—I'm not Koontz exactly, but I'm travelling with the fullest line of rods you ever saw."'

'And what happened?' I asked breathlessly.

'I shut the door. He was not Ben Koontz—

exactly—not my old school-fellow, but I had shaken him by both hands in love, and . . I had been boarded by a lightning-rod man in my own house.

'As I was saying, I do very little work in Hartford. I come here for three months every year, and I work four or five hours a day in a study down the garden of that little house on the hill. Of course, I do not object to two or three interruptions. When a man is in the full swing of his work these little things do not affect him. Eight or ten or twenty interruptions retard composition.'

I was burning to ask him all manner of impertinent questions, as to which of his works he himself preferred, and so forth; but, standing in awe of his eyes, I dared not. He spoke on, and I listened, grovelling.

It was a question of mental equipment that was on the carpet, and I am still wondering whether he meant what he said.

'Personally I never care for fiction or story-books. What I like to read about are facts and statistics of any kind. If they are only facts about the raising of radishes, they interest me. Just now, for instance, before you came in'—he pointed to an encyclopædia on the shelves—'I was reading an article about "Mathematics." Perfectly pure mathematics.

'My own knowledge of mathematics stops at "twelve times twelve," but I enjoyed that article immensely. I didn't understand a word of it; but facts, or what a man believes to be facts, are always delightful. That mathematical fellow believed in his facts. So do I. Get your facts first, and'—the voice dies away to an almost inaudible drone—'then you can distort 'em as much as you please.'

Bearing this precious advice in my bosom, I left; the great man assuring me with gentle kindness that I had not interrupted him in the least. Once outside the door, I yearned to go back and ask some questions—it was easy enough to think of them now—but his time was his own, though his books belonged to me.

I should have ample time to look back to that meeting across the graves of the days. But it was sad to think of the things he had not spoken about.

In San Francisco the men of *The Call* told me many legends of Mark's apprenticeship in their paper five-and-twenty years ago; how he was a reporter delightfully incapable of reporting according to the needs of the day He preferred, so they said, to coil himself into a heap and meditate until the last minute. Then he would produce copy bearing no sort of relationship to his legitimate work—copy that made the editor swear horribly, and the readers of *The Call* ask for more.

I should like to have heard Mark's version of that, with some stories of his joyous and variegated past. He has been journeyman-printer (in those days he wandered from the banks of the Missouri even to Philadelphia), pilot-cub and full-blown pilot, soldier of the South (that was for three weeks only), private secretary to a Lieutenant-Governor of Nevada (that displeased him), miner, editor, special correspondent in the Sandwich Islands, and the Lord only knows what else. If so experienced a man could by any means be made drunk, it would be a glorious thing to fill him up with composite liquors, and, in the language of his own country, 'let him retrospect.' But these eyes will never see that orgy fit for the gods!

CITY OF DREADFUL NIGHT

City of Dreadful Night

JAN.-FEB., 1888

CHAPTER I

A REAL LIVE CITY

WE are all backwoodsmen and barbarians together—we others dwelling beyond the Ditch, in the outer darkness of the Mofussil. There are no such things as Commissioners and heads of departments in the world, and there is only one city in India. Bombay is too green, too pretty, and too stragglesome; and Madras died ever so long ago. Let us take off our hats to Calcutta, the many-sided, the smoky, the magnificent, as we drive in over the Hughli Bridge in the dawn of a still February morning. We have left India behind us at Howrah Station, and now we enter foreign parts. No, not wholly foreign. Say rather too familiar.

All men of a certain age know the feeling of caged irritation—an illustration in the *Graphic*, a bar of music or the light words of a friend from home may set it ablaze—that comes from the knowledge of our lost heritage of London. At Home they, the other men, our equals, have at their disposal all that Town can supply—the roar of the streets, the lights, the music, the pleasant places, the millions of their own kind, and a wilderness full of pretty, fresh-coloured Englishwomen, theatres and restaurants. It is their right. They accept it as such, and even affect to look upon it with contempt. And we—we have nothing except the few amusements that we painfully build up for ourselves—the dolorous dissipations of gymkhanas where every one knows everybody else, or the chastened intoxication of dances where all engagements are booked, in ink, ten days ahead, and where everybody's antecedents are as patent as his or her method of waltzing. We have been deprived of our inheritance. The men at home are enjoying it all, not knowing how fair and rich it is, and we at the most can only fly westward for a few months and gorge what, properly speaking, should take seven or eight or ten luxurious years. That is the lost heritage of London; and the knowledge of the forfeiture, wilful or forced, comes to most men at times and seasons, and they get cross.

Calcutta holds out false hopes of some return. The dense smoke hangs low, in the chill of the morning, over an ocean of roofs, and, as the city wakes, there goes up to the smoke a deep, full-throated boom of life and motion and humanity. For this reason does he who sees Calcutta for the first time hang joyously out of the *ticca-gharri* and sniff the smoke, and turn his face toward the tumult, saying: 'This is, at last, some portion of my heritage returned to me. This is a city. There is life here, and there should be all manner of pleasant things for the having, across the river and under the smoke.'

The litany is an expressive one and exactly describes the first emotions of a wandering savage adrift in Calcutta. The eye has lost its sense of proportion, the focus has contracted through overmuch residence in up-country stations—twenty minutes' canter from hospital to parade-ground, you know—and the mind has shrunk with the eye. Both say together, as they take in the sweep of shipping above and below the Hughli Bridge: 'Why, this is London! This is the docks. This is Imperial. This is worth coming across India to see!'

Then a distinctly wicked idea takes possession of the mind: 'What a divine—what a heavenly place to *loot!*' This gives place to a much worse devil—that of Conservatism. It seems not only a wrong but a criminal thing to allow natives to have any voice in the control of such a city—adorned, docked, wharfed, fronted, and reclaimed by Englishmen, existing only because England lives, and dependent for its life on England. All India knows of the Calcutta Municipality; but has any one thoroughly investigated the Big Calcutta Stink? There is only one. Benares is fouler in point of concentrated, pent-up muck, and there are local stenches in Peshawar which are stronger than the B. C. S.; but, for diffused, soul-sickening expansiveness, the reek of Calcutta beats both Benares and Peshawar. Bombay cloaks her stenches with a veneer of assafœtida and tobacco; Calcutta is above pretence. There is no tracing back the Calcutta plague to any one source. It is faint, it is sickly, and it is indescribable; but Americans at the Great Eastern Hotel say that it is something like the smell of the Chinese quarter in San Francisco. It is certainly not an Indian smell. It resembles the essence of corruption that has rotted for the second time—the clammy odour of blue slime. And there is no escape from it. It blows across the *maidan;* it comes in gusts into the corridors of the Great Eastern Hotel; what they are pleased to call the 'Palaces of Chowringhi' carry it; it swirls round the Bengal Club; it pours out of by-streets with sickening intensity, and the breeze of the morning is laden with it. It is first found, in spite of the fume of the engines, in Howrah Station. It seems to be worst in the little lanes at the back of Lal Bazar where the drinking-shops are, but it is nearly as bad opposite Government House and in the Public Offices. The thing is intermittent. Six moderately pure mouthfuls of air may be drawn without offence. Then comes the seventh wave and the queasiness of an uncultured stomach. If you live long enough in Calcutta you grow used to it. The regular residents admit the disgrace, but their answer is: 'Wait till the wind blows off the Salt Lakes where all the sewage goes, and *then* you'll smell something.' That is their defence! Small wonder that they consider Calcutta is a fit place till they know through their purses the measure of their neglect in the past, and when a little of the smell has been abolished, let us bring them back again to talk and take the credit of enlightenment. The better classes own their broughams and barouches; the worse can shoulder an Englishman into the kennel and talk to him as though he were a cook. They can refer to an English lady as an *aurat*; they are permitted a freedom—not to put it too coarsely—of speech which, if used by an Englishman toward an Englishman, would end in serious trouble. They are fenced and protected and made inviolate. Surely they might be content with all those things without entering into matters which they cannot, by the nature of their birth, understand.

Now, whether all this genial diatribe be the outcome of an unbiassed mind or the result first of sickness caused by that ferocious stench, and secondly of headache due to day-long smoking to drown the stench, is an open question. Anyway, Calcutta is a fearsome place for a man not educated up to it.

A word of advice to other barbarians. Do not bring a north-country servant into Calcutta. He is sure to get into trouble, because he does not understand the customs of the city. A Punjabi in this place for the first time esteems it his bounden duty to go to the *Ajaib-ghar*—the Museum. Such an one has gone and is even now returned very angry and troubled in the spirit. 'I went to the Museum,' says he, 'and no one gave me any abuse. I went to the market to buy my food, and then I

CHAPTER II

THE REFLECTIONS OF A SAVAGE

MORNING brings counsel. *Does* Calcutta smell so pestiferously after all? Heavy rain has fallen in the night. She is newly washed, and the clear sunlight shows her at her best. Where, oh where, in all this wilderness of life shall a man go?

The Great Eastern hums with life through all its hundred rooms. Doors slam merrily, and all the nations of the earth run up and down the staircases. This alone is refreshing, because the passers bump you and ask you to stand aside. Fancy finding any place outside the Levée-room where Englishmen are crowded together to this extent! Fancy sitting down seventy strong to *table d'hôte* and with a deafening clatter of knives and forks! Fancy finding a real bar whence drinks may be obtained! and, joy of joys, fancy stepping out of the hotel into the arms of a live, white, helmeted, buttoned, truncheoned Bobby! What would happen if one spoke to this Bobby? Would he be offended? He is not offended. He is affable. He has to patrol the pavement in front of the Great Eastern and to see that pretty ladies, who live anywhere within a reasonable distance, come down to do their shopping personally.

'Look here. If you want to be respectable you mustn't smoke in the streets. Nobody does it.' This is advice kindly tendered by a friend in a black coat. There is no Levée or Lieutenant-Governor in sight; but he wears the frock-coat because it is daylight, and he can be seen. He refrains from smoking for the same reason. He admits that Providence built the open air to be smoked in, but he says that 'it isn't the thing.' This man has a brougham, a remarkably natty little pill-box with a curious wabble about the wheels. He steps into the brougham and puts on—a top-hat, a shiny black 'plug.'

There was a man up-country once who owned a top-hat. He leased it to amateur theatrical companies for some seasons until the nap wore off. Then he threw it into a tree and wild bees hived in it. Men were wont to come and look at the hat, in its palmy days, for the sake of feeling homesick. It interested all the station, and died with two seers of *babul*-flower honey in its bosom. But top-hats are not intended to be worn in India. They are as sacred as home letters and old rose-buds. The friend cannot see this. He allows that if he stepped out of his brougham and walked about in the sunshine for ten minutes he would get a bad headache. In half an hour he would probably die of sunstroke. He allows all this, but he keeps to his Hat and cannot see why a barbarian is moved their spaciousness they are Oriental, but those service-staircases do not look healthy. We will form an amateur sanitary commission and call upon Chowringhi.

A first introduction to the Calcutta *durwân* or door-keeper is not nice. If he is chewing *pân*, he does not take the trouble to get rid of his quid. If he is sitting on his cot chewing sugar-cane, he does not think it worth his while to rise. He has to be taught those things, and he cannot understand why he should be reproved. Clearly he is a survival of a played-out system. Providence never intended that any native should be made a *concierge* more insolent than any of the French variety. The people of Calcutta put a man in a little lodge close to the gate of their house, in order that loafers may be turned away, and the houses protected from theft. The natural result is that the *durwân* treats everybody whom he does not know as a loafer, has an intimate and vendible knowledge of all the outgoings and incomings in that house, and controls, to a large extent, the nomination of the servants. They say that one of the estimable class is now suing a bank for about three lakhs of rupees. Up-country, a Lieutenant-Governor's servant has to work for thirty years before he can retire on seventy thousand rupees of savings. The Calcutta *durwân* is a great institution. The head and front of his offence is that he will insist upon trying to talk English. How he protects the houses Calcutta only knows. He can be frightened out of his wits by severe is sound and produces figures to prove it; at the same time admitting that healthy cut flesh will not readily heal. Further evidence may be dispensed with.

Here come pouring down Park Street on the *maidân* a rush of broughams, neat buggies, the lightest of gigs, trim office brownberrys, shining victorias, and a sprinkling of veritable hansom cabs. In the broughams sit men in top-hats. In the other carts, young men, all very much alike, and all immaculately turned out. A fresh stream from Chowringhi joins the Park Street detachment, and the two together stream away across the *maidân* toward the business quarter of the city. This is Calcutta going to office—the civilians to the Government Buildings and the young men to their firms and their blocks and their wharves. Here one sees that Calcutta has the best turn-out in the Empire. Horses and traps alike are enviably perfect, and—mark the touchstone of civilisation—*the lamps are in their sockets!* The country-bred is a rare beast here; his place is taken by the Waler, and the Waler, though a ruffian at heart, can be made to look like a gentleman. It would be indecorous to applaud the winking harness, the perfectly lacquered panels, and the liveried *saises*. They show well in the outwardly fair roads shadowed by the Palaces.

How many sections of the complex society of the place do the carts carry? *First*, the Bengal Civilian who goes to Writers' Buildings and sits in a perfect office and speaks flippantly of 'sending things into India,' meaning thereby he refers

CHAPTER III

THE COUNCIL OF THE GODS

He set up conclusions to the number of nine thousand seven hundred and sixty-four . . . he went afterwards to the Sorbonne, where he maintained argument against the theologians for the space of six weeks, from four o'clock in the morning till six in the evening, except for an interval of two hours to refresh themselves and take their repasts, and at this were present the greatest part of the lords of the court, the masters of request, presidents, counsellors, those of the accompts, secretaries, advocates, and others ; as also the sheriffs of the said town.—*Pantagruel.*

'THE Bengal Legislative Council is sitting now. You will find it in an octagonal wing of Writers' Buildings : straight across the *maidân*. It's worth seeing.' 'What are they sitting on ?' 'Municipal business. No end of a debate.' So much for trying to keep low company. The long-shore loafers must stand over. Without doubt this Council is going to hang some one for the state of the City, and Sir Steuart Bayley will be chief executioner. One does not come across councils every day.

Writers' Buildings are large. You can trouble the busy workers of half a dozen departments before you stumble upon the black-stained staircase that leads to an upper chamber looking out over a populous street. Wild orderlies block the way. The Councillor Sahibs are sitting, but any one can enter. 'To the right of the Lât Sahib's chair, and go quietly.' Ill-mannered minion! Does he expect the awe-stricken spectator to prance in with a war-whoop or turn Catherine-wheels round that sumptuous octagonal room with the blue-domed roof? There are gilt capitals to the half pillars and an Egyptian-patterned lotus-stencil makes the walls gay. A thick-piled carpet covers all the floor, and must be delightful in the hot weather. On a black wooden throne, comfortably cushioned in green leather, sits Sir Steuart Bayley, Ruler of Bengal. The rest are all great men, or else they would not be there. Not to know them argues oneself unknown. There are a dozen of them, and sit six aside at two slightly curved lines of beautifully polished desks. Thus Sir Steuart Bayley occupies the frog of a badly made horse-shoe split at the toe. In front of him, at a table covered with books and pamphlets and papers, toils a secretary. There is a seat for the Reporters, and that is all. The place enjoys a chastened gloom, and its very atmosphere fills one with awe. This is the heart of Bengal, and uncommonly well upholstered. If the work matches the first-class furniture, the inkpots, the carpet, and the resplendent ceilings, there will be something worth seeing. But where is the criminal who is to be hanged for the stench that runs up and down Writers' Buildings staircases; for the rubbish heaps in the Chitpore Road; for the sickly savour of Chowringhi; for the dirty little tanks at the back of Belvedere; for the street full of smallpox; for the reeking gharri-stand outside the Great Eastern; for the state of the stone and dirt pavements; for the condition of the gullies of Shampooker, and for a hundred other things?

'This, I submit, is an artificial scheme in supersession of Nature's unit, the individual.' The speaker is a slight, spare native in a flat hat-turban, and a black alpaca frock-coat. He looks like a scribe to the boot-heels, and, with his unvarying smile and regulated gesticulation, recalls memories of up-country courts. He never hesitates, is never at a loss for a word, and never in one sentence repeats himself. He talks and talks and talks in a level voice, rising occasionally half an octave when a point has to be driven home. Some of his periods sound very familiar. This, for instance, might be a sentence from the *Mirror*: 'So much for the principle. Let us now examine how far it is supported by precedent.' This sounds bad. When a fluent native is discoursing of 'principles' and 'precedents,' the chances are that he will go on for some time. Moreover, where is the criminal, and what is all this talk about abstractions? They want shovels not sentiments, in this part of the world.

A friendly whisper brings enlightenment: 'They are ploughing through the Calcutta Municipal Bill—plurality of votes, you know. Here are the papers.' And so it is! A mass of motions and amendments on matters relating to ward votes. Is quotes one John Stuart Mill to prove it. There steals over the listener a numbing sense of nightmare. He has heard all this before somewhere—yea; even down to J. S. Mill and the references to the 'true interests of the ratepayers.' He sees what is coming next. Yes, there is the old Sabha, Anjuman, journalistic formula: 'Western education is an exotic plant of recent importation.' How on earth did this man drag Western education into this discussion? Who knows? Perhaps Sir Steuart Bayley does. He seems to be listening. The others are looking at their watches. The spell of the level voice sinks the listener yet deeper into a trance. He is haunted by the ghosts of all the cant of all the political platforms of Great Britain. He hears all the old, old vestry phrases, and once more he smells the Smell. *That* is no dream. Western education is an exotic plant. It is the upas tree, and it is all our fault. We brought it out from England exactly as we brought out the ink-bottles and the patterns for the chairs. We planted it and it grew—monstrous as a banian. Now we are choked by the roots of it spreading so thickly in this fat soil of Bengal. The speaker continues. Bit by bit we builded this dome, visible and invisible, the crown of Writers' Buildings, as we have built and peopled the buildings. Now we have gone too far to retreat, being 'tied and bound with the chain of our own sins.' The speech continues. We made that florid sentence. That torrent of verbiage is Ours. We taught him what was constitutional and what was unconstitutional in the days when Calcutta smelt. Calcutta smells essaying the well-known 'cuttle-fish trick' of the West?

He abandons England for a while, and *now* we get a glimpse of the cloven hoof in a casual reference to Hindus and Mahometans. The Hindus will lose nothing by the complete establishment of plurality of votes. They will have the control of their own wards as they used to have. So there is race-feeling, to be explained away, even among these beautiful desks. Scratch the Council, and you come to the old, old trouble. The black frock-coat sits down, and a keen-eyed, black-bearded Englishman rises with one hand in his pocket to explain his views on an alteration of the vote qualification. The idea of an amendment seems to have just struck him. He hints that he will bring it forward later on. He is academical like the others, but not half so good a speaker. All this is dreary beyond words. Why do they talk and talk about owners and occupiers and burgesses in England and the growth of autonomous institutions when the city, the great city, is here crying out to be cleansed? What has England to do with Calcutta's evil, and why should Englishmen be forced to wander through mazes of unprofitable argument against men who cannot understand the iniquity of dirt?

A pause follows the black-bearded man's speech. Rises another native, a heavily built Babu, in a black gown and a strange head-dress. A snowy white strip of cloth is thrown duster-wise over his shoulders. His voice is high, and not always under control. He begins, 'I will to vote! He has yet to learn how to drive.) Hereon the gentleman with the white cloth: 'Then the complaint is that influential voters will not take the trouble to vote? In my humble opinion, if that be so, adopt voting-papers. *That* is the way to meet them. In the same way—the Calcutta Trades' Association—you abolish all plurality of votes: and that is the way to meet *them*.' Lucid, is it not? Up flies the irresponsible voice, and delivers this statement, 'In the election for the House of Commons plurality are allowed for persons having interest in different districts.' Then hopeless, hopeless fog. It is a great pity that India ever heard of anybody higher than the heads of the Civil Service. Once more a whiff of the Stink. The gentleman gives a defiant jerk of his shoulder-cloth, and sits down.

Then Sir Steuart Bayley: 'The question before the Council is,' etc. There is a ripple of 'Ayes' and 'Noes,' and the 'Noes' have it, whatever it may be. The black-bearded gentleman springs his amendment about the voting qualifications. A large senator in a white waistcoat, and with a most genial smile, rises and proceeds to smash up the amendment. Can't see the use of it. Calls it in effect rubbish. The black dressing-gown, he who spoke first of all, speaks again, and talks of the 'sojourner who comes here for a little time, and then leaves the land.' Well it is for the black gown that the sojourner does come, or there would be no comfy places wherein to talk about the power that can be measured by

CHAPTER IV

ON THE BANKS OF THE HUGHLI

THE clocks of the city have struck two. Where can a man get food? Calcutta is not rich in respect of dainty accommodation. You can stay your stomach at Peliti's or Bonsard's, but their shops are not to be found in Hastings Street, or in the places where brokers fly to and fro in office-jauns, sweating and growing visibly rich. There must be some sort of entertainment where sailors congregate. 'Honest Bombay Jack' supplies nothing but Burma cheroots and whisky in liqueur-glasses, but in Lal Bazar, not far from 'The Sailors' Coffee-rooms,' a board gives bold advertisement that 'officers and seamen can find good quarters.' In evidence a row of neat officers and seamen are sitting on a bench by the 'hotel' door smoking. There is an almost military likeness in their clothes. Perhaps 'Honest Bombay Jack' only keeps one kind of felt hat and one brand of suit. When Jack of the mercantile marine is sober, he is very sober. When he is drunk he is—but ask the river police what a lean, mad opinion without heat or passion. No one seems to resent the garnish.

Let us get down to the river and see this stamp of men more thoroughly. Clark Russell has told us that their lives are hard enough in all conscience. What are their pleasures and diversions? The Port Office, where live the gentlemen who make improvements in the Port of Calcutta, ought to supply information. It stands large and fair, and built in an orientalised manner after the Italians at the corner of Fairlie Place upon the great Strand Road, and a continual clamour of traffic by land and by sea goes up throughout the day and far into the night against its windows. This is a place to enter more reverently than the Bengal Legislative Council, for it controls the direction of the uncertain Hughli down to the Sandheads; owns enormous wealth; and spends huge sums on the frontaging of river banks, the expansion of jetties, and the manufacture of docks costing two hundred lakhs of rupees. Two million tons of sea-going shippage yearly find their way up and down the river by the guidance of the Port Office, and the men of the Port Office know more than it is good for men to hold in their heads. They can without reference to telegraphic bulletins give the position of all the big steamers, coming up or going down, from the Hughli to the sea, day by day, with their tonnage, the names of their captains and the nature of their cargo. Looking out from the verandah of their office over a lancer-regiment of masts, they can declare truthfully the name of every ship within eye-scope, and the day and hour when she will depart.

end of one month exactly thirty rupees. This is a grievance with them; and it seems well-founded.

In the flats above the pilots' room are hushed and chapel-like offices, all sumptuously fitted, where Englishmen write and telephone and telegraph, and deft Babus for ever draw maps of the shifting Hughli. Any hope of understanding the work of the Port Commissioners is thoroughly dashed by being taken through the Port maps of a quarter of a century past. Men have played with the Hughli as children play with a gutter-runnel, and, in return, the Hughli once rose and played with men and ships till the Strand Road was littered with the raffle and the carcasses of big ships. There are photos on the walls of the cyclone of '64, when the *Thunder* came inland and sat upon an American barque, obstructing all the traffic. Very curious are these photos, and almost impossible to believe. How can a big, strong steamer have her three masts razed to deck-level? How can a heavy country-boat be pitched on to the poop of a high-walled liner? and how can the side be bodily torn out of a ship? The photos say that all these things are possible, and men aver that a cyclone may come again and scatter the craft like chaff. Outside the Port Office are the export and import sheds, buildings that can hold a ship's cargo apiece, all standing on reclaimed ground. Here be several strong smells, a mass of railway lines, and a multitude of men. 'Do you see where that trolly is standing, behind the big P. and O. berth? In that place as nearly as may be the whites, Burmese, Burma-whites, Burma-native-whites; Italians with gold ear-rings and a thirst for gambling; Yankees of all the States, with Mulattoes and pure buck-niggers; red and rough Danes, Cingalese, Cornish boys fresh taken from the plough-tail, 'corn-stalks' from colonial ships where they got four pound ten a month as seamen; tun-bellied Germans, Cockney mates keeping a little aloof from the crowd and talking in knots together; unmistakable 'Tommies' who have tumbled into seafaring life by some mistake; cockatoo-tufted Welshmen spitting and swearing like cats; broken-down loafers, grey-headed, penniless and pitiful, swaggering boys, and very quiet men with gashes and cuts on their faces. It is an ethnological museum where all the specimens are playing comedies and tragedies. The head of it all is the 'Deputy Shipping,' and he sits, supported by an English policeman whose fists are knobby, in a great Chair of State. The 'Deputy Shipping' knows all the iniquity of the river-side, all the ships, all the captains, and a fair amount of the men. He is fenced off from the crowd by a strong wooden railing behind which are gathered the unemployed of the mercantile marine. They have had their spree—poor devils!—and now they will go to sea again on as low a wage as three pound ten a month, to fetch up at the end in some Shanghai stew or San Francisco hell. They have turned their backs on the seductions of the Howrah boarding-houses and the delights of Colootollah. If Fate will, 'Nightingale's' will know them no more for a season. But what skipper will take some of these battered, shattered wrecks whose hands shake and whose eyes are red?

Enter suddenly a bearded captain, who has made his selection from the crowd on a previous day, and now wants to get his men passed. He is not fastidious in his choice. His eleven seem a tough lot for such a mild-eyed, civil-spoken man to manage. But the captain in the Shipping Office and the captain on his ship are two different things. He brings his crew up to the 'Deputy Shipping's' bar, and hands in their greasy, tattered discharges. But the heart of the 'Deputy Shipping' is hot within him, because, two days ago, a Howrah crimp stole a whole crew from a down-dropping ship, insomuch that the captain had to come back and whip up a new crew at one o'clock in the day. Evil will it be if the 'Deputy Shipping' finds one of these bounty-jumpers in the chosen crew of the *Blenkindoon*.

The 'Deputy Shipping' tells the story with heat. 'I didn't know they did such things in Calcutta,' says the captain. 'Do such things! They'd steal the eye-teeth out of your head there, Captain' He picks up a discharge and calls for Michael Donelly, a loose-knit, vicious-looking Irish-American who chews. 'Stand up, man, stand up!' Michael Donelly wants to lean against the desk, and the English policeman won't have it. 'What was your last ship?' '*Fairy Queen.*' 'When did you leave her?' ''Bout 'leven days.' 'Captain's name?' 'Flahy.' 'That'll do. Next man: Jules Anderson.' Jules Anderson is a Dane. His statements tally with the discharge-certificate of the United States, as the Eagle attesteth. He is passed and falls back. Slivey, the Englishman, and David, a huge plum-coloured negro who ships as cook, are also passed. Then comes Bassompra, a little Italian, who speaks English. 'What's your last ship?' '*Ferdinand.*' 'No, after that?' 'German barque.' Bassompra does not look happy. 'When did she sail?' 'About three weeks ago.' 'What's her name?' '*Haidée.*' 'You deserted from her?' 'Yes, but she's left port.' The 'Deputy Shipping' runs rapidly through a shipping-list, throws it down with a bang. ''Twon't do. No German barque *Haidée* here for three months. How do I know you don't belong to the *Jackson's* crew? Cap'en, I'm afraid you'll have to ship another man. He must stand over. Take the rest away and make 'em sign.'

The bead-eyed Bassompra seems to have lost his chance of a voyage, and his case will be inquired into. The captain departs with his men and they sign articles for the voyage, while the 'Deputy Shipping' tells strange tales of the sailor-man's life. 'They'll quit a good ship for the sake of a spree, and catch on again at three pound ten, and by Jove, they'll let their skippers pay 'em at ten rupees to the sovereign—poor beggars! As soon as the money's gone they'll ship, but not before. Every one under rank of captain engages here. The competition makes first mates ship sometimes for five pounds or as low as four ten a month.' (The gentleman in the boarding-house was right, you see.) 'A first mate's wages are seven ten or eight, and foreign captains ship for twelve pounds a month and bring their own small stores — everything, that is to say, except beef, peas, flour, coffee, and molasses.'

These things are not pleasant to listen to while the hungry-eyed men in the bad clothes lounge and scratch and loaf behind the railing. What comes to them in the end? They die, it seems, though that is not altogether strange. They die at sea in strange and horrible ways; they die, a few of them, in the Kintals, being lost and suffocated in the great sink of Calcutta; they die in strange places by the water-side, and the Hughli takes them away under the mooring-chains and the buoys, and casts them up on the sands below, if the River Police have missed the capture. They sail the sea because they must live; and there is no end to their toil. Very, very few find haven of any kind, and the earth, whose ways they do not understand, is cruel to them, when they walk upon it to drink and be merry after the manner of beasts. Jack ashore is a pretty thing when he is in a book or in the blue jacket of the Navy. Mercantile Jack is not so lovely. Later on, we will see where his 'sprees' lead him.

CHAPTER V

WITH THE CALCUTTA POLICE

The City was of Night—perchance of Death,
But certainly of Night.

The City of Dreadful Night.

In the beginning, the Police were responsible. They said in a patronising way that they would prefer to take a wanderer round the great city themselves, sooner than let him contract a broken head on his own account in the slums. They said that there were places and places where a white man, unsupported by the arm of the Law, would be robbed and mobbed ; and that there were other places were drunken seamen would make it very unpleasant for him.

'Come up to the fire look-out in the first place, and then you'll be able to see the city.' This was at No. 22 Lal Bazar, which is the headquarters of the Calcutta Police, the centre of the great web of telephone wires where Justice sits all day and all night looking after one million people and a floating population of one hundred thousand. But her work shall be dealt with later on. The fire look-out is a little sentry-box on the top of the three-storied police offices. Here a native watchman waits to give warning to the brigade below if the smoke rises by day or the flames by night in any ward of the city. From this eyrie, in the warm night, one hears the heart of Calcutta beating. Northward, the city stretches away three long miles, with three more miles of suburbs beyond, to Dum-Dum and Barrackpore The lamplit dusk on this side is full of noises and shouts and smells. Close to the Police Office, jovial mariners at the sailors' coffee-shop are roaring hymns. Southerly, the city's confused lights give place to the orderly lamp-rows of the *maidân* and Chowringhi, where the respectabilities live and the Police have very little to do. From the east goes up to the sky the clamour of Sealdah, the rumble of the trams, and the voices of all Bow Bazar chaffering and making merry. Westward are the business quarters, hushed now; the lamps of the shipping on the river; and the twinkling lights on the Howrah side. 'Does the noise of traffic go on all through the hot weather?' 'Of course. The hot months are the busiest in the year and money's tightest. You should see the brokers cutting about at that season. Calcutta *can't* stop, my dear sir.' 'What happens then?' 'Nothing happens; the death-rate goes up a little. That's all!' Even in February, the weather would, up-country, be called muggy and stifling, but Calcutta is convinced that it is her cold season. The noises of the city grow perceptibly; it is the night side of Calcutta waking up and going abroad. Jack in the sailors' coffee-shop is singing joyously: 'Shall we gather at the River

—the beautiful, the beautiful, the River?' There is a clatter of hoofs in the courtyard below. Some of the Mounted Police have come in from somewhere or other out of the great darkness. A clog-dance of iron hoofs follows, and an Englishman's voice is heard soothing an agitated horse who seems to be standing on his hind-legs. Some of the Mounted Police are going out into the great darkness. 'What's on?' 'A dance at Government House. The Reserve men are being formed up below. They're calling the roll.' The Reserve men are all English, and big English at that. They form up and tramp out of the courtyard to line Government Place, and see that Mrs. Lollipop's brougham does not get smashed up by Sirdar Chuckerbutty Bahadur's lumbering C-spring barouche with the two raw Walers. Very military men are the Calcutta European Police in their set-up, and he who knows their composition knows some startling stories of gentlemen-rankers and the like. They are, despite the wearing climate they work in and the wearing work they do, as fine a five-score of Englishmen as you shall find east of Suez.

Listen for a moment from the fire look-out to the voices of the night, and you will see why they must be so. Two thousand sailors of fifty nationalities are adrift in Calcutta every Sunday, and of these perhaps two hundred are distinctly the worse for liquor. There is a mild row going on, even now, somewhere at the back of Bow Bazar, which at nightfall fills with sailormen who have a wonderful gift of falling foul of the native population. To keep the Queen's peace is of course only a small portion of Police duty, but it is trying. The burly president of the lock-up for European drunks—Calcutta central lock-up is worth seeing—rejoices in a sprained thumb just now, and has to do his work left-handed in consequence. But his left hand is a marvellously persuasive one, and when on duty his sleeves are turned up to the shoulder that the jovial mariner may see that there is no deception. The president's labours are handicapped in that the road of sin to the lock-up runs though a grimy little garden—the brick paths are worn deep with the tread of many drunken feet—where a man can give a great deal of trouble by sticking his toes into the ground and getting mixed up with the shrubs. A straight run-in would be much more convenient both for the president and the drunk. Generally speaking—and here Police experience is pretty much the same all over the civilised world—a woman-drunk is a good deal worse than a man-drunk. She scratches and bites like a Chinaman and swears like several fiends. Strange people may be unearthed in the lock-ups. Here is a perfectly true story, not three weeks old. A visitor, an unofficial one, wandered into the native side of the spacious accommodation provided for those who have gone or done wrong. A wild-eyed Babu rose from the fixed charpoy and said in the best of English, 'Good morning, sir.' '*Good* morning. Who are you, and what are you in for?' Then the Babu, in one breath: 'I would have you know that I do not go to prison as a criminal but as a reformer. You've read the *Vicar of Wakefield?*' 'Ye-es.' 'Well, *I* am the Vicar of Bengal—at least that's what I call myself.' The visitor collapsed. He had not nerve enough to continue the conversation. Then said the voice of the authority: 'He's down in connection with a cheating case at Serampore. May be shamming insane, but he'll be seen to in time.'

The best place to hear about the Police is the fire look-out. From that eyrie one can see how difficult must be the work of control over the great, growling beast of a city. By all means let us abuse the Police, but let us see what the poor wretches have to do with their three thousand natives and one hundred Englishmen. From Howrah and Bally and the other suburbs at least a hundred thousand people come in to Calcutta for the day and leave at night. Then, too, Chandernagore is handy for the fugitive law-breaker, who can enter in the evening and get away before the noon of the next day, having marked his house and broken into it.

'But how can the prevalent offence be housebreaking in a place like this? 'Easily enough. When you've seen a little of the city you'll see. Natives sleep and lie about all over the place, and whole quarters are just so many rabbit-warrens. Wait till you see the Machua Bazar. Well, besides the petty theft and burglary, we have heavy cases of forgery and fraud, that leave us with our wits pitted against a Bengali's. When a Bengali criminal is working a fraud of the sort he loves, he is about the cleverest soul you could wish for. He gives us cases a year long to unravel. Then there are the murders in the low houses—very curious things they are. You'll see the house where Sheikh Babu was murdered presently, and you'll understand. The Burra Bazar and Jora Bagan sections are the two worst ones for heavy cases; but Colootollah is the most aggravating. There's Colootollah over yonder—that patch of darkness beyond the lights. That section is full of tuppenny-ha'penny petty cases, that keep the men up all night and make 'em swear. You'll see Colootollah, and then perhaps you'll understand. Bamun Bustee is the quietest of all, and Lal Bazar and Bow Bazar, as you can see for yourself, are the rowdiest. You've no notion what the natives come to the police station for. A man will come in and want a summons against his master for refusing him half-an-hour's leave. I suppose it *does* seem rather revolutionary to an up-country man, but they try to do it here. Now wait a minute, before we go down into the city and see the Fire Brigade turned out. Business is slack with them just now, but you time 'em and see.' An order is given, and a bell strikes softly thrice. There is a rush of men, the click of a bolt, a red fire-engine, spitting and swearing with the sparks flying from the furnace, is dragged out of its shelter. A huge brake, which holds supplementary horses, men, and hatchets, follows, and a hose-cart is the third on the list. The men push the heavy things about as though they were pith toys. The men clamber up, some one says softly, 'All ready there,' and with an angry whistle the fire-engine, followed by the other two, flies out into Lal Bazar. Time—1 min. 40 secs. 'They'll find out it's a false alarm, and come back again in five minutes.' 'Why?' 'Because there will be no constables on the road to give 'em the direction of the fire, and because the driver wasn't told the ward of the outbreak when he went out!' 'Do you mean to say that you can from this absurd pigeon-loft locate the wards in the night-time?' 'What would be the good of a look-out if the man couldn't tell where the fire was?' 'But it's all pitchy black, and the lights are so confusing.'

'You'll be more confused in ten minutes. You'll have lost your way as you never lost it before. You're going to go round Bow Bazar section.'

'And the Lord have mercy on my soul!' Calcutta, the darker portion of it, does not look an inviting place to dive into at night.

CHAPTER VI

THE CITY OF DREADFUL NIGHT

And since they cannot spend or use aright
  The little time here given them in trust,
But lavish it in weary undelight
  Of foolish toil, and trouble, strife and lust—
They naturally clamour to inherit
The Everlasting Future—that their merit
  May have full scope. . . . As surely is most just.

The City of Dreadful Night.

THE difficulty is to prevent this account from growing steadily unwholesome. But one cannot rake through a big city without encountering muck.

The Police kept their word. In five short minutes, as they had prophesied, their charge was lost as he had never been lost before. 'Where are we now?' 'Somewhere off the Chitpore Road, but you wouldn't understand if you were told. Follow now, and step pretty much where we step—there's a good deal of filth hereabouts.'

The thick, greasy night shuts in everything. We have gone beyond the ancestral houses of the Ghoses and the Boses, beyond the lamps, the smells, and the crowd of Chitpore Road, and have come to a great wilderness of packed houses—just such mysterious, conspiring tenements as Dickens would have loved. There is no breeze here, and the air is perceptibly warmer. If Calcutta keeps such luxuries as Commissioners of Sewers and Paving, they die before they reach this place. The air is heavy with a faint, sour stench—the essence of long-neglected abominations—and it cannot escape from among the tall, three-storied houses. 'This, my dear Sir, is a *perfectly* respectable quarter as quarters go. That house at the head of the alley, with the elaborate stucco-work round the top of the door, was built long ago by a celebrated midwife. Great people used to live here once. Now it's the—. Aha! Look out for that carriage.' A big mail-phaeton crashes out of the darkness and, recklessly driven, disappears. The wonder is how it ever got into this maze of narrow streets, where nobody seems to be moving, and where the dull throbbing of the city's life only comes faintly and by snatches. 'Now it's the what?' 'The St. John's Wood of Calcutta—for the rich Babus. That "fitton" belonged to one of them.' 'Well, it's not much of a place to look at!' 'Don't judge by appearances. About here live the women who have beggared kings. We aren't going to let you down into unadulterated vice all at once. You must see it first with the gilding on—and mind that rotten board.'

Stand at the bottom of a lift-shaft and look upwards. Then you will get both the size and the design of the tiny courtyard round which one of these big dark houses is built. The central square may be perhaps ten feet every way, but the balconies that run inside it overhang, and seem to cut away half the available space. To reach the square a man must go round many corners, down a covered-in way, and up and down two or three baffling and confused steps. 'Now you will understand,' say the Police kindly, as their charge blunders, shin-first, into a well-dark winding staircase, 'that these are not the sort of places to visit alone.' 'Who wants to? Of all the disgusting, inaccessible dens—Holy Cupid, what's this?'

A glare of light on the stair-head, a clink of innumerable bangles, a rustle of much fine gauze, and the Dainty Iniquity stands revealed, blazing—literally blazing—with jewellery from head to foot. Take one of the fairest miniatures that the Delhi painters draw, and multiply it by ten; throw in one of Angelica Kaufmann's best portraits, and add anything that you can think of from Beckford to Lalla Rookh, and you will still fall short of the merits of that perfect face! For an instant, even the grim, professional gravity of the Police is relaxed in the presence of the Dainty Iniquity with the gems, who so prettily invites every one to be seated, and proffers such refreshments as she conceives the palates of the barbarians would prefer. Her maids are only one degree less gorgeous than she. Half a lakh, or fifty thousand pounds' worth—it is easier to credit the latter statement than the former—are disposed upon her little body. Each hand carries five jewelled rings which are connected by golden chains to a great jewelled boss of gold in the centre of the back of the hand. Ear-rings weighted with emeralds and pearls, diamond nose-rings, and how many other hundred articles make up the list of adornments. English furniture of a gorgeous and gimcrack kind, unlimited chandeliers, and a collection of atrocious Continental prints are scattered about the house, and on every landing squats or loafs a Bengali who can talk English with unholy fluency. The recurrence suggests—only suggests, mind—a grim possibility of the affectation of excessive virtue by day, tempered with the sort of unwholesome enjoyment after dusk—this loafing and lobbying and chattering and smoking, and unless the bottles lie, tippling, among the foul-tongued handmaidens of the Dainty Iniquity. How many men follow this double, deleterious sort of life? The Police are discreetly dumb.

'Now don't go talking about "domiciliary visits" just because this one happens to be a pretty woman. We've *got* to know these creatures. They make the rich man and the poor spend their money; and when a man can't get money for 'em honestly, he comes under *our* notice. Now do you see? If there was any "domiciliary visit" about it, the whole houseful would be hidden past our finding as soon as we turned up in the courtyard. We're friends—to a certain extent.' And, indeed, it seemed no difficult thing to be friends to any extent with the Dainty Iniquity who was so surpassingly different from all that experience taught of the beauty of the East. Here was the face from which a man could write *Lalla Rookhs* by the dozen, and believe every ord that he wrote. Hers was the beauty that yron sang of when he wrote . . .

'Remember, if you come here alone, the chances ·e that you'll be clubbed, or stuck, or, anyhow, ıobbed You'll understand that thıs part of the ʼorld is shut to Europeans—absolutely. Mind ıe steps, and follow on.' The vısion dies out ı the smells and gross darkness of the night, ı evil, time-rotten brickwork, and another wilder-ess of shut-up houses.

Follows, after another plunge into a passage of courtyard, and up a staircase, the apparition of Fat Vice, in whom is no sort of romance, nor ›eauty, but unlimited coarse humour. She too ; studded with jewels, and her house is even finer han the house of the other, and more infested vith the extraordinary men who speak such good English and are so deferentıal to the Police. The Fat Vice has been a great leader of fashion n her day, and stripped a zemindar Raja to his ast acre—insomuch that he ended in the House of Correction for a theft commıtted for her sake. Native opinion has it that she is a 'monstrous well-preserved woman.' On this point, as on some others, the races will agree to differ.

The scene changes suddenly as a slide in a magic-lantern. Dainty Inıquity and Fat Vice slide away on a roll of streets and alleys, each more squalid than its predecessor. We are 'somewhere at the back of the Machua Bazar,' well in the heart of the city. There are no houses here —nothing but acres and acres, it seems, of foul wattle-and-dab huts, any one of which would be a disgrace to a frontier village. The whole arrangement is a neatly contrived germ and fire trap, reflecting great credit upon the Calcutta Municipality.

'What happens when these pig-sties catch fire?' 'They're built up again,' say the Police, as though this were the natural order of things. 'Land is immensely valuable here.' All the more reason, then, to turn several Haussmanns loose into the city, with instructions to make barracks for the population that cannot find room in the huts and sleeps in the open ways, cherishing dogs and worse, much worse, in its unwashen bosom. 'Here is a licensed coffee-shop. This is where your servants go for amusement and to see nautches.' There is a huge thatch shed, ingeniously ornamented with insecure kerosene lamps, and crammed with drivers, cooks, small store-keepers and the like. Never a sign of a European. Why? 'Because if an Englishman messed about here, he'd get into trouble. Men don't come here unless they're drunk or have lost their way.' The hack-drivers —they have the privilege of voting, have they not?—look peaceful enough as they squat on tables or crowd by the doors to watch the nautch that is going forward. Five pitiful draggle-tails are huddled together on a bench under one of the lamps, while the sixth is squirming and shrieking before the impassive crowd. She sings of love as understood by the Oriental—the love that dries the heart and consumes the liver. In this place, the words that would look so well on paper have an evil and ghastly significance. The men stare or sup tumblers and cups of a filthy decoction, and the *kunchenee* howls with renewed vigour in the presence of the Police. Where the Dainty Iniquity was hung with gold and gems, she is trapped with pewter and glass; and where there was heavy embroidery on the Fat Vice's dress, defaced, stamped tinsel faithfully reduplicates the pattern on the tawdry robes of the *kunchenee.*

Two or three men with uneasy consciences have quietly slipped out of the coffee-shop into the mazes of the huts. The Police laugh, and those nearest in the crowd laugh applausively, as in duty bound. Thus do the rabbits grin uneasily when the ferret lands at the bottom of the burrow and begins to clear the warren.

'The *chandoo*-shops shut up at six, so you'll have to see opium-smoking before dark some day. No, you won't, though.' The detective makes for a half-opened door of a hut whence floats the fragrance of the Black Smoke. Those of the inhabitants who are able promptly clear out—they have no love for the Police—and there remain only four men lying down and one standing up. This latter has a pet mongoose coiled round his neck. He speaks English fluently. Yes, he has no fear. It was a private smoking party and—'No business to-night—show how you smoke opium.' 'Aha! You want to see. Very good, I show. Hiya! you'—he kicks a man on the floor—'show how opium-smoke.' The kickee grunts lazily and turns on his elbow. The mongoose, always keeping to the man's neck, erects every hair of its body like an angry cat, and chatters in its owner's ear. The lamp for the opium-pipe is the only one in the room, and lights a scene as wild as anything in the witches' revel; the mongoose acting as the familiar spirit. A voice from the ground says, in tones of infinite weariness: 'You take *afim*, so'—a long, long pause, and another kick from the man possessed of the devil—the mongoose. 'You take *afim?*' He takes a pellet of the black, treackly stuff on the end of a knitting-needle. 'And light *afim*.' He plunges the pellet into the night-light, where it swells and fumes greasily. 'And then you put it in your pipe.' The smoking pellet is jammed into the tiny bowl of the thick, bamboo-stemmed pipe, and all speech ceases, except the unearthly chitter of the mongoose. The man on the ground is sucking at his pipe, and when the smoking pellet has ceased to smoke will be halfway to *Nibban*. 'Now you go,' says the man with the mongoose. 'I am going smoke.' The hut door closes upon a red-lit view of huddled legs and bodies, and the man with the mongoose sinking, sinking on to his knees, his head bowed forward, and the little hairy devil chattering on the nape of his neck.

After this the fetid night air seems almost cool, for the hut is as hot as a furnace. 'Now for Colootollah. Come through the huts. There is no decoration about *this* vice.'

The huts now gave place to houses very tall and spacious and very dark. But for the narrowness of the streets we might have stumbled upon Chowringhi in the dark. An hour and a half has passed, and up to this time we have not crossed our trail once. 'You might knock about the city for a night and never cross the same line. Recollect Calcutta isn't one of your poky up-country cities of a lakh and a half of people.' 'How long does it take to know it then?' 'About a lifetime, and even then some of the streets puzzle you.' 'How much has the head of a ward to know?' 'Every house in his ward if he can, who owns it, what sort of character the inhabitants are, who are their friends, who go out and in, who loaf about the place at night, and so on and so on.' 'And he knows all this by night as well as by day?' 'Of course. Why shouldn't he?' 'No reason in the world. Only it's pitchy black just now, and I'd like to see where this alley is going to end.' 'Round the corner beyond that dead wall. There's a lamp there. Then you'll be able to see.' A shadow flits out of a gully and disappears. 'Who's that?' 'Sergeant of Police just to see where we're going in case of accidents.' Another shadow staggers into the darkness. 'Who's *that?*' 'Soldier from the Fort or a sailor from the ships. I couldn't quite see.' The Police open a shut door in a high wall, and stumble unceremoniously among a gang of women cooking their food. The floor is of beaten earth, the steps that lead into the upper stories are unspeakably grimy, and the heat is the heat of April. The women rise hastily, and the light of the bull's eye—for the Police have now lighted a lantern in regular London fashion—shows six bleared faces—one a half-native half-Chinese one, and the others Bengali. 'There are no men here!' they cry. 'The house is empty.' Then they grin and jabber and chew *pan* and spit, and hurry up the steps into the darkness. A range of three big rooms has been knocked into one here, and there is some sort of arrangement of mats. But an average country-bred is more sumptuously accommodated in an Englishman's stable. A horse would snort at the accommodation.

'Nice sort of place, isn't it?' say the Police genially. 'This is where the sailors get robbed and drunk.' 'They must be blind drunk before they come.' 'Na—na! Na sailor men ee—yah!' chorus the women, catching at the one word they understand. 'Arl gone!' The Police take no notice, but tramp down the big room with the mat loose-boxes. A woman is shivering in one of these. 'What's the matter?' 'Fever. Seek. Vary, *vary* seek.' She huddles herself into a heap on the *charpoy* and groans.

A tiny, pitch-black closet opens out of the long room, and into this the Police plunge. 'Hullo! What's here?' Down flashes the lantern, and a white hand with black nails comes out of the gloom. Somebody is asleep or drunk in the cot. The ring of lantern-light travels slowly up and down the body. 'A sailor from the ships. He'll be robbed before the morning most likely.' The man is sleeping like a little child, both arms thrown over his head, and he is not unhandsome. He is shoeless, and there are huge holes in his stockings. He is a pure-blooded white, and carries the flush of innocent sleep on his cheeks.

The light is turned off, and the Police depart; while the woman in the loose-box shivers, and moans that she is 'seek; vary, *vary* seek.'

CHAPTER VII

DEEPER AND DEEPER STILL

I built myself a lordly pleasure-house,
  Wherein at ease for aye to dwell.
I said, 'O Soul, make merry and carouse,
  Dear soul, for all is well.'

The Palace of Art.

'AND where next? I don't like Colootollah.' The Police and their charge are standing in the interminable waste of houses under the starlight. 'To the lowest sink of all, but you wouldn't know if you were told.' They lead till they come to the last circle of the Inferno — a long, quiet, winding road. 'There you are; you can see for yourself.'

But there is nothing to be seen. On one side are houses — gaunt and dark, naked and devoid of furniture; on the other, low, mean stalls, lighted, and with shamelessly open doors, where women stand and mutter and whisper one to another. There is a hush here, or at least the busy silence of an office or counting-house in working hours. One look down the street is sufficient. Lead on, gentlemen of the Calcutta

Police. We do not love the lines of open doors, the flaring lamps within, the glimpses of the tawdry toilet-tables adorned with little plaster dogs, glass balls from Christmas-trees, and—for religion must not be despised though women be fallen—pictures of the saints and statuettes of the Virgin. The street is a long one, and other streets, full of the same pitiful wares, branch off from it.

'Why are they so quiet? Why don't they make a row and sing and shout, and so on?' 'Why should they, poor devils?' say the Police, and fall to telling tales of horror, of women decoyed and shot into this trap. Then other tales that shatter one's belief in all things and folk of good repute. 'How can you Police have faith in humanity?'

'That's because you're seeing it all in a lump for the first time, and it's not nice that way. Makes a man jump rather, doesn't it? But, recollect, you've *asked* for the worst places, and you can't complain.' 'Who's complaining? Bring on your atrocities. Isn't that a European woman at that door? 'Yes. Mrs. D——, widow of a soldier, mother of seven children.' 'Nine, if you please, and good evening to you,' shrills Mrs. D——, leaning against the door-post, her arms folded on her bosom. She is a rather pretty, slightly made Eurasian, and whatever shame she may have owned she has long since cast behind her. A shapeless Burmo-native trot, with high cheek-bones and mouth like a shark, calls Mrs. D—— 'Mem-Sahib.' The word jars unspeakably. Her life is a matter between herself and her Maker, but in that she—the widow of a soldier of the Queen—has stooped to this common foulness in the face of the city, she has offended against the White race. 'You're from up-country, and of course you don't understand. There are any amount of that lot in the city,' say the Police. Then the secret of the insolence of Calcutta is made plain. Small wonder the natives fail to respect the Sahib, seeing what they see and knowing what they know. In the good old days, the Honourable the Directors deported him or her who misbehaved grossly, and the white man preserved his face. He may have been a ruffian, but he was a ruffian on a large scale. He did not sink in the presence of the people. The natives are quite right to take the wall of the Sahib who has been at great pains to prove that he is of the same flesh and blood.

All this time Mrs. D—— stands on the threshold of her room and looks upon the men with unabashed eyes. Mrs. D—— is a lady with a story. She is not averse to telling it. 'What was—ahem —the case in which you were—er—hmn—concerned, Mrs. D——?' 'They said I'd poisoned my husband by putting something into his drinking water.' This is interesting. 'And—ah—*did* you?' ''Twasn't proved,' says Mrs. D—— with a laugh, a pleasant, lady-like laugh that does infinite credit to her education and upbringing. Worthy Mrs. D——! It would pay a novelist—a French one let us say—to pick you out of the stews and make you talk.

The Police move forward, into a region of Mrs.

D——'s. Everywhere are the empty houses, and the babbling women in print gowns. The clocks in the city are close upon midnight, but the Police show no signs of stopping. They plunge hither and thither, like wreckers into the surf; and each plunge brings up a sample of misery, filth and woe.

A woman—Eurasian—rises to a sitting position on a cot and blinks sleepily at the Police. Then she throws herself down with a grunt. 'What's the matter with you?' 'I live in Markiss Lane and'—this with intense gravity—'I'm *so* drunk.' She has a rather striking gipsy-like face, but her language might be improved.

'Come along,' say the Police, 'we'll head back to Bentinck Street, and put you on the road to the Great Eastern.' They walk long and steadily, and the talk falls on gambling hells. 'You ought to see our men rush one of 'em. When we've marked a hell down, we post men at the entrances and carry it. Sometimes the Chinese bite, but as a rule they fight fair. It's a pity we hadn't a hell to show you. Let's go in here—there may be something forward.' 'Here' appears to be in the heart of a Chinese quarter, for the pigtails—do they ever go to bed?—are scuttling about the streets. 'Never go into a Chinese place alone,' say the Police, and swing open a postern gate in a strong, green door. Two Chinamen appear.

'What are we going to see?' 'Japanese gir—— No, we aren't, by Jove! Catch that Chinaman, *quick*.' The pigtail is trying to double back across a courtyard into an inner chamber; but a large hand on his shoulder spins him round and puts him in rear of the line of advancing Englishmen, who are, be it observed, making a fair amount of noise with their boots. A second door is thrown open, and the visitors advance into a large, square room blazing with gas. Here thirteen pigtails, deaf and blind to the outer world, are bending over a table. The captured Chinaman dodges uneasily in the rear of the procession. Five—ten—fifteen seconds pass, the Englishmen standing in the full light less than three paces from the absorbed gang who see nothing. Then the burly Superintendent brings his hand down on his thigh with a crack like a pistol-shot and shouts: 'How do, John?' Follows a frantic rush of scared Celestials, almost tumbling over each other in their anxiety to get clear. One pigtail scoops up a pile of copper money, another a chinaware soup-bowl, and only a little mound of accusing cowries remains on the white matting that covers the table. In less than half a minute two facts are forcibly brought home to the visitor. First, that a pigtail is largely composed of silk, and rasps the palm of the hand as it slides through; and secondly, that the forearm of a Chinaman is surprisingly muscular and well-developed. 'What's going to be done?' 'Nothing. There are only three of us, and all the ringleaders would get away. We've got 'em safe any time we want to catch 'em, if this little visit doesn't make 'em shift their quarters. Hi! John. No pidgin to-night. Show how you makee play. That fat youngster there is our informer.'

Half the pigtails have fled into the darkness, but the remainder assured and trebly assured that he Police really mean 'no pidgin,' return to the able and stand round while the croupier manipuates the cowries, the little curved slip of bamboo, ınd the soup-bowl. They never gamble, these nnocents. They only come to look on, and smoke ɔpium in the next room. Yet as the game progresses heir eyes light up, and one by one put their money ɔn odd or even—the number of the cowries that ıre covered and left uncovered by the little soupɔowl. *Mythan* is the name of the amusement, and, vhatever may be its demerits, it is clean. The Police look on while their charge plays and loots a ɔarchment-skinned horror—one of Swift's Struldɔrugs, strayed from Laputa—of the enormous sum ɔf two annas. The return of this wealth, doubled, ıets the loser beating his forehead against the table from sheer gratitude.

'Most immoral game this. A man might drop ive whole rupees, if he began playing at sun-down ınd kept it up all night. Don't you ever play whist ɔccasionally?'

'Now, we didn't bring you round to make un of this department. A man can lose as much ıs ever he likes and he can fight as well, and f he loses all his money he steals to get more. A Chinaman is insane about gambling, and half his crime comes from it. It *must* be kept down. Here we are in Bentinck Street and you can be driven to the Great Eastern in a few minutes. Joss-houses? Oh yes. If you want more horrors, Superintendent Lamb will take you round with him to-morrow ıfternoon at five. Good night.'

The Police depart, and in a few minutes the

silent respectability of Old Council House Street, with the grim Free Kirk at the end of it, is reached. All good Calcutta has gone to bed, the last tram has passed, and the peace of the night is upon the world. Would it be wise and rational to climb the spire of that Kirk, and shout: 'O true believers! Decency is a fraud and a sham. There is nothing clean or pure or wholesome under the Stars, and we are all going to perdition together. Amen!' On second thoughts it would not; for the spire is slippery, the night is hot, and the Police have been specially careful to warn their charge that he must not be carried away by the sight of horrors that cannot be written or hinted at.

'Good morning,' says the Policeman tramping the pavement in front of the Great Eastern, and he nods his head pleasantly to show that he is the representative of Law and Peace and that the city of Calcutta is safe from itself at the present.

CHAPTER VIII

CONCERNING LUCIA

TIME must be filled in somehow till five this afternoon, when Superintendent Lamb will reveal more horrors. Why not, the trams aiding, go to the Old Park Street Cemetery?

'You want go Park Street? No trams going Park Street. You get out here.' Calcutta tram conductors are not polite. The car shuffles unsympathetically down the street, and the evicted is stranded in Dhurrumtollah, which may be the Hammersmith Highway of Calcutta. Providence arranged this mistake, and paved the way to a Great Discovery now published for the first time. Dhurrumtollah is full of the People of India, walking in family parties and groups and confidential couples. And the people of India are neither Hindu nor Mussulman—Jew, Ethiop, Gueber, or expatriated British. They are the Eurasians, and there are hundreds and hundreds of them in Dhurrumtollah now. There is Papa with a shining black hat fit for a counsellor of the Queen, and Mamma, whose silken dress is tight upon her portly figure, and The Brood made up of straw-hatted, olive-cheeked, sharp-eyed little boys, and leggy maidens wearing white, open-work stockings calculated to show dust. There are the young men who smoke bad cigars and carry themselves lordily—such as have incomes. There are also the young women with the beautiful eyes and the wonderful dresses which always fit so badly across the shoulders. And they carry prayer-books or baskets, because they are either going to mass or the market. Without doubt, these are the People of India. They were born in it, bred in it, and will die in it. The Englishman only comes to the country, and the natives of course were there from the first, but these people have been made here, and no one has done anything for them except talk and write about them. Yet they belong, some of them, to old and honourable families, hold houses in Sealdah, and are rich, a few of them. They all look prosperous and contented, and they chatter eternally in that curious dialect that no one has yet reduced to print. Beyond what little they please to reveal now and again in the newspapers, we know nothing about their life which touches so intimately the White on the one hand and the Black on the other. It must be interesting—more interesting than the colourless Anglo-Indian article; but who has treated of it? There was one novel once in which the second heroine was an Eurasienne. She was a strictly subordinate character and came to a sad end. The poet of the race, Henry Derozio,—he of whom Mr. Thomas Edwards wrote a history,—

was bitten with Keats and Scott and Shelley, and overlooked in his search for material things that lay nearest to him. All this mass of humanity in Dhurrumtollah is unexploited and almost unknown. Wanted, therefore, a writer from among the Eurasians, who shall write so that men shall be pleased to read a story of Eurasian life; then outsiders will be interested in the People of India, and will admit that the race has possibilities.

A futile attempt to get to Park Street from Dhurrumtollah ends in the market—the Hogg Market men call it. Perhaps a knight of that name built it. It is not one-half as pretty as the Crawford Market, in Bombay, but . . . it appears to be the trysting-place of Young Calcutta. The natural inclination of youth is to lie abed late, and to let the seniors do all the hard work. Why, therefore, should Pyramus, who has to be ruling account forms at ten, and Thisbe, who *cannot* be interested in the price of second-quality beef, wander, in studiously correct raiment, round and about the stalls before the sun is well clear of the earth? Pyramus carries a walking-stick with imitation silver straps upon it, and there are cloth tops to his boots; but his collar has been two days worn. Thisbe crowns her dark head with a blue velvet Tam-o'-Shanter; but one of her boots lacks a button, and there is a tear in the left-hand glove. Mamma, who despises gloves, is rapidly filling a shallow basket, that the coolie-boy carries, with vegetables, potatoes, purple brinjals, and—O Pyramus! Do you ever kiss Thisbe when Mamma is not by?—garlic—yea, *lusson* of the bazaar. Mamma is generous in her views on garlic. Pyramus comes round the corner of the stall looking for nobody in particular — not he — and is elaborately polite to Mamma. Somehow, he and Thisbe drift off together, and Mamma, very portly and very voluble, is left to chaffer and sort and select alone. In the name of the Sacred Unities do not, young people, retire to the meat-stalls to exchange confidences! Come up to this end, where the roses are arriving in great flat baskets, where the air is heavy with the fragrance of flowers, and the young buds and greenery are littering all the floor. They won't —they prefer talking by the dead, unromantic muttons, where there are not so many buyers. There must have been a quarrel to make up. Thisbe shakes the blue velvet Tam-o'-Shanter and says, 'Oah yess!' scornfully. Pyramus answers: 'No-a, no-a. Do-ant say thatt.' Mamma's basket is full and she picks up Thisbe hastily. Pyramus departs. *He* never came here to do any marketing. He came to meet Thisbe, who in ten years will own a figure very much like Mamma's. May their ways be smooth before them, and after honest service of the Government, may Pyramus retire on 250 rupees per mensem, into a nice little house somewhere in Monghyr or Chunar!

From love by natural sequence to death. Where *is* the Park Street Cemetery? A hundred hack-drivers leap from their boxes and invade the market, and after a short struggle one of them uncarts his capture in a burial-ground—a ghastly new place, close to a tramway. This is not what is wanted. The living dead are here—the people whose names are not yet altogether perished and whose tombstones are tended. 'Where are the *old* dead?' 'Nobody goes there,' says the driver. 'It is up that road.' He points up a long and utterly deserted thoroughfare, running between high walls. This is the place, and the entrance to it, with its gardener waiting with one brown, battered rose for the visitor, its grilled door and its professional notices, bears a hideous likeness to the entrance of Simla churchyard. But, once inside, the sightseer stands in the heart of utter desolation—all the more forlorn for being swept up. Lower Park Street cuts a great graveyard in two. The guide-books will tell you when the place was opened and when it was closed. The eye is ready to swear that it is as old as Herculaneum and Pompeii. The tombs are small houses. It is as though we walked down the streets of a town, so tall are they and so closely do they stand—a town shrivelled by fire, and scarred by frost and siege. Men must have been afraid of their friends rising up before the due time that they weighted them with such cruel mounds of masonry. Strong man, weak woman, or somebody's 'infant son aged fifteen months,' for each the squat obelisk, the defaced classic temple, the cellaret of chunam, or the candlestick of brickwork—the heavy slab, the rust-eaten railings, whopper-jawed cherubs, and the apoplectic angels. Men were rich in those days and could afford to put a hundred cubic feet of masonry into the grave of even so humble a person as 'Jno. Clements, Captain of the Country Service, 1820.' When the 'dearly beloved' had held rank answering to that of Commissioner, the efforts are still more sumptuous and the verse . . . Well, the following speaks for itself :—

> Soft on thy tomb shall fond Remembrance shed
> The warm yet unavailing tear,
> And purple flowers that deck the honoured dead
> Shall strew the loved and honoured bier.

Failure to comply with the contract does not, let us hope, entail forfeiture of the earnest-money; or the honoured dead might be grieved. The slab is out of his tomb, and leans foolishly against it; the railings are rotted, and there are no more lasting ornaments than blisters and stains, which are the work of the weather, and not the result of the 'warm yet unavailing tear.'

Let us go about and moralise cheaply on the tombstones, trailing the robe of pious reflection up and down the pathways of the grave. Here is a big and stately tomb sacred to 'Lucia,' who died in 1776 A.D., aged 23. Here also be lichened verses which an irreverent thumb can bring to light. Thus they wrote, when their hearts were heavy in them, one hundred and sixteen years ago:—

> What needs the emblem, what the plaintive strain,
> What all the arts that sculpture e'er expressed,
> To tell the treasure that these walls contain?
> Let those declare it most who knew her best.

The tender pity she would oft display
  Shall be with interest at her shrine returned,
Connubial love, connubial tears repay,
  And Lucia loved shall still be Lucia mourned.

Though closed the lips, though stopped the tuneful breath,
  The silent, clay-cold monitress shall teach—
In all the alarming eloquence of death
  With double pathos to the heart shall preach.

Shall teach the virtuous maid, the faithful wife,
  If young and fair, that young and fair was she,
Then close the useful lesson of her life,
  And tell them what she is, they soon must be.

That goes well, even after all these years, does it not? and seems to bring Lucia very near, in spite of what the later generation is pleased to call the stiltedness of the old-time verse.

Who will declare the merits of Lucia—dead in her spring before there was even a *Hickey's Gazette* to chronicle the amusements of Calcutta, and publish, with scurrilous asterisks, the *liaisons* of heads of departments? What pot-bellied East Indiaman brought the 'virtuous maid' up the river, and did Lucia 'make her bargain' as the cant of those times went, on the first, second, or third day after her arrival? Or did she, with the others of the batch, give a spinsters' ball as a last trial—following the custom of the country? No. She was a fair Kentish maiden, sent out, at a cost of five hundred pounds, English money, under the captain's charge, to wed the man of her choice, and *he* knew Clive well, had had dealings with Omichand, and talked to men who had lived through the terrible night in the Black Hole. He was a rich man, Lucia's battered tomb proves it, and he gave Lucia all that her heart could wish: a green-painted boat to take the air in on the river of evenings, Coffree slave-boys who could play on the French horn, and even a very elegant, neat coach with a genteel rutlan roof ornamented with flowers very highly finished, ten best polished plate glasses, ornamented with a few elegant medallions enriched with mother-o'-pearl, that she might take her drive on the course as befitted a factor's wife. All these things he gave her. And when the convoys came up the river, and the guns thundered, and the servants of the Honourable the East India Company drank to the king's health, be sure that Lucia before all the other ladies in the Fort had her choice of the new stuffs from England and was cordially hated in consequence. Tilly Kettle painted her picture a little before she died, and the hot-blooded young writers did duel with small-swords in the Fort ditch for the honour of piloting her through a minuet at the Calcutta theatre or the Punch House. But Warren Hastings danced with her instead, and the writers were confounded —every man of them. She was a toast far up the river. And she walked in the evening on the bastions of Fort William, and said, 'La! I protest!' It was there that she exchanged congratulations with all her friends on the 20th of October, when those who were alive gathered together to felicitate themselves on having come through another hot season; and the men—even the sober factor saw no wrong here—got most royally and Britishly drunk on Madeira that had twice rounded the Cape. But Lucia fell sick, and the doctor—he who went home after seven years with five lakhs and a half, and a corner of this vast graveyard to his account—said that it was a pukka or putrid fever, and the system required strengthening. So they fed Lucia on hot curries, and mulled wine worked up with spirits and fortified with spices, for nearly a week; at the end of which time she closed her eyes on the weary river and the Fort for ever, and a gallant, with a turn for *belles-lettres*, wept openly as men did then and had no shame of it, and composed the verses above set, and thought himself a neat hand at the pen—stap his vitals! But the factor was so grieved that he could write nothing at all—could only spend his money—and he counted his wealth by lakhs—on a sumptuous grave. A little later on he took comfort, and when the next batch came out—

But this has nothing whatever to do with the story of Lucia, the 'virtuous maid, the faithful wife.' Her ghost went to a big Calcutta powder ball that very night, and looked very beautiful. I met her.

AMONG THE RAILWAY FOLK

Among the Railway Folk

CHAPTER I

A RAILWAY SETTLEMENT

JAMALPUR is the headquarters of the East India Railway. This in itself is not a startling statement. The wonder begins with the exploration of Jamalpur, which is a station entirely made by, and devoted to, the use of those untiring servants of the public, the railway folk. They have towns of their own at Toondla and Assensole ; a sun-dried sanitarium at Bandikui ; and Howrah, Ajmir, Allahabad, Lahore, and Pindi know their colonies. But Jamalpur is unadulteratedly 'Railway,' and he who has nothing to do with the E. I. Railway in some shape or another feels a stranger and an interloper. Running always east and southerly, the train carries him from the torments of the North-west into the wet, woolly warmth of Bengal, where may be found the hothouse heat that has ruined the temper of the good people of Calcutta. The land is fat and greasy with good living, and the wealth of the bodies of innumerable dead things; and here—just above Mokameh—may be seen fields stretching, without stick, stone, or bush to break the view, from the railway line to the horizon.

Up-country innocents must look at the map to learn that Jamalpur is near the top left-hand corner of the big loop that the E. I. R. throws out round Bhagalpur and part of the Bara-Banki districts. Northward of Jamalpur, as near as may be, lies the Ganges and Tirhoot, and eastward an off-shoot of the volcanic Rajmehal range blocks the view.

A station which has neither Judge, Commissioner, Deputy, or 'Stunt, which is devoid of law courts, *ticca-gharries*, District Superintendents of Police, and many other evidences of an over-cultured civilisation, is a curiosity. 'We administer ourselves,' says Jamalpur proudly, 'or we did—till we had local self-government in—and now the racket-marker administers us.' This is a solemn fact. The station, which had its beginnings thirty odd years ago, used, till comparatively recent times, to control its own roads, sewage, conservancy, and the like. But, with the introduction of local self-government, it was ordained that the 'inestimable boon' should be extended to a place made by, and maintained for, Europeans, and a brand-new municipality was created and nominated according to the many rules of the game. In the skirmish that ensued, the Club racket-marker fought his way to the front, secured a place on a board largely composed of Babus, and since that day Jamalpur's views on government have not been fit for publication. To understand the magnitude of the insult, one must study the city —for station, in the strict sense of the word, it is not. Crotons, palms, mangoes, wellingtonias, teak, and bamboos adorn it, and the poinsettia and bougainvillea, the railway creeper and the *Bignonia venusta*, make it gay with many colours. It is laid out with military precision; to each house its just share of garden, its red-brick path, its growth of trees, and its neat little wicket gate. Its general aspect, in spite of the Dutch formality, is that of an English village, such a thing as enterprising stage-managers put on the theatres at home. The hills have thrown a protecting arm round nearly three sides of it, and on the fourth it is bounded by what are locally known as the 'sheds'; in other words, the station, offices, and workshops of the Company. The E. I. R. only exists for outsiders. Its servants speak of it reverently, angrily, despitefully, or enthusiastically as 'The Company'; and they never omit the big, big C. Men must have treated the Honourable the East India Company in something the same fashion ages ago. 'The Company' in Jamalpur is Lord Dufferin, all the Members of Council, the Body-Guard, Sir Frederick Roberts, Mr. Westland, whose name is at the bottom of the currency notes, the Oriental Life Assurance Company, and the Bengal Government all rolled into one. At first when a stranger enters this life, he is inclined to scoff and ask, in his ignorance, '*What* is this Company that you talk so much about?' Later on, he ceases to scoff; for the Company is a 'big' thing—almost big enough to satisfy an American.

Ere beginning to describe its doings, let it be written, and repeated several times hereafter, that the E. I. R. passenger carriages, and especially the second-class, are just now horrid—being filthy and unwashen, dirty to look at, and dirty to live in. Having cast this small stone, we will examine Jamalpur. When it was laid out, in or before the Mutiny year, its designers allowed room for growth, and made the houses of one general design—some of brick, some of stone, some three, four, and six roomed, some single men's barracks and some two-storied—all for the use of the employés. King's Road, Prince's Road, Queen's Road, and Victoria Road—Jamalpur is loyal—cut the breadth of the station; and Albert Road, Church Street, and Steam Road the length of it. Neither on these roads, or on any of the cool-shaded smaller ones is anything unclean or unsightly to be found. There is a dreary village in the neighbourhood which is said to make the most of any cholera that may be going, but Jamalpur itself is specklessly and spotlessly neat. From St. Mary's Church to the railway station, and from the buildings where they print daily about half a lakh of tickets, to the ringing, roaring, rattling workshops, everything has the air of having been cleaned up at ten that very morning and put under a glass case. There is a holy calm about the roads—totally unlike anything in an English manufacturing town. Wheeled conveyances are few, because every man's bungalow is close to his work, and when the day has begun and the offices of the 'Loco.' and 'Traffic' have soaked up their thousands of natives and hundreds of Europeans, you shall pass under the dappled shadows of the trees, hearing nothing louder than the croon of some bearer playing with a child in the verandah or the faint tinkle of a piano. This is pleasant, and produces an impression of Watteau-like refinement tempered with Arcadian simplicity. The dry, anguished howl of the 'buzzer,' the big steam-whistle, breaks the hush, and all Jamalpur is alive with the tramping of tiffin-seeking feet. The Company gives one hour for meals between eleven and twelve. On the stroke of noon there is another rush back to the works or the offices, and Jamalpur sleeps through the afternoon till four or half-past, and then rouses for tennis at the institute.

In the hot weather it splashes in the swimming bath, or reads, for it has a library of several thousand books. One of the most flourishing lodges in the Bengal jurisdiction—'St. George in the East'—lives at Jamalpur, and meets twice a month. Its members point out with justifiable pride that all the fittings were made by their own hands; and the lodge in its accoutrements and the energy of the craftsmen can compare with any in India. But the institute is the central gathering place, and its half-dozen tennis-courts and neatly-laid-out grounds seem to be always full. Here, if a stranger could judge, the greater part of the flirtation of Jamalpur is carried out, and here the dashing apprentice—the apprentices are the liveliest of all—learns that there are problems harder than any he studies at the night school, and that the heart of a maiden is more inscrutable than the mechanism of a locomotive. On Tuesdays and Fridays the volunteers parade. A and B Companies, 150 strong in all, of the E. I. R. Volunteers, are stationed here with the band. Their uniform, grey with red facings, is not lovely, but they know how to shoot and drill. They have to. The 'Company' makes it a condition of service that a man must be a volunteer; and volunteer in something more than name he must be, or some one will ask the reason why. Seeing that there are no regulars between Howrah and Dinapore, the 'Company' does well in exacting this toll. Some of the old soldiers are wearied of drill, some of the youngsters don't like it, but—the way they entrain and detrain is worth seeing. They are as mobile a corps as can be desired, and perhaps ten or twelve years hence the Government may possibly be led to take a real interest in them and spend a few thousand rupees in providing them with real soldiers' kits—not uniform and rifle merely. Their ranks include all sorts and conditions of men—heads of the 'Loco.' and 'Traffic,'—the Company is no respecter of rank—clerks in the 'audit,' boys from mercantile firms at home, fighting with the intricacies of time, fare, and freight tables; guards who have grown grey in the service of the Company; mail and passenger drivers with nerves of cast-iron, who can shoot through a long afternoon without losing temper or flurrying; light-blue East Indians; Tyne-side men, slow of speech and uncommonly strong in the arm; lathy apprentices who have not yet 'filled out'; fitters, turners, foremen, full, assistant, and sub-assistant stationmasters, and a host of others. In the hands of the younger men the regulation Martini-Henry naturally goes off the line occasionally on hunting expeditions.

There is a twelve hundred yards range running down one side of the station, and the condition of the grass by the firing butts tells its own tale. Scattered in the ranks of the volunteers are a fair number of old soldiers, for the Company has a weakness for recruiting from the Army for its guards who may, in time, become stationmasters. A good man from the Army, with his papers all correct and certificates from his commanding officer, can, after depositing twenty pounds to pay his home passage, in the event of his services being dispensed with, enter the Company's service on something less than one hundred rupees a month and rise in time to four hundred as a station-master. A railway bungalow—and they are as substantially built as the engines—will cost him more than one-ninth of the pay of his grade, and the Provident Fund provides for his latter end.

Think for a moment of the number of men that a line running from Howrah to Delhi must use, and you will realise what an enormous amount of patronage the Company holds in its hands. Naturally a father who has worked for the line expects the line to do something for the son; and the line is not backward in meeting his wishes where possible. The sons of old servants may be taken on at fifteen years of age, or thereabouts, as apprentices in the 'shops,' receiving twenty rupees in the first and fifty in the last year of their indentures. Then they come on the books as full 'men' on perhaps Rs. 65 a month, and the road is open to them in many ways. They may become foremen of departments on Rs. 500 a month, or drivers earning with overtime Rs. 370; or if they have been brought into the audit or the traffic, they may control innumerable Babus and draw several hundreds of rupees monthly; or, at eighteen or nineteen, they may be ticket-collectors, working up to the grade of guard, etc. Every rank of the huge, human hive has a desire to see its sons placed properly, and the native workmen, about three thousand, in the locomotive department only, are, said one man, 'making a family affair of it altogether. You see all those men turning brass and looking after the machinery? They've all got relatives, and a lot of 'em own land out Monghyr-way close to us. They bring on their sons as soon as they are old enough to do anything, and the Company rather encourages it. You see the father is in a way responsible for his son, and he'll teach him all he knows, and in that way the Company has a hold on them all. You've no notion how sharp a native is when he's working on his own hook. All the district round here, right up to Monghyr, is more or less dependent on the railway.'

The Babus in the traffic department, in the stores' issue department, in all the departments where men sit through the long, long Indian day among ledgers, and check and pencil and deal in figures and items and rupees, may be counted by hundreds. Imagine the struggle among them to locate their sons in comfortable cane-bottomed chairs, in front of a big pewter inkstand and stacks of paper! The Babus make beautiful accountants, and if we could only see it, a merciful Providence has made the Babu for figures and detail. Without him, the dividends of any company would be eaten up by the expenses of English or city-bred clerks. The Babu is a great man, and, to respect him, you must see five score or so of him in a room a hundred yards long, bending over ledgers, ledgers, and yet more ledgers—silent as the Sphinx and busy as a bee. He is the lubricant of the great machinery of the Company whose ways and works cannot be dealt with in a single scrawl.

CHAPTER II

THE SHOPS

THE railway folk, like the army and civilian castes, have their own language and life, which an outsider cannot hope to understand. For instance, when Jamalpur refers to itself as being 'on the long siding,' a lengthy explanation is necessary before the visitor grasps the fact that the whole of the two hundred and thirty odd miles of the loop from Luckeeserai to Kanu-Junction *via* Bhagalpur is thus contemptuously treated. Jamalpur insists that it is out of the world, and makes this an excuse for being proud of itself and all its institutions. But in one thing it is badly, disgracefully provided. At a moderate estimate there must be about two hundred Europeans with their families in this place. They can, and do, get their small supplies from Calcutta, but they are dependent on the tender mercies of the bazaar for their meat, which seems to be hawked from door to door. There is a Raja who owns or has an interest in the land on which the station stands, and he is averse to cow-killing. For these reasons, Jamalpur is not too well supplied with good meat, and what it wants is a decent meat-market with cleanly controlled slaughtering arrangements. The 'Company,' who gives grants to the schools and builds the institute and throws the shadow of its protection all over the place, might help this scheme forward.

The heart of Jamalpur is the 'shops,' and here a visitor will see more things in an hour than he can understand in a year. Steam Street very appropriately leads to the forty or fifty acres that the 'shops' cover, and to the busy silence of the loco. superintendent's office, where a man must put down his name and his business on a slip of paper before he can penetrate into the Temple of Vulcan. About three thousand five hundred men are in the 'shops,' and, ten minutes after the day's work has begun, the assistant superintendent knows exactly how many are 'in.' The heads of departments—silent, heavy-handed men, captains of five hundred or more—have their names fairly printed on a board which is exactly like a pool-marker. They 'star a life' when they come in, and their few names alone represent salaries to the extent of six thousand a month. They are men worth hearing deferentially. They hail from Manchester and the Clyde, and the great ironworks of the North: pleasant as cold water in a thirsty land is it to hear again the full Northumbrian burr or the long-drawn Yorkshire 'aye.' Under their great gravity of demeanour—a man who is in charge of a few lakhs' worth of plant cannot afford to be riotously mirthful—lurks melody and humour. They can sing like north-countrymen, and in their hours of ease go back to the speech of the iron countries they have left behind, when 'Ab o' th' yate' and all 'Ben Briarly's' shrewd wit shakes the warm air of Bengal with deep-chested laughter. Hear 'Ruglan' Toon,' with a chorus as true as the fall of trip-hammers, and fancy that you are back again in the smoky, rattling North!

But this is the 'unofficial' side. Go forward through the gates under the mango trees, and set foot at once in sheds which have as little to do with mangoes as a locomotive with Lakshmi. The 'buzzer' howls, for it is nearly tiffin time. There is a rush from every quarter of the shops, a cloud of flying natives, and a procession of more sedately pacing Englishmen, and in three short minutes you are left absolutely alone among arrested wheels and belts, pulleys, cranks, and cranes—in a silence only broken by the soft sigh of a far-away steam-valve or the cooing of pigeons. You are, by favour freely granted, at liberty to wander anywhere you please through the deserted works. Walk into a huge, brick-built, tin-roofed stable, capable of holding twenty-four locomotives under treatment, and see what must be done to the Iron Horse once in every three years if he is to do his work well. On reflection, Iron Horse is wrong. An engine is a she—as distinctly feminine as a ship or a mine. Here stands the *Echo*, her wheels off, resting on blocks, her underside machinery taken out, and her side scrawled with mysterious hieroglyphics in chalk. An enormous green-painted iron harness-rack bears her piston and eccentric rods, and a neatly painted board shows that such and such Englishmen are the fitter, assistant, and apprentice engaged in editing that *Echo.* An engine seen from the platform and an engine viewed from underneath are two very different things. The one is as unimpressive as a cart; the other as imposing as a man-of-war in the yard.

In this manner is an engine treated for navicular, laminitis, back-sinew, or whatever it is that engines most suffer from. No. 607, we will say, goes wrong at Dinapore, Assensole, Buxar, or wherever it may be, after three years' work. The place she came from is stencilled on the boiler, and the foreman examines her. Then he fills in a hospital sheet, which bears one hundred and eighty printed heads under which an engine can come into the shops. No. 607 needs repair in only one hundred and eighteen particulars, ranging from mud-hole-flanges and blower-cocks to lead-plugs, and platform brackets which have shaken loose. This certificate the foreman signs, and it is framed near the engine for the benefit of the three Europeans and the eight or nine natives who have to mend No. 607. To the ignorant the superhuman wisdom of the examiner seems only equalled by the audacity of the two men and the boy who are to undertake what is frivolously called the 'job.' No. 607 is in a sorely mangled condition, but 403 is much worse. She is reduced to a shell—is a very elle-woman of an engine, bearing only her funnel, the iron frame and the saddle that supports the boiler.

Four-and-twenty engines in every stage of decomposition stand in one huge shop. A travelling crane runs overhead, and the men have hauled up one end of a bright vermilion loco. The effect is the silence of a scornful stare—just such a look as a colonel's portly wife gives through her *pince-nez* at the audacious subaltern. Engines are the 'livest' things that man ever made. They glare through their spectacle-plates, they tilt their noses contemptuously, and when their insides are gone they adorn themselves with red lead, and leer like decayed beauties; and in the Jamalpur works there is no escape from them. The shops can hold fifty without pressure, and on occasion as many again. Everywhere there are engines, and everywhere brass domes lie about on the ground like huge helmets in a pantomime. The silence is the weirdest touch of all. Some sprightly soul—an apprentice be sure—has daubed in red lead on the end of an iron tool-box a caricature of some friend who is evidently a riveter. The picture has all the interest of an Egyptian cartouche, for it shows that men have been here, and that the engines do not have it all their own way.

And so, out in the open, away from the three great sheds, between and under more engines, till we strike a wilderness of lines all converging to one turn-table. Here be elephant-stalls ranged round a half-circle, and in each stall stands one engine, and each engine stares at the turn-table.

A stolid and disconcerting company is this ring-of-eyes monsters; 324, 432, and 8 are shining like toys. They are ready for their turn of duty, and are as spruce as hansoms. Lacquered chocolate, picked out with black, red, and white, is their dress, and delicate lemon graces the ceilings of the cabs. The driver should be a gentleman in evening dress with white kid gloves, and there should be gold-headed champagne bottles in the spick-and-span tenders. Huckleberry Finn says of a timber raft, 'It amounted to something being captain of that raft.' Thrice enviable is the man who, drawing Rs. 220 a month, is allowed to make Rs. 150 overtime out of locos. Nos. 324, 432, or 8. Fifty yards beyond this gorgeous trinity are ten to twelve engines who have put in to Jamalpur to bait. They are alive, their fires are lighted, and they are swearing and purring and growling one at another as they stand alone. Here is evidently one of the newest type—No. 25, a giant who has just brought the mail in and waits to be cleaned up preparatory to going out afresh.

The tiffin hour has ended. The buzzer blows, and with a roar, a rattle, and a clang the shops take up their toil. The hubbub that followed on the Prince's kiss to the sleeping beauty was not so loud or sudden. Experience, with a foot-rule in his pocket, authority in his port, and a merry twinkle in his eye, comes up and catches Ignorance walking gingerly round No. 25. 'That's one of the best we have,' says Experience, 'a four-wheeled coupled bogie they call her. She's by Dobbs. She's done her hundred and fifty miles to-day;

and she'll run in to Rampore Haut this afternoon; then she'll rest a day and be cleaned up. Roughly, she does her three hundred miles in the four-and-twenty hours. She's a beauty. She's out from home, but we can build our own engines—all except the wheels. We're building ten locos. now, and we've got a dozen boilers ready if you care to look at them. How long does a loco. last? That's just as may be. She will do as much as her driver lets her. Some men play the mischief with a loco. and some handle 'em properly. Our drivers prefer Hawthorne's old four-wheeled coupled engines because they give the least bother. There is one in that shed, and it's a good 'un to travel. But eighty thousand miles generally sees the gloss off an engine, and she goes into the shops to be overhauled and refitted and replaned, and a lot of things that you wouldn't understand if I told you about them. No. 1, the first loco. on the line, is running still, but very little of the original engine must be left by this time. That one there came out in the Mutiny year. She's by Slaughter and Grunning, and she's built for speed in front of a light load. French-looking sort of thing, isn't she? That's because her cylinders are on a tilt. We used her for the mail once, but the mail has grown heavier and heavier, and now we use six-wheeled coupled eighteen-inch, inside cylinder, 45-ton locos. to shift thousand-ton trains. *No!* All locos. aren't alike. It isn't merely pulling a lever. The Company likes its drivers to know their locos., and a man will keep his Hawthorne for two or three years. The more mileage he gets out of her before she has to be overhauled the better man he is. It pays to let a man have his fancy engine. A man must take an interest in his loco., and that means she must belong to him. Some locos. won't do anything, even if you coax and humour them. I don't think there are any unlucky ones now, but some years ago No. 31 wasn't popular. The drivers went sick or took leave when they were told off for her. She killed her driver on the Jubbulpore line, she left the rails at Kajra, she did something or other at Rampur Haut, and Lord knows what she didn't do or try to do in other places! All the drivers fought shy of her, and in the end she disappeared. They said she was condemned, but I shouldn't wonder if the Company changed her number quietly, and changed the luck at the same time. You see, the Government Inspector comes and looks at our stock now and again, and when an engine's condemned he puts his dhobi-mark on her, and she's broken up. Well, No. 31 was condemned, but there was a whisper that they only shifted her number, and ran her out again. When the drivers didn't know, there were no accidents. I don't think we've got an unlucky one running now. Some are different from others, but there are no man-eaters. Yes, a driver of the mail *is* somebody. He can make Rs. 370 a month if he's a covenanted man. We get a lot of our drivers in the country, and we don't import from England as much as we did. 'Stands to reason that, now there's more competition both among lines and in the labour market, the Company can't afford to be as generous as it used to be. It doesn't cheat a man though. It's this way with the drivers. A native driver gets about Rs. 20 a month, and in his way he's supposed to be good enough for branch work and shunting and such. Well, an English driver'll get from Rs. 80 to Rs. 220, and overtime. The English driver knows what the native gets, and in time they tell the driver that the native'll improve. The driver has that to think of. You see? That's competition!'

Experience returns to the engine-sheds, now full of clamour, and enlarges on the beauties of sick locomotives. The fitters and the assistants and the apprentices are hammering and punching and gauging, and otherwise technically disporting themselves round their enormous patients, and their language, as caught in snatches, is beautifully unintelligible.

But one flying sentence goes straight to the heart. It is the cry of Humanity over the Task of Life, done into unrefined English. An apprentice, grimed to his eyebrows, his cloth cap well on the back of his curly head and his hands deep in his pockets, is sitting on the edge of a tool-box ruefully regarding the very much disorganised engine whose slave is he. A handsome boy, this apprentice, and well made. He whistles softly between his teeth, and his brow puckers. Then he addresses the engine, half in expostulation and half in despair, 'Oh, you condemned old female dog!' He puts the sentence more crisply—much more crisply—and Ignorance chuckles sympathetically.

Ignorance also is puzzled over these engines.

CHAPTER III

VULCAN'S FORGE

In the wilderness of the railway shops — and machinery that planes and shaves, and bevels and stamps, and punches and hoists and nips — the first idea that occurs to an outsider, when he has seen the men who people the place, is that it must be the birthplace of inventions—a pasture-ground of fat patents. If a writing-man, who plays with shadows and dresses dolls that others may laugh at their antics, draws help and comfort and new methods of working old ideas from the stored shelves of a library, how, in the name of Commonsense, his god, can a doing-man, whose mind is set upon things that snatch a few moments from flying Time or put power into weak hands, refrain from going forward and adding new inventions to the hundreds among which he daily moves?

Appealed to on this subject, Experience, who had served the E. I. R. loyally for many years, held his peace. 'We don't go in much for patents; but,' he added, with a praiseworthy attempt to turn the conversation, 'we can build you any mortal thing you like. We've got the

Bradford Leslie steamer for the Sahibgunge ferry. Come and see the brass-work for her bows. It's in the casting-shed.'

It would have been cruel to have pressed Experience further, and Ignorance, to foredate matters a little, went about to discover why Experience shied off this question, and why the men of Jamalpur had not each and all invented and patented something. He won his information in the end, but it did not come from Jamalpur. *That* must be clearly understood. It was found anywhere you please between Howrah and Hoti Mardan; and here it is that all the world may admire a prudent and far-sighted Board of Directors. Once upon a time, as every one in the profession knows, two men invented the D. and O. sleeper—cast-iron, of five pieces, very serviceable. The men were in the Company's employ, and their masters said: 'Your brains are ours. Hand us over those sleepers.' Being of pay and position, D. and O. made some sort of resistance and got a royalty or a bonus. At any rate, the Company had to pay for its sleepers. But thereafter, and the condition exists to this day, they caused it to be written in each servant's covenant, that if by chance he invented aught, his invention was to belong to the Company. Providence has mercifully arranged that no man or syndicate of men can buy the 'holy spirit of man' outright without suffering in some way or another just as much as the purchase. America fully, and Germany in part, recognises this law. The E. I. Railway's breach of it is thoroughly

English. They say, or it is said of them that they say, 'We are afraid of our men, who belong to us, wasting their time on trying to invent.'

Is it wholly impossible, then, for men of mechanical experience and large sympathies to check the mere patent-hunter and bring forward the man with an idea? Is there no supervision in the 'shops,' or have the men who play tennis and billiards at the institute not a minute which they can rightly call their very own? Would it ruin the richest Company in India to lend their model-shop and their lathes to half a dozen, or, for the matter of that, half a hundred, abortive experiments? A Massachusetts organ factory, a Racine buggy shop, an Oregon lumber-yard, would laugh at the notion. An American toy-maker might swindle an employé after the invention, but he would in his own interests help the man to 'see what comes of the thing.' Surely a wealthy, a powerful and, as all Jamalpur bears witness, a considerate Company might cut that clause out of the covenant and await the issue. There would be quite enough jealousy between man and man, grade and grade, to keep down all but the keenest souls; and, with due respect to the steam-hammer and the rolling-mill, we have not yet made machinery perfect. The 'shops' are not likely to spawn unmanageable Stephensons or grasping Brunels; but in the minor turns of mechanical thought that find concrete expressions in links, axle-boxes, joint packings, valves, and spring-stirrups something might—something would—be done were the practical prohibition removed.

Will a North-countryman give you anything but warm hospitality for nothing? Or if you claim from him overtime service as a right, will he work zealously? 'Onything but t' brass,' is his motto, and his ideas are his 'brass.'

Gentlemen in authority, if this should meet your august eyes, spare it a minute's thought, and, clearing away the floridity, get to the heart of the mistake and see if it cannot be rationally put right. Above all, remember that Jamalpur supplied no information. It was as mute as an oyster. There is no one within your jurisdiction to—ahem—'drop upon.'

Let us, after this excursion into the offices, return to the shops and only ask Experience such questions as he can without disloyalty answer.

'We used once,' says he, leading to the foundry, 'to sell our old rails and import new ones. Even when we used 'em for roof beams and so on, we had more than we knew what to do with. Now we have got rolling-mills, and we use the rails to make tie-bars for the D. and O. sleepers and all sorts of things. We turn out five hundred D. and O. sleepers a day. Altogether, we use about seventy-five tons of our own iron a month here. Iron in Calcutta costs about five-eight a hundred-weight; ours costs between three-four and three-eight, and on that item alone we save three thousand a month. Don't ask me how many miles of rails we own. There are fifteen hundred miles of line, and you can make your own calculation. All those things like babies' graves, down in that shed, are the moulds for the D. and O.

sleepers. We test them by dropping three hundredweight and three hundred quarters of iron on top of them from a height of seven feet, or eleven sometimes. They don't often smash. We have a notion here that our iron is as good as the Home stuff.'

A sleek white and brindled pariah thrusts himself into the conversation. His house appears to be on the warm ashes of the bolt-maker. This is a horrible machine, which chews red-hot iron bars and spits them out perfect bolts. Its manners are disgusting, and it gobbles over its food.

'Hi, Jack!' says Experience, stroking the interloper, 'you've been trying to break your leg again. That's the dog of the works. At least he makes believe that the works belong to him. He'll follow any one of us about the shops as far as the gate, but never a step further. You can see he's in first-class condition. The boys give him his ticket, and, one of these days, he'll try to get on to the Company's books as a regular worker. He's too clever to live.' Jack heads the procession as far as the walls of the rolling-shed and then returns to his machinery room. He waddles with fatness and despises strangers.

'How would you like to be hot-potted there?' says Experience, who has read and who is enthusiastic over *She*, as he points to the great furnaces whence the slag is being dragged out by hooks. 'Here is the old material going into the furnace in that big iron bucket. Look at the scraps of iron. There's an old D. and O. sleeper, there's a lot of clips from a cylinder, there's a lot of snipped-up rails, there's a driving-wheel block, there's an old hook, and a sprinkling of boiler-plates and rivets.'

The bucket is tipped into the furnace with a thunderous roar and the slag below pours forth more quickly. 'An engine,' says Experience reflectively, 'can run over herself so to say. After she's broken up she is made into sleepers for the line. You'll see how she's broken up later.' A few paces further on, semi-nude demons are capering over strips of glowing hot iron which are put into a mill as rails and emerge as thin, shapely tie-bars. The natives wear rough sandals and some pretence of aprons, but the greater part of them is 'all face.' 'As I said before,' says Experience, 'a native's cuteness when he's working on ticket is something startling. Beyond occasionally hanging on to a red-hot bar too long and so letting their pincers be drawn through the mills, these men take precious good care not to go wrong. Our machinery is fenced and guard-railed as much as possible, and these men don't get caught up in the belting. In the first place, they're careful—the father warns the son and so on—and in the second, there's nothing about 'em for the belting to catch on unless the man shoves his hand in. Oh, a native's no fool! He knows that it doesn't do to be foolish when he's dealing with a crane or a driving-wheel. You're looking at all those chopped rails? We make our iron as they blend baccy. We mix up all sorts to get the required quality. Those rails have just been chopped by this tobacco-cutter thing.' Experience bends down and sets a vicious-looking, parrot-headed beam to work. There is a quiver—a snap—and a dull smash and a heavy rail is nipped in two like a stick of barley-sugar.

Elsewhere, a bull-nosed hydraulic cutter is rail-cutting as if it enjoyed the fun. In another shed stand the steam-hammers ; the unemployed ones murmuring and muttering to themselves, as is the uncanny custom of all steam-souled machinery. Experience, with his hand on a long lever, makes one of the monsters perform : and though Ignorance knows that a man designed and men do continually build steam-hammers, the effect is as though Experience were maddening a chained beast. The massive block slides down the guides, only to pause hungrily an inch above the anvil, or restlessly throb through a foot and a half of space, each motion being controlled by an almost imperceptible handling of the levers. 'When these things are newly overhauled, you can regulate your blow to within an eighth of an inch,' says Experience. 'We had a foreman here once who could work 'em beautifully. He had the touch. One day a visitor, no end of a swell in a tall, white hat, came round the works, and our foreman borrowed the hat and brought the hammer down just enough to press the nap and no more. "How wonderful!" said the visitor, putting his hand carelessly upon this lever rod here.' Experience suits the action to the word and the hammer thunders on the anvil. 'Well, you can guess for yourself. Next minute there wasn't enough left of that tall, white hat to make a postage-stamp of. Steam-hammers aren't things to play with. Now we'll go over to the stores. . . .

Whatever apparent disorder there might have been in the works, the store department is as clean as a new pin, and stupefying in its naval order. Copper plates, bar, angle, and rod iron, duplicate cranks and slide bars, the piston rods of the *Bradford Leslie* steamer, engine grease, files, and hammer-heads—every conceivable article, from leather laces of beltings to head-lamps, necessary for the due and proper working of a long line, is stocked, stacked, piled, and put away in appropriate compartments. In the midst of it all, neck deep in ledgers and indent forms, stands the many-handed Babu, the steam of the engine whose power extends from Howrah to Ghaziabad.

The Company does everything, and knows everything. The gallant apprentice may be a wild youth with an earnest desire to go occasionally 'upon the bend.' But three times a week, between 7 and 8 P.M., he must attend the night-school and sit at the feet of M. Bonnaud, who teaches him mechanics and statics so thoroughly that even the awful Government Inspector is pleased. And when there is no night-school the Company will by no means wash its hands of its men out of working-hours. No man can be violently restrained from going to the bad if he insists upon it, but in the service of the Company a man has every warning; his escapades are known, and a judiciously arranged transfer sometimes keeps a good fellow clear of the down-grade. No one can flatter himself that in the multitude he is overlooked, or believe that between 4 P.M. and 9 A.M. he is at liberty to misdemean himself. Sooner or later, but generally sooner, his goings-on are known, and he is reminded that 'Britons never shall be slaves'—to things that destroy good work as well as souls. Maybe the Company acts only in its own interest, but the result is good.

Best and prettiest of the many good and pretty things in Jamalpur is the institute of a Saturday when the Volunteer Band is playing and the tennis courts are full and the babydom of Jamalpur—fat, sturdy children—frolic round the band-stand. The people dance—but big as the institute is, it is getting too small for their dances—they act, they play billiards, they study their newspapers, they play cards and everything else, and they flirt in a sumptuous building, and in the hot weather the gallant apprentice ducks his friend in the big swimming-bath. Decidedly the railway folk make their lives pleasant.

Let us go down southward to the big Giridih colleries and see the coal that feeds the furnace that smelts the iron that makes the sleeper that bears the loco. that pulls the carriage that holds the freight that comes from the country that is made richer by the Great Company Bahadur, the East Indian Railway.

THE GIRIDIH COAL-FIELDS

The Giridih Coal-Fields

CHAPTER I

ON THE SURFACE

SOUTHWARD, always southward and easterly, runs the Calcutta Mail from Luckeeserai, till she reaches Madapur in the Sonthal Parganas. From Madapur a train, largely made up of coal-trucks, heads westward into the Hazaribagh district and toward Giridih. A week would not have exhausted 'Jamalpur and its environs,' as the guide-books say. But since time drives and man must e'en be driven, the weird, echoing bund in the hills above Jamalpur, where the owls hoot at night and hyenas come down to laugh over the grave of 'Quillem Roberts, who died from the effects of an encounter with a tiger near this place, A.D. 1864,' goes undescribed. Nor is it possible to deal with Monghyr, the headquarters of the district, where one sees for the first time the age of Old Bengal in the sleepy, creepy station, built in a time-eaten fort, which runs out into the Ganges, and is full of quaint houses, with fat-legged balustrades on the roofs. Pensioners certainly, and probably a score of ghosts, live in Monghyr. All the country seems haunted. Is there not at Pir Bahar a lonely house on a bluff, the grave of a young lady, who, thirty years ago, rode her horse down the cliff and perished? Has not Monghyr a haunted house in which tradition says sceptics have seen much more than they could account for? And is it not notorious throughout the countryside that the seven miles of road between Jamalpur and Monghyr are nightly paraded by tramping battalions of spectres—phantoms of an old-time army, massacred who knows how long ago? The common voice attests all these things, and an eerie cemetery packed with blackened, lichened, candle-extinguisher tomb-stones persuades the listener to believe all that he hears. Bengal is second—or third is it?—in order of seniority among the Provinces, and like an old nurse, she tells many witch-tales.

But ghosts have nothing to do with collieries, and that ever-present 'Company,' the E. I. R., has more or less made Giridih—principally more. 'Before the E. I. R. came,' say the people, 'we had one meal a day. Now we have two.' Stomachs do not tell fibs, whatever mouths may say. That 'Company,' in the course of business, throws about five lakhs a year into the Hazaribagh district in the form of wages alone, and Giridih Bazar has to supply the wants of twelve thousand men, women, and children. But we have now the authority of a number of high-souled and intelligent native prints that the Sahib of all grades spends his time in 'sucking the blood out of the country,' and 'flying to England to spend his ill-gotten gains.'

Giridih is perfectly mad—quite insane! Geologically, 'the country is in the metamorphic higher grounds that rise out of the alluvial flats of Lower Bengal between the Osri and the Barakar rivers.' Translated, this sentence means that you can twist your ankle on pieces of pure white, pinky, and yellowish granite, slip over weather-worn sandstone, grievously cut your boots over flakes of trap, and throw hornblende pebbles at the dogs. Never was such a place for stone-throwing as Giridih. The general aspect of the country is falsely park-like, because it swells and sinks in a score of grass-covered undulations, and is adorned with plantation-like jungle. There are low hills on every side, and twelve miles away bearing south the blue bulk of the holy hill of Parasnath, greatest of the Jain Tirthankars, overlooks the world. In Bengal they consider four thousand five hundred feet good enough for a Dagshai or Kasauli, and once upon a time they tried to put troops on Parasnath. There was a scarcity of water, and Thomas of those days found the silence and seclusion prey upon his spirits. Since twenty years, therefore, Parasnath has been abandoned by Her Majesty's Army.

As to Giridih itself, the last few miles of train bring up the reek of the 'Black Country.' Memory depends on smell. A noseless man is devoid of sentiment, just as a noseless woman, in this country, must be devoid of honour. That first breath of the coal should be the breath of the murky, clouded tract between Yeadon and Dale—or Barnsley, rough and hospitable Barnsley—or Dewsbury and Batley and the Derby Canal on a Sunday afternoon when the wheels are still and the young men and maidens walk stolidly in pairs. Unfortunately, it is nothing more than Giridih—seven thousand miles away from Home and blessed with a warm and genial sunshine, soon to turn into something very much worse. The insanity of the place is visible at the station door. A G.B.T. cart once married a bathing-machine, and they called the child *tum-tum*. You who in flannel and Cawnpore harness drive bamboo-carts about up-country roads, remember that a Giridih *tum-tum* is painfully pushed by four men, and must be entered crawling on all-fours, head first. So strange are the ways of Bengal!

They drive mad horses in Giridih—animals that become hysterical as soon as the dusk falls and the country-side blazes with the fires of the great coke ovens. If you expostulate tearfully, they produce another horse, a raw, red fiend whose ear has to be screwed round and round, and round and round, before she will by any manner of means consent to start. The roads carry neat little eighteen-inch trenches at their sides, admirably adapted to hold the flying wheel. Skirling about this savage land in the dark, the white population beguile the time by rapturously recounting past accidents, insisting throughout on the super-equine 'steadiness' of their cattle. Deep and broad and wide is their jovial hospitality; but somebody—the Tirhoot planters for choice—ought to start a ıission to teach the men of Giridih what to drive. 'hey know *how*, or they would be severally and :parately and many times dead, but they do not, ıey do not indeed, know that animals who stand n one hind leg and beckon with all the rest, or ·y to pigstick in harness, are not trap-horses 'orthy of endearing names, but things to be pole-xed! Their feelings are hurt when you say this. Sit tight,' say the men of Giridih; 'we're insured! Ve can't be hurt.'

And now with grey hairs, dry mouth, and chat-ering teeth to the collieries. The E. I. R. estate, ıought or leased in perpetuity from the Serampore ℜaja, may be about four miles long and between ıne and two miles across. It is in two pieces, the ierampore field being separated from the Karhar-ıari (or Kurhurballi or Kabarbari) field by the ıroperty of the Bengal Coal Company. The ℜaneegunge Coal Association lies to the east of all ıther workings. So we have three companies at vork on about eleven square miles of land.

There is no such thing as getting a full view of he whole place. A short walk over a grassy down ;ives on to an outcrop of very dirty sandstone, which in the excessive innocence of his heart the visitor naturally takes to be the coal lying neatly on the surface. Up to this sandstone the path seems to be made of crushed sugar, so white and shiny is the quartz. Over the brow of the down comes in sight the old familiar pit-head wheel, spinning for the dear life, and the eye loses itself in a maze of pumping sheds, red-tiled, mud-walled miners' huts, dotted all over the landscape, and railway lines that run on every kind of gradient. There are lines that dip into valleys and disappear round the shoulders of slopes, and lines that career on the tops of rises and disappear over the brow of the slopes. Along these lines whistle and pant metre-gauge engines, some with trucks at their tail, and others rattling back to the pit-bank with the absurd air of a boy late for school that an unemployed engine always assumes. There are six engines in all, and as it is easiest to walk along the lines one sees a good deal of them. They bear not altogether unfamiliar names. Here, for instance, passes the 'Cockburn' whistling down a grade with thirty tons of coal at her heels; while the 'Whitly' and the 'Olpherts' are waiting for their complement of trucks. Now a Mr. T. F. Cockburn was superintendent of these mines nearly thirty years ago, in the days before the chord-lines from Kanu to Luckeeserai were built, and all the coal was carted to the latter place; and surely Mr. Olpherts was an engineer who helped to think out a new sleeper. What may these things mean?

'Apotheosis of the Manager,' is the reply. 'Christen the engines after the managers. You'll find Cockburn, Dunn, Whitly, Abbot, Olpherts, and Saise knocking about the place. Sounds funny, doesn't it? Doesn't sound so funny when one of these idiots does his best to derail Saise, though, by putting a line down anyhow. Look at that line! Laid out in knots—by Jove!' To the unprofessional eye the rail seems all correct; but there must be something wrong, because 'one of those idiots' is asked why in the name of all e considers sacred he does not ram the ballast roperly.

'What would happen if you threw an engine ff the line! Can't say that I know exactly. 'ou see, our business is to keep them *on*, and we o that. Here's rather a curiosity. You see that ointsman! They say he's an old mutineer, and vhen he relaxes he boasts of the Sahibs he has illed. He's glad enough to eat the Company's alt now.' Such a withered old face was the face f the pointsman at No. 11 point! The informa-ion suggested a host of questions, and the answers vere these: 'You won't be able to understand till ou've been down into a mine. We work our nen in two ways: some by direct payment—under our own hand, and some by contractors. The contractor undertakes to deliver us the coal, sup-plying his own men, tools, and props. He's re-sponsible for the safety of his men, and of course he Company knows and sees his work. Just fancy, among these five thousand people, what sort of effect the news of an accident would produce! It would go all through the Sonthal Parganas. We have any amount of Sonthals besides Maho-metans and Hindus of every possible caste, down to those Musahers who eat pig. They don't require much administering in the civilian sense of the word. On Sundays, as a rule, if any man has had his daughter eloped with, or anything of that kind, he generally comes up to the manager's bungalow to get the matter put straight. If a man is disabled through accident he knows that as long as he's in the hospital he gets full wages, and the Company pays for the food of any of his women-folk who come to look after him. *One*, of course; not the whole clan. That makes our service popular with the people. Don't you believe that a native is a fool. You can train him to everything except responsibility. There's a rule in the workings that if there is any dangerous work—we haven't choke-damp; I will show you when we get down—no gang must work without an Englishman to look after them. A native wouldn't be wise enough to understand what the danger was, or where it came in. Even if he did, he'd shirk the responsibility. We can't afford to risk a single life. All our output is just as much as the Company want—about a thousand tons per working day. Three hundred thousand in the year. We could turn out more? Yes—a little. Well, yes, twice as much. I won't go on, because you wouldn't believe me. There's the coal under us, and we work it at any depth from following up an outcrop down to six hundred feet. That is our deepest shaft. We have no necessity to go deeper. At home the mines are sometimes fifteen hundred feet down. Well, the thickness of this coal here varies from anything you please to anything you please. There's enough of it to last your time and one or two hundred years longer. Perhaps even longer than that. Look at that stuff. That's big coal from the pit.'

It was aristocratic-looking coal, just like the picked lumps that are stacked in baskets of coal agencies at home with the printed legend atop 'Only 23s. a ton.' But there was no picking in this case The great piled banks were all equal to sample, and beyond them lay piles of small, broken, 'smithy' coal. 'The Company doesn't sell to the public. This small, broken coal is an exception. That is sold, but the big stuff is for the engines and the shops. It doesn't cost much to get out, as you say; but our men can earn as much as twelve rupees a month. Very often when they've earned enough to go on with they retire from the concern till they've spent their money and then come on again. It's piece-work and they are improvident. If some of them only lived like other natives they would have enough to buy land and cows with. When there's a press of work they make a good deal by overtime, but they don't seem to keep it. You should see Giridih Bazar on a Sunday if you want to know where the money goes. About ten thousand rupees change hands once a week there. If you want to get at the number of people who are indirectly dependent or profit by the E. I. R. you'll have to conduct a census of your own. After Sunday is over the men generally lie off on Monday and take it easy on Tuesday. Then they work hard for the next four days and make it up. Of course there's nothing in the wide world to prevent a man from resigning and going away to wherever he came from—behind those hills if he's a Sonthal. He loses his employment, that's all. But they have their own point of honour. A man hates to be told by his friends that he has been guilty of shirking. And now we'll go to breakfast. You shall be "pitted" to-morrow to any depth you like.'

CHAPTER II

IN THE DEPTHS

'PITTED to any extent you please.' The only difficulty was for Joseph to choose his pit. Giridih was full of them. There was an arch in the side of a little hill, a blackened brick arch leading into thick night. A stationary engine was hauling a procession of coal-laden trucks—'tubs' is the technical word—out of its depths. The tubs were neither pretty nor clean. 'We are going down in those when they are emptied. Put on your helmet and keep it on, and keep your head down.'

There is nothing mirth-provoking in going down a coal-mine—even though it be only a shallow incline running to one hundred and forty feet vertical below the earth 'Get into the tub and lie down. Hang it, no! This is not a railway carriage: you can't see the country out of the windows. Lie down in the dust and don't lift your head. Let her go!'

The tubs strain on the wire rope and slide down fourteen hundred feet of incline, at first through a chastened gloom, and then through darkness. An absurd sentence from a trial report rings in the head: 'About this time prisoner expressed a desire for the consolations of religion.' A hand with a reeking flare-lamp hangs over the edge of the tub, and there is a glimpse of a blackened hat near it, for those accustomed to the pits have a merry trick of going down sitting or crouching on the coupling of the rear tub. The noise is deafening, and the roof is very close indeed. The tubs bump, and the occupant crouches lovingly in the coal dust. What would happen if the train went off the line? The desire for the 'consolations of religion' grows keener and keener as the air grows closer and closer. The tubs stop in darkness spangled by the light of the flare-lamps which many black devils carry. Underneath and on both sides is the greasy blackness of the coal, and, above, a roof of grey sandstone, smooth as the flow of a river at evening. 'Now, remember that if you don't keep your hat on, you'll get your head broken, because you will forget to stoop. If you hear any tubs coming up behind you step off to one side. There's a tramway under your feet: be careful not to trip over it.'

The miner has a gait as peculiarly his own as Tommy's measured pace or the bluejacket's roll. Big men who slouch in the light of day become almost things of beauty underground. Their foot is on their native heather; and the slouch is a very necessary act of homage to the great earth, which if a man observe not, he shall without doubt have his hat—bless the man who invented pith hats!—grievously cut.

The road turns and winds and the roof becomes

lower, but those accursed tubs still rattle by on the tramways. The roof throws back their noises, and when all the place is full of a grumbling and a growling, how under earth is one to know whence danger will turn up next? The air brings to the unacclimatised a singing in the ears, a hotness of the eyeballs, and a jumping of the heart. 'That's because the pressure here is different from the pressure up above. It'll wear off in a minute. *We* don't notice it. Wait till you get down a four-hundred-foot pit. *Then* your ears will begin to sing, if you like.'

Most people know the One Night of each hot weather—that still, clouded night just before the Rains break, when there seems to be no more breathable air under the bowl of the pitiless skies, and all the weight of the silent, dark house lies on the chest of the sleep-hunter. This is the feeling in a coal-mine—only more so—much more so, for the darkness is the 'gross darkness of the inner sepulchre.' It is hard to see which is the black coal and which the passage driven through it. From far away, down the side galleries, comes the regular beat of the pick—thick and muffled as the beat of the labouring heart. 'Six men to a gang, and they aren't allowed to work alone. They make six-foot drives through the coal—two and sometimes three men working together. The rest clear away the stuff and load it into the tubs. We have no props in this gallery because we have a roof as good as a ceiling. The coal lies under the sandstone here. It's beautiful sandstone.' It *was* beautiful sandstone—as hard as a billiard table and devoid of any nasty little bumps and jags.

There was a roaring down one road—the roaring of infernal fires. This is not a pleasant thing to hear in the dark. It is too suggestive. 'That's our ventilating shaft. Can't you feel the air getting brisker? Come and look.'

Imagine a great iron-bound crate of burning coal, hanging over a gulf of darkness faintly showing the brickwork of the base of a chimney. 'We're at the bottom of the shaft. That fire makes a draught that sucks up the foul air from the bottom of the pit. There's another down-draw shaft in another part of the mine where the clean air comes in. We aren't going to set the mines on fire. There's an earth and brick floor at the bottom of the pit the crate hangs over. It isn't so deep as you think.' Then a devil—a naked devil—came in with a pitchfork and fed the spouting flames. This was perfectly in keeping with the landscape.

More trucks, more muffled noises, more darkness made visible, and more devils—male and female—coming out of darkness and vanishing. Then a picture to be remembered. A great Hall of Eblis, twenty feet from inky-black floor to grey roof, upheld by huge pillars of shining coal, and filled with flitting and passing devils. On a shattered pillar near the roof stood a naked man, his flesh olive-coloured in the light of the lamps, hewing down a mass of coal that still clove to the roof. Behind him was the wall of darkness, and when the lamps shifted he disappeared like a ghost.

The devils were shouting directions, and the man howled in reply, resting on his pick and wiping the sweat from his brow. When he smote the coal crushed and slid and rumbled from the darkness into the darkness, and the devils cried *Shabash!* The man stood erect like a bronze statue, he twisted and bent himself like a Japanese grotesque, and anon threw himself on his side after the manner of the dying gladiator. Then spoke the still small voice of fact: 'A first-class workman if he would only stick to it. But as soon as he makes a little money he lies off and spends it. That's the last of a pillar that we've knocked out. See here. These pillars of coal are square, about thirty feet each way. As you can see, we make the pillar first by cutting out all the coal between. Then we drive two square tunnels, about seven feet wide, through and across the pillar, propping it with balks. There's one fresh cut.'

Two tunnels crossing at right angles had been driven through a pillar which in its under-cut condition seemed like the rough draft of a statue for an elephant. 'When the pillar stands only on four legs we chip away one leg at a time from a square to an hour-glass shape, and then either the whole of the pillar crashes down from the roof or else a quarter or a half. If the coal lies against the sandstone it carries away clear, but in some places it brings down stone and rubbish with it. The chipped-away legs of the pillars are called stooks.'

'Who has to make the last cut that breaks a leg through?'

'Oh! Englishmen, of course. We can't trust natives for the job unless it's very easy. The natives take kindly to the pillar-work though. They are paid just as much for their coal as though they had hewed it out of the solid. Of course we take very good care to see that the roof doesn't come in on us. You would never understand how and why we prop our roofs with those piles of sleepers. Anyway, you can see that we cannot take out a whole line of pillars. We work 'em *en échelon*, and those big beams you see running from floor to roof are our indicators. They show when the roof is going to give. Oh! dear no, there's no dramatic effect about it. No splash, you know. Our roofs give plenty of warning by cracking and then collapse slowly. The parts of the work that we have cleared out and allowed to fall in are called goafs. You're on the edge of a goaf now. All that darkness there marks the limit of the mine. We have worked that out piece-meal, and the props are gone and the place is down. The roof of any pillar-working is tested every morning by tapping—pretty hard tapping.'

'Hi yi! yi!' shout all the devils in chorus, and the Hall of Eblis is full of rolling sound. The olive man has brought down an avalanche of coal. 'It is a sight to see the whole of one of the pillars come away. They make an awful noise. It would startle you out of your wits. But there's not an atom of risk.'

('Not an atom of risk.' Oh, genial and courteous host, when you turned up next day blacker than any sweep that ever swept, with a neat half-inch gash on your forehead — won by cutting a 'stook' and getting caught by a bounding coal-knob — how long and earnestly did you endeavour to show that 'stook-cutting' was an employment as harmless and unexciting as wool-samplering!)

'Our ways are rather primitive, but they're cheap, and safe as houses. Doms and Bauris, Kols and Beldars, don't understand refinements in mining. They'd startle an English pit where there was fire-damp. Do you know it's a solemn fact that if you drop a Davy lamp or snatch it quickly you can blow a whole English pit inside out with all the miners? Good for us that we don't know what fire-damp is here. We can use flare-lamps.'

After the first feeling of awe and wonder is worn out, a mine becomes monotonous. There is only the humming, palpitating darkness, the rumble of the tubs, and the endless procession of galleries to arrest the attention. And one pit to the uninitiated is as like to another as two peas. Tell a miner this and he laughs—slowly and softly. To him the pits have each distinct personalities, and each must be dealt with differently.

CHAPTER III

THE PERILS OF THE PITS

An engineer, who has built a bridge, can strike you nearly dead with professional facts; the captain of a seventy-horse-power Ganges river-steamer can, in one hour, tell legends of the Sandheads and the James and Mary shoal sufficient to fill half a *Pioneer*, but a couple of days spent on, above, and in a coal-mine yields more mixed information than two engineers and three captains. It is hopeless to pretend to understand it all.

When your host says, 'Ah, such an one is a thundering good fault-reader!' you smile hazily, and by way of keeping up the conversation, adventure on the statement that fault-reading and palmistry are very popular amusements. Then men explain.

Every one knows that coal-strata, in common with women, horses, and official superiors, have 'faults' caused by some colic of the earth in the days when things were settling into their places. A coal-seam is suddenly sliced off as a pencil is cut through with one slanting blow of the penknife, and one-half is either pushed up or pushed down any number of feet. The miners work the seam till they come to this break-off, and then call for an expert to 'read the fault.' It is sometimes very hard to discover whether the sliced-off seam has gone up or down. Theoretically, the end of the broken piece should show the direction. Practically its indications are not always clear. Then a good 'fault-reader,' who must more than know geology, is a useful man, and is much prized; for the Giridih fields are full of faults and 'dykes.' Tongues of what was once molten lava thrust themselves sheer into the coal, and the disgusted miner finds that for about twenty feet on each side of the tongue all coal has been burnt away.

The head of the mine is supposed to foresee these things and more. He can tell you, without looking at the map, what is the geological formation of any thousand square miles of India; he knows as much about brickwork and the building of houses, arches, and shafts as an average P.W.D. man; he has not only to know the intestines of a pumping or winding engine, but must be able to take them to pieces with his own hands, indicate on the spot such parts as need repair, and make drawings of anything that requires renewal; he knows how to lay out and build railways with a grade of one in twenty-seven; he has to carry in his head all the signals and points between and over which his locomotive engines work; he must be an electrician capable of controlling the apparatus that fires the dynamite charges in the pits, and must thoroughly understand boring operations with thousand-foot drills. He must know by ıame, at least, one thousand of the men on the vorks, and must fluently speak the vernaculars of he low castes. If he has Sonthalı, which is more elaborate than Greek, so much the better for him. He must know how to handle men of all grades, ınd, while holding himself aloof, must possess ufficient grip of the men's private lives to be able o see at once the merits of a charge of attempted bduction preferred by a clucking, croaking Kol gainst a fluent English-speaking Brahmin. For ie is literally the Light of Justice, and to him the njured husband and the wrathful father look for edress. He must be on the spot and take all esponsibility when any specially risky job is under vay in the pit, and he can claim no single hour of he day or the night for his own. From eight in he morning till one in the afternoon he is coated vith coal-dust and oil From one till eight in the vening he has office work. After eight o'clock ıe is free to attend to anything that he may be vanted for.

This is a soberly drawn picture of a life that ahibs on the mines actually enjoy. They are pared all private socio-official worry, for the Comany, in its mixture of State and private interest, is s perfectly cold-blooded and devoid of bias as any reat Department of the Empire. If certain things e done, well and good. If certain things be not one the defaulter goes, and his place is filled by nother. The conditions of service are graven on tone. There may be generosity; there undoubtedly justice, but above all, there is freedom within road limits. No irrepressible shareholder cripples the executive arm with suggestions and restrictions, and no private piques turn men's blood to gall within them. They work like horses and are happy.

When he can snatch a free hour, the grimy, sweating, cardigan-jacketed, ammunition-booted, pick-bearing ruffian turns into a well-kept English gentleman, who plays a good game of billiards, and has a batch of new books from England every week. The change is sudden, but in Giridih nothing is startling. It is right and natural that a man should be alternately Valentine and Orson, specially Orson. It is right and natural to drive—always behind a mad horse—away and away towards the lonely hills till the flaming coke ovens become glow-worms on the dark horizon, and in the wilderness to find a lovely English maiden teaching squat, filthy Sonthal girls how to become Christians. Nothing is strange in Giridih, and the stories of the pits, the raffle of conversation that a man picks up as he passes, are quite in keeping with the place. Thanks to the law, which enacts that an Englishman must look after the native miners, and if any one be killed must explain satisfactorily that the accident was not due to preventable causes, the death-roll is kept astoundingly low. In one 'bad' half-year, six men out of the five thousand were killed, in another four, and in another none at all. As has been said before, a big accident would scare off the workers, for, in spite of the age of the mines—nearly thirty years—the hereditary pitman has not yet been evolved. But to small accidents the men are orientally apathetic. Read of a death among the five thousand——

A gang has been ordered to cut clay for the ıting of the coke furnaces. The clay is piled in a uge bank in the open sunlight. A coolie hacks ıd hacks till he has hewn out a small cave with venty foot of clay above him. Why should he ouble to climb up the bank and bring down the ıve of the cave? It is easier to cut in The Sirdar f the gang is watching round the shoulder of the ank. The coolie cuts lazily as he stands. Sunday very near, and he will get gloriously drunk in iridih Bazar with his week's earnings. He digs is own grave stroke by stroke, for he has not ense enough to see that undercut clay is danger-ıs. He is a Sonthal from the hills. There is a nash and a dull thud, and his grave has shut down pon him in an avalanche of heavy-caked clay.

The Sirdar calls to the Babu of the Ovens, and ith the promptitude of his race the Babu loses his ead. He runs puffily, without giving orders, any-here, everywhere. Finally he runs to the Sahib's ouse. The Sahib is at the other end of the collieries. [e runs back. The Sahib has gone home to wash. hen his indiscretion strikes him. He should have nt runners—fleet-footed boys from the coal-reening gangs. He sends them and they fly. One tches the Sahib just changed after his bath. There is a man dead at such a place'—he gasps, nitting to say whether it is a surface or a pit cident. On goes the grimy pit-kit, and in three inutes the Sahib's dogcart is flying to the place dicated.

They have dug out the Sonthal. His head is ıashed in, spine and breastbone are broken, and the gang-Sirdar, bowing double, throws the blame of the accident on the poor, shapeless, battered dead. 'I had warned him, but he would not listen! *Twice* I warned him! These men are witnesses.'

The Babu is shaking like a jelly. 'Oh, sar, I have never seen a man killed before! Look at that eye, sar! I should have sent runners. I ran everywhere! I ran to your house. You were not in. I was running for hours. It was not my fault! It was the fault of the gang-Sirdar.' He wrings his hands and gurgles. The best of accountants, but the poorest of coroners is he. No need to ask how the accident happened. No need to listen to the Sirdar and his 'witnesses.' The Sonthal had been a fool, but it was the Sirdar's business to protect him against his own folly. 'Has he any people here?'

'Yes, his *rukni*,—his kept-woman,—and his sister's brother-in-law. His home is far-off.'

The sister's brother-in-law breaks through the crowd howling for vengeance on the Sirdar. He will send for the police, he will have the price of his brother's blood full tale. The windmill arms and the angry eyes fall, for the Sahib is making the report of the death.

'Will the Government give me *pensin?* I am his wife,' a woman clamours, stamping her pewter-ankleted feet. 'He was killed in your service. Where is his *pensin?* I am his wife.'

'You lie! You're his *rukni*. Keep quiet! Go! The pension comes to *us*.'

The sister's brother-in-law is not a refined man, but the *rukni* is his match. They are silenced. The

Sahib takes the report, and the body is borne away. Before to-morrow's sun rises the gang-Sirdar may find himself a simple 'surface-coolie,' earning nine *pice* a day; and in a week some Sonthal woman behind the hills may discover that she is entitled to draw monthly great wealth from the coffers of the Sirkar. But this will not happen if the sister's brother-in-law can prevent it. He goes off swearing at the *rukni.*

In the meantime, what have the rest of the dead man's gang been doing? They have, if you please, abating not one stroke, dug out all the clay, and would have it verified. They have seen their comrade die. He is dead. *Bus!* Will the Sirdar take the tale of clay? And yet, were twenty men to be crushed by their own carelessness in the pit, these same impassive workers would scatter like panic-stricken horses.

Turning from this sketch, let us set in order a few stories of the pits. In some of the mines the coal is blasted out by the dynamite which is fired by electricity from a battery on the surface. Two men place the charges, and then signal to be drawn up in the cage which hangs in the pit-eye. Once two natives were entrusted with the job. They performed their parts beautifully till the end, when the vaster idiot of the two scrambled into the cage, gave signal, and was hauled up before his friend could follow.

Thirty or forty yards up the shaft all possible danger for those in the cage was over, and the charge was accordingly exploded. Then it occurred to the man in the cage that his friend stood a very good chance of being, by this time, riven to pieces and choked.

But the friend was wise in his generation. He had missed the cage, but found a coal-tub—one of the little iron trucks—and turning this upside down, crawled into it. When the charge went off, his shelter was battered in so much, that men had to hack him out, for the tub had made, as it were, a tinned sardine of its occupant. He was absolutely unhurt, but for his feelings. On reaching the pit-bank his first words were, 'I do not desire to go down to the pit with *that* man any more.' His wish had been already gratified, for 'that man' had fled. Later on, the story goes, when 'that man' found that the guilt of murder was not at his door, he returned, and was made a mere surface-coolie, and his brothers jeered at him as they passed to their better-paid occupations.

Occasionally there are mild cyclones in the pits. An old working, perhaps a mile away, will collapse: a whole gallery sinking bodily. Then the displaced air rushes through the inhabited mine, and, to quote their own expression, blows the pitmen about 'like dry leaves.' Few things are more amusing than the spectacle of a burly Tyneside foreman who, failing to dodge round a corner in time, is 'put down' by the wind, sitting-fashion, on a knobby lump of coal.

But most impressive of all is a tale they tell of a fire in a pit many years ago. The coal caught light. They had to send earth and bricks down the shaft and build great dams across the galleries to choke the fire. Imagine the scene, a few hundred feet underground, with the air growing hotter and hotter each moment, and the carbonic acid gas trickling through the dams. After a time the rough dams gaped, and the gas poured in afresh, and the Englishmen went down and leeped the cracks between roof and dam-sill with anything they could get. Coolies fainted, and had to be taken away, but no one died, and behind the first dams they built great masonry ones, and bested that fire; though for a long time afterwards, whenever they pumped water into it, the steam would puff out from crevices in the ground above.

It is a queer life that they lead, these men of the coal-fields, and a 'big' life to boot. To describe one half of their labours would need a week at the least, and would be incomplete then. 'If you want to see anything,' they say, 'you should go over to the Baragunda copper-mines; you should look at the Barakar ironworks; you should see our boring operations five miles away; you should see how we sink pits; you should, above all, see Giridih Bazar on a Sunday. Why, you haven't seen anything. There's no end of a Sonthal Mission hereabouts. All the little dev—dears have gone on a picnic. Wait till they come back, and see 'em learning to read.'

Alas! one cannot wait. At the most one can but thrust an impertinent pen skin-deep into matters only properly understood by specialists.

IN AN OPIUM FACTORY

In an Opium Factory

On the banks of the Ganges, forty miles below Benares as the crow flies, stands the Ghazipur Factory, an opium mint as it were, whence issue he precious cakes that are to replenish the coffers of the Indian Government. The busy season is etting in, for with April the opium comes up from he districts after having run the gauntlet of the listrict officers of the Opium Department, who vill pass it as fit for use. Then the really serious vork opens, under a roasting sun. The opium urrives by *challans*, regiments of one hundred jars, ach holding one maund, and each packed in a basket and sealed atop. The district dficer ubmits forms—never was such a place for forms s the Ghazipur Factory—showing the quality and veight of each pot, and with the jars comes a erson responsible for the safe carriage of the tring, their delivery, and their virginity. If any ots are broken or tampered with, an unfortunate ndividual called the import-officer, and appointed o work like a horse from dawn till dewy eve, nust examine the man in charge of the *challan* and educe his statement to writing. Fancy getting any native to explain how a jar has been smashed! But the Perfect Flower is about as valuable as silver.

Then all the pots have to be weighed, and the weight of each pot is recorded on the pot, in a book, and goodness knows where else, and every one has to sign certificates that the weighing is correct. The pots have been weighed once in the district and once in the factory. None the less a certain number of them are taken at random and weighed afresh before they are opened. This is only the beginning of a long series of checks. Then the testing begins. Every single pot has to be tested for quality. A native, called the *purkhea*, drives his fist into the opium, rubs and smells it, and calls out the class for the benefit of the opium examiner. A sample picked between finger and thumb is thrown into a jar, and if the opium examiner thinks the *purkhea* has said sooth, the class of that jar is marked in chalk, and everything is entered in a book. Every ten samples are put in a locked box with duplicate keys, and sent over to the laboratory for assay. With the tenth boxful—and this marks the end of the *challan* of a hundred jars—the Englishman in charge of the testing signs the test-paper, and enters the name of the native tester and sends it over to the laboratory. For convenience' sake, it may be as well to say that, unless distinctly stated to the contrary, every single thing in Ghazipur is locked, and every operation is conducted under more than police supervision.

In the laboratory each set of ten samples is

horoughly mixed by hand : a quarter-ounce lump
; then tested for starch adulteration by iodine,
rhich turns the decoction blue, and, if necessary,
or gum adulteration by alcohol, which makes the
ecoction filmy. If adulteration be shown, all the
en pots of that set are tested separately till the
inful pot is discovered. Over and above this
est, three samples of one hundred grains each are
aken from the mixed set of ten samples, dried on
steam-table, and then weighed for consistence.
heresult is written down in a ten-columned form in
he assay register, and by the mean result are those
en pots paid for. This, after everything has been
one in duplicate and countersigned, completes
he test and assay. If a district officer has classed
he opium in a glaringly wrong way, he is thus
aught and reminded of his error. No one trusts
ny one in Ghazipur. They are always weighing,
esting, and assaying.

Before the opium can be used it must be
alligated' in big vats. The pots are emptied
ito these, and special care is taken that none of
ie drug sticks to the hands of the coolies. Opium
as a knack of doing this, and therefore coolies
re searched at most inopportune moments. There
re a good many Mahometans in Ghazipur, and
ley would all like a little opium. The pots after
mptying are smashed up and scraped, and heaved
own the steep river-bank of the factory, where
ley help to keep the Ganges in its place, so many
e they and the little earthen bowls in which the
pium cakes are made. People are forbidden
wander about the river-front of the factory

in search of remnants of opium on the shards. There are no remnants, but people will not credit this. After vatting, the big vats, holding from one to three thousand maunds, are probed with test-rods, and the samples are treated just like the samples of the *challans*, everybody writing everything in duplicate and signing it. Having secured the mean consistence of each vat, the requisite quantity of each blend is weighed out, thrown into an alligating vat, of 250 maunds, and worked up by the feet of coolies.

This completes the working of the opium. It is now ready to be made into cakes after a final assay. Man has done nothing to improve it since it streaked the capsule of the poppy — this mysterious drug. April, May, and June are the months for receiving and manufacturing opium, and in the winter months come the packing and the despatch.

At the beginning of the cold weather Ghazipur holds, locked up, a trifle, say, of three and a half millions sterling in opium. Now, there may be only a paltry three-quarters of a million on hand, and that is going out at the rate per diem of one Viceroy's salary for two and a half years.

There are ranges and ranges of gigantic godowns, huge barns that can hold over half a million pounds' worth of opium. There are acres of bricked floor, regiments on regiments of chests; and yet more godowns and more godowns. The heart of the whole is the laboratory, which is full of the sick faint smell of an opium-joint where they sell *chandu*. This makes Ghazipur indignant.

That's the smell of pure opium. We don't need *handu* here. You don't know what real opium nells like. *Chandu - khana* indeed! That's efined opium under treatment for morphia, and ocaine, and perhaps narcotine.' 'Very well, let's ee some of the real opium made for the China narket.' 'We shan't be making any for another x weeks at earliest; but we can show you one ake made, and you must imagine two hundred nd fifty men making 'em as hard as they can— ne every four minutes.'

A Sirdar of cake-makers is called, and appears rith a miniature wash-board, on which he sets a ttle square box of dark wood, a tin cup, an arthen bowl, and a mass of poppy-petal cakes. A irger earthen bowl holds what looks like bad Cape obacco.

'What's that?'

'Trash—dried poppy-leaves, not petals, broken p and used for packing the cakes in. You'll see resently.' The cake-maker sits down and eceives a lump of opium, weighed out, of one eer seven chittacks and a half, neither more nor ess. 'That's pure opium of seventy consistence.' Every allowance is weighed.

'What are they weighing that brown water for?'

'That's *lewa*—thin opium at fifty consistence. t's the paste. He gets four chittacks and a half f it.' 'And do they weigh the petal-cakes?' Of course.' The Sirdar takes a brass hemispheri-al cup and wets it with a rag. Then he tears a etal-cake, which resembles a pancake, across so hat it fits into the cup without a wrinkle, and pastes it with the thin opium, the *lewa*. After this his actions become incomprehensible, but there is evidently a deep method in them. Pancake after pancake is torn across, dressed with *lewa*, and pressed down into the cup; the fringes hanging over the edge of the bowl. He takes half-pancakes and fixes them skilfully, picking now first-class and now second-class ones, for there are three kinds of them. Everything is gummed on to everything else with the *lewa*, and he presses all down by twisting his wrists inside the bowl till the bowl is lined half an inch deep with them, and they all glisten with the greasy *lewa*. He now takes up an ungummed pancake and fits it carefully all round. The opium is dropped tenderly upon this, and a curious washing motion of the hand follows. The mass of opium is drawn up into a cone as, one by one, the Sirdar picks up the overlapping portions of the cakes that hung outside the bowl and plasters them against the drug for an outside coat. He tucks in the top of the cone with his thumbs, brings the fringe of cake over to close the opening, and pastes fresh leaves upon all. The cone has now taken a spherical shape, and he gives it the finishing touch by gumming a large *chupatti*, one of the 'moon' kind, set aside from the first, on the top, so deftly that no wrinkle is visible. The cake is now complete, and all the Celestials of the Middle Kingdom shall not be able to disprove that it weighs two seers one and three-quarter chittacks, with a play of half a chittack for the personal equation.

The Sirdar takes it up and rubs it in the bran-like poppy trash of the big bowl, so that two-thirds of it are powdered with the trash and one-third is fair and shiny poppy-petal. 'That is the difference between a Ghazipur and a Patna cake. Our cakes have always an unpowdered head. The Patna ones are rolled in trash all over. You can tell them anywhere by that mark. Now we'll cut this one open and you can see how a section looks.' One-half of an inch, as nearly as may be, is the thickness of the shell all round the cake, and even in this short time so firmly has the *lewa* set that any attempt at sundering the skin is followed by the rending of the poppy-petals that compose the *chupatti*. 'Now you've seen in detail what a cake is made of—that is to say, pure opium 70 consistence, poppy-petal pancakes, *lewa* of 52.50 consistence, and a powdering of poppy trash.'

'But why are you so particular about the shell?'

'Because of the China market. The Chinaman likes every inch of the stuff we send him, and uses it. He boils the shell and gets out every grain of the *lewa* used to gum it together. He smokes that after he has dried it. Roughly speaking, the value of the cake we've just cut open is two pound ten. All the time it is in our hands we have to look after it and check it, and treat as it though it were gold. It mustn't have too much moisture in it, or it will swell and crack, and if it is too dry John Chinaman won't have it. He values his opium for qualities just the opposite of those in Smyrna opium. Smyrna opium gives as much as ten per cent of morphia, and if nearly solid—90 consistence. Our opium does not give more than three or three and a half per cent of morphia on the average, and, as you know, it is only 70, or in Patna 75, consistence. That is the drug the Chinaman likes. He can get the maximum of extract out of it by soaking it in hot water, and he likes the flavour. He knows it is absolutely pure too, and it comes to him in good condition.'

'But has nobody found out any patent way of making these cakes and putting skins on them by machinery?'

'Not *yet*. Poppy to poppy. There's nothing better. Here are a couple of cakes made in 1849, when they tried experiments in wrapping them in paper and cloth. You can see that they are beautifully wrapped and sewn like cricket balls, but it would take about half an hour to make one cake, and we could not be sure of keeping the aroma in them. There is nothing like poppy plant for poppy drug.'

And this is the way the drug, which yields such a splendid income to the Indian Government, is prepared.

THE SMITH ADMINISTRATION

The Smith Administration[1]

THE COW-HOUSE JIRGA

How does a King feel when he has kept peace in his borders, by skilfully playing off people against people, sect against sect, and kin against kin? Does he go out into the back verandah, take off his terai-crown, and rub his hands softly, chuckling the while—as I do now? Does he pat himself on the back and hum merry little tunes as he walks up and down his garden? A man who takes no delight in ruling men—dozens of them—is no man. Behold! India has been squabbling over the Great Cow Question any time these four hundred years, to the certain knowledge of history and successive governments. I, Smith, have settled it. That is all!

The trouble began, in the ancient and well-established fashion, with a love-affair across the Border, that is to say, in the next compound. Peroo, the cow-boy, went a-courting, and the innocent had not sense enough to keep to his

[1] The following are newspaper articles written between 1887 and 1888 for my paper.—R. K.

own creed. He must needs make love to Baktawri, Corkler's *coachwan's* (coachman) little girl, and she being betrothed to Ahmed Buksh's son, *ætat* nine, very properly threw a cow-dung cake at his head. Peroo scrambled back, hot and dishevelled, over the garden wall, and the vendetta began. Peroo is in no sense chivalrous. He saved Chukki, the *ayah's* (maid) little daughter, from a big pariah dog once; but he made Chukki give him half a *chupatti* for his services, and Chukki cried horribly. Peroo threw bricks at Baktawri when next he saw her, and said shameful things about her birth and parentage. 'If she be not fair to me, I will heave a rock at she,' was Peroo's rule of life after the cow-dung incident. Baktawri naturally objected to bricks, and she told her father.

Without, in the least, wishing to hurt Corkler's feelings, I must put on record my opinion that his *coachwan* is a *chamar*-Mahometan, not too long converted. The lines on which he fought the quarrel lead me to this belief, for he made a Creed-question of the brick-throwing, instead of waiting for Peroo and smacking that young cateran when he caught him. Once beyond my borders, my people carry their lives in their own hand—the Government is not responsible for their safety. Corkler's *coachwan* did not complain to me. He sent out an Army—Imam Din, his son—with general instructions to do Peroo a mischief in the eyes of his employer. This brought the fight officially under my cognisance; and was a direct breach of the neutrality existing between myself and Corkler, who has 'Punjab head,' and declares that his servants are the best in the Province. I know better. They are the tailings of my compound—'casters' for dishonesty and riotousness. As an Army, Imam Din was distinctly inexperienced. As a General, he was beneath contempt. He came in the night with a hoe, and chipped a piece out of the dun heifer, —Peroo's charge,—fondly imagining that Peroo would have to bear the blame. Peroo was discovered next morning weeping salt tears into the wound, and the mass of my Hindu population were at once up and in arms. Had I headed them, they would have descended upon Corkler's compound and swept it off the face of the earth. But I calmed them with fair words and set a watch for the cow-hoer. Next night, Imam Din came again with a bamboo and began to hit the heifer over her legs. Peroo caught him—caught him by the leg—and held on for the dear vengeance, till Imam Din was locked up in the gram-godown, and Peroo told him that he would be led out to death in the morning. But with the dawn, the Clan Corkler came over, and there was pulling of turbans across the wall, till the Supreme Government was dressed and said, 'Be silent!' Now Corkler's *coachwan's* brother was my *coachwan*, and a man much dreaded by Peroo. He was not unaccustomed to speak the truth at intervals, and, by virtue of that rare failing, I, the Supreme Government, appointed him head of the *jirga* (committee) to try the case of Peroo's unauthorised love-making. The other members were my bearer (Hindu), Corkler's bearer (Mahometan), with the *ticca-dharzi* (hired tailor), Mahometan, for Standing Counsel. Baktawri and Baktawri's father were witnesses, but Baktawri's mother came all unasked and seriously interfered with the gravity of the debate by abuse. But the *dharzi* upheld the dignity of the Law, and led Peroo away by the ear to a secluded spot near the well.

Imam Din's case was an offence against the Government, raiding in British territory and maiming of cattle, complicated with trespass by night—all heinous crimes for which he might have been sent to gaol. The evidence was deadly conclusive, and the case was tried summarily in the presence of the heifer. Imam Din's counsel was Corkler's *sais*, who, with great acumen, pointed out that the boy had only acted under his father's instructions. Pressed by the Supreme Government, he admitted that the letters of marque did not specify cows as an object of revenge, but merely Peroo. The hoeing of a heifer was a piece of spite on Imam Din's part. This was admitted. The penalties of failure are dire. A *chowkidar* (watchman) was deputed to do justice on the person of Imam Din, but sentence was deferred pending the decision of the *jirga* on Peroo. The *dharzi* announced to the Supreme Government that Peroo had been found guilty of assaulting Baktawri, across the Border in Corkler's compound, with bricks, thereby injuring the honour and dignity of Corkler's *coachwan*. For this offence, the *jirga* submitted, a sentence of a dozen stripes was necessary, to be followed by two hours of ear-holding. The Corkler *chowkidar* was deputed to do sentence on the person of Peroo, and the Smith *chowkidar* on that of Imam Din. They laid on together with justice and discrimination, and seldom have two small boys been better trounced. Followed next a dreary interval of 'ear-holding' side by side. This is a peculiarly Oriental punishment, and should be seen to be appreciated. The Supreme Government then called for Corkler's *coachwan* and pointed out the bleeding heifer, with such language as seemed suitable to the situation. Local knowledge in a case like this is invaluable. Corkler's *coachwan* was notoriously a wealthy man, and so far a bad Mussulman in that he lent money at interest. As a financier he had few friends among his co-servants. On the other hand, in the Smith quarters, the Mahometan element largely predominated; because the Supreme Government considered the minds of Mahometans more get-at-able than those of Hindus. The sin of inciting an illiterate and fanatic family to go forth and do a mischief was duly dwelt upon by the Supreme Government, together with the dangers attending the vicarious *jehad* (religious war). Corkler's *coachwan* offered no defence beyond the general statement that the Supreme Government was his father and his mother. This carried no weight. The Supreme Government touched lightly on the inexpediency of reviving an old creed-quarrel, and pointed out at venture, that the birth and education of a *chamar* (low-caste Hindu), three months converted, did not justify such extreme sectarianism. Here the populace shouted like the men of Ephesus, and sentence was passed amid tumultuous applause. Corkler's *coachwan* was ordered to give a dinner, not only to the Hindus whom he had insulted, but also to the Mahometans of the Smith compound, and also to his own fellow-servants. His brother, the Smith *coachwan*, unconverted *chamar*, was to see that he did it. Refusal to comply with these words entailed a reference to Corkler and the 'Inspector Sahib,' who would send in his constables, and, with the connivance of the Supreme Government, would harry and vex all the Corkler compound. Corkler's *coachwan* protested, but was overborne by Hindus and Mahometans alike, and his brother, who hated him with a cordial hatred, began to discuss the arrangements for the dinner. Peroo, by the way, was not to share in the feast, nor was Imam Din. The proceedings then terminated, and the Supreme Government went in to breakfast.

Ten days later the dinner came off and was continued far into the night. It marked a new era in my political relations with the outlying states, and was graced for a few minutes by the presence of the Supreme Government. Corkler's *coachwan* hates me bitterly, but he can find no one to back him up in any scheme of annoyance that he may mature; for have I not won for my Empire a free dinner, with oceans of sweetmeats? And in this, gentlemen all, lies the secret of Oriental administration. My throne is set where it should be—on the stomachs of many people.

A BAZAR DHULIP

I and the Government are roughly in the same condition; but modesty forces me to say that the Smith Administration is a few points better than the Imperial. Corkler's *coachwan*, you may remember, was fined a caste-dinner by me for sending his son, Imam Din, to mangle my dun heifer. In my last published administration report, I stated that Corkler's *coachwan* bore me a grudge for the fine imposed upon him, but among my servants and Corkler's, at least, could find no one to support him in schemes of vengeance. I was quite right—right as an administration with prestige to support should always be.

But I own that I had never contemplated the possibility of Corkler's *coachwan* going off to take service with Mr. Jehan Concepcion Fernandez de Lisboa Paul—a gentleman semi-orientalised, possessed of several dwelling-houses and an infamous temper. Corkler was an Englishman, and any attempt on his *coachwan's* part to annoy me would have been summarily stopped. Mr. J. C. F. de L. Paul, on the other hand . . . but no matter. The business is now settled, and there is no necessity for importing a race-question into the story.

Once established in Mr. Paul's compound, Corkler's *coachwan* sent me an insolent message demanding a refund, with interest, of all the money spent on the caste-dinner. The Government, in a temperately framed reply, refused point-blank, and pointed out that a Mahometan by his religion could not ask for interest. As I have stated in my last report, Corkler's *coachwan* was a renegade *chamar*, converted to Islam for his wife's sake. The impassive attitude of the Government had the effect of monstrously irritating Corkler's *coachwan*, who sat on the wall of Mr. Paul's compound and flung highly flavoured vernacular at the servants of the State as they passed. He said that it was his intention to make life a burden to the Government—profanely called Eschmitt Sahib. The Government went to office as usual and made no sign. Then Corkler's *coachwan* formulated an indictment to the effect that Eschmitt Sahib had, on the occasion of the caste-dinner, pulled him vehemently by the ears, and robbed him of one rupee nine annas four pie. The charge was shouted from the top of Mr. Paul's compound wall to the four winds of Heaven. It was disregarded by the Government, and the refugee took more daring measures. He came by night, and wrote upon the whitewashed walls with charcoal disgraceful sentences which made the Smith servants grin.

Now it is bad for any Government that its servants should grin at it. Rebellion is as the sin of witchcraft; and irreverence is the parent of rebellion. Not content with writing, Corkler's *coachwan* began to miscall the State—always from the top of Mr. Paul's wall. He informed intending *mussalchis* (scullions) that Eschmitt Sahib invariably administered his pantry with a polo-stock; possible *saises* (grooms) were told that wages in the Smith establishment were paid yearly; while *khitmatgars* (butlers) learnt that their family honour was not safe within the gate-posts of the house of 'Eschmitt.' No real harm was done, for the character of my rule is known among all first-class servants. Still, the vituperation and all its circumstantial details made men laugh; and I choose that no one shall laugh.

My relations with Mr. Paul had always—for reasons connected with the incursions of hens—been strained. In pursuance of a carefully matured plan of campaign I demanded of Mr. Paul the body of Corkler's *coachwan*, to be dealt with after my own ideas. Mr. Paul said that the man was a good *coachwan* and should not be given up. I then temperately—always temperately—gave him a sketch of the ruffian's conduct. Mr. Paul announced his entire freedom from any responsibility in this matter, and requested that the correspondence might cease. It was vitally necessary to the well-being of my administration that Corkler's *coachwan* should come into my possession. He was daily growing a greater nuisance, and had drawn unto him a disaffected dog-boy, lately in my employ.

Mr. Paul was deaf to my verbal, and blind to my written entreaties. For these reasons I was reluctantly compelled to take the law into my own hands—and break it. A *khitmatgar* was sent down the length of Mr. Paul's wall to 'draw the fire' of Corkler's *coachwan*, and while the latter cursed him by his gods for ever entering Eschmitt

Sahib's service, Eschmitt Sahib crept subtilely behind the wall and thrust the evil-speaker into the moonlit road, where he was pinioned, in strict silence, by the ambushed population of the Smith compound. Once collared, I regret to say, Cockler's *coachwan* was seized with an unmanly panic; for the memory of the lewd sentences on the wall, the insults shouted from the top of Mr. Paul's wall, and the warnings to wayfaring table-servants, came back to his mind. He wept salt tears and demanded the protection of the law and of Mr. Paul. He received neither. He was paraded by the State through the quarters, that all men and women and little children might look at him. He was then formally appointed last and lowest of the carriage-grooms—*nauker-ke-nauker* (servant of servants)—in perpetuity, on a salary which would never be increased. The entire Smith people—Hindu and Mussulman alike—were made responsible for his safe-keeping under pain of having all the thatch additions to their houses torn down, and the Light of the Favour of the State—the Great *Hazur-ki-Mehrbani*—darkened for ever.

Legally the State was wrongfully detaining Corkler's *coachwan*. Practically, it was avenging itself for a protracted series of insults to its dignity.

Days rolled on, and Corkler's *coachwan* became carriage-*sais*. Instead of driving two horses, it was his duty to let down the steps for the State to tread upon. When the other servants received cold-weather coats, he was compelled to buy one, and all extra lean-to huts round his house were strictly forbidden. That he did not run away, I ascribe solely to the exertions of the domestic police—that is to say, every man, woman, and child of the Smith Kingdom. He was delivered into their hands, for a prey and a laughing-stock; and in their hands, unless I am much mistaken, they intend that he shall remain. I learn that my *khansamah* (head-butler) has informed Mr. Paul that his late servant is in gaol for robbing the Roman Catholic Chapel, of which Mr. Paul is a distinguished member; consequently that gentleman has relaxed his attempts to unearth what he called his 'so good *coachwan*.' That *coachwan* is now a living example and most lively presentment of the unrelaxing wrath of the State. However well he may work, however earnestly strive to win my favour, there is no human chance of his ever rising from his present position so long as Eschmitt Sahib and he are above the earth together. For reasons which I have hinted at above, he remains cleaning carriage-wheels, and will so remain to the end of the chapter; while the story of his fall and fate spreads through the bazars, and fills the ranks of servantdom with an intense respect for Eschmitt Sahib.

A broad-minded Oriental administration would have allowed me to nail up the head of Corkler's *coachwan* over the hall door; a narrow-souled public may consider my present lenient treatment of him harsh and illegal. To this I can only reply that I know how to deal with my own people. I will never, never part with Corkler's *coachwan*.

THE HANDS OF JUSTICE

Be pleased to listen to a story of domestic trouble connected with the Private Services Commission in the back verandah, which did good work, though I, the Commission, say so, but it could not guard against the Unforeseen Contingency. There was peace in all my borders till Peroo, the cow-keeper's son, came yesterday and paralysed the Government. He said his father had told him to gather sticks—dry sticks—for the evening fire. I would not check parental authority in any way, but I did not see why Peroo should mangle my *sirris*-trees. Peroo wept copiously, and, promising never to despoil my garden again, fled from my presence.

To-day I have caught him in the act of theft, and in the third fork of my white Doon *sirris*, twenty feet above ground. I have taken a chair and established myself at the foot of the tree, preparatory to making up my mind.

The situation is a serious one, for if Peroo be led to think that he can break down my trees unharmed, the garden will be a wilderness in a week. Furthermore, Peroo has insulted the Majesty of the Government. Which is Me. Also he has insulted my *sirris* in saying that it is dry. He deserves a double punishment.

On the other hand, Peroo is very young, very small, and very, very naked. At present he is penitent, for he is howling in a dry and husky fashion, and the squirrels are frightened.

The question is—how shall I capture Peroo?

There are three courses open to me. I can shin up the tree and fight him on his own ground. I can shell him with clods of earth till he makes submission and comes down; or, and this seems the better plan, I can remain where I am, and cut him off from his supplies until the rifles—sticks I mean—are returned.

Peroo, for all practical purposes, is a marauding tribe from the Hills—head-man, fighting-tail and all. I, once more, am the State, cool, collected, and impassive. In half an hour or so Peroo will be forced to descend. He will then be smacked: that is, if I can lay hold of his wriggling body. In the meantime, I will demonstrate.

'Bearer, bring me the *tum-tum ki chabuq* (carriage-whip).'

It is brought and laid on the ground, while Peroo howls afresh. I will overawe this child. He has an armful of stolen sticks pressed to his stomach.

'Bearer, bring also the *chota mota chabuq* (the little whip)—the one kept for the *punnia kutta* (spaniel).'

Peroo has stopped howling. He peers through the branches and breathes through his nose very hard. Decidedly, I am impressing him with a show of armed strength. The idea of that cruel whip-thong curling round Peroo's fat little brown stomach is not a pleasant one. But I must be firm.

'Peroo, come down and be hit for stealing the Sahib's wood.'

Peroo scuttles up to the fourth fork, and waits developments.

'Peroo, will you come down?'

'No. The Sahib will hit me.'

Here the *goalla* appears, and learns that his son is in disgrace. 'Beat him well, Sahib,' says the *goalla*. 'He is a *budmash*. I never told him to steal your wood. Peroo, descend and be very much beaten.'

There is silence for a moment. Then, crisp and clear from the very top of the *sirris*, floats down the answer of the treed dacoit.

'*Kubbi*, *kubbi nahin* (Never—never—No!).'

The *goalla* hides a smile with his hand and departs, saying: 'Very well. This night I will beat you dead.'

There is a rustle in the leaves as Peroo wriggles himself into a more comfortable seat.

'Shall I send a *punkha-coolie* after him?' suggests the bearer.

This is not good. Peroo might fall and hurt himself. Besides I have no desire to employ native troops. They demand too much batta. The *punkha-coolie* would expect four annas for capturing Peroo. I will deal with the robber myself. He shall be treated judicially, when the excitement of wrong-doing shall have died away, as befits his tender years, with an old bedroom slipper, and the bearer shall hold him. Yes, he shall be smacked three times,—once gently, once moderately, and once severely. After the punishment shall come the fine. He shall help the *malli* (gardener) to keep the flower-beds in order for a week, and then—

'Sahib! Sahib! Can I come down?'

The rebel treats for terms.

'Peroo, you are a *nut-cut* (a young imp).'

'It was my father's order. He told me to get sticks.'

'From this tree?'

'Yes; Protector of the Poor. He said the Sahib would not come back from office till I had gathered many sticks.'

'Your father didn't tell me that.'

'My father is a liar. Sahib! Sahib! Are you going to hit me?'

'Come down and I'll think about it.'

Peroo drops as far as the third fork, sees the whip, and hesitates.

'If you will take away the whips I will come down.'

There is a frankness in this negotiation that I respect. I stoop, pick up the whips, and turn to throw them into the verandah.

Follows a rustle, a sound of scraped bark, and a thud. When I turn, Peroo is down, off and over the compound wall. He has not dropped the stolen firewood, and I feel distinctly foolish.

My prestige, so far as Peroo is concerned, is gone.

This Administration will now go indoors for a drink.

THE SERAI CABAL

Upon the evidence of a scullion, I, the State, rose up and made sudden investigation of the crowded *serai*. There I found and dismissed, as harmful to public morals, a lady in a pink *saree* who was masquerading as somebody's wife. The utter and abject loneliness of the *mussalchi*, that outcaste of the cook-room, should, Orientally speaking, have led him to make a favourable report to his fellow-servants. That he did not do so I attributed to a certain hardness of character brought out by innumerable kickings and scanty fare. Therefore I acted on his evidence and, in so doing, brought down the wrath of the entire *serai*, not on my head,—for they were afraid of me,—but on the humble head of Karim Baksh, *mussalchi*. He had accused the bearer of inaccuracy in money matters, and the *khansamah* of idleness; besides bringing about the ejectment of fifteen people—men, women, and children—related by holy and unholy ties to all the servants. Can you wonder that Karim Baksh was a marked boy? Departmentally, he was under the control of the *khansamah*, I myself taking but small interest in the subordinate appointments on my staff. Two days after the evidence had been tendered, I was not surprised to learn that Karim Baksh had been dismissed by his superior; reason given, that he was personally unclean. It is a fundamental maxim of my administration that all power delegated is liable to sudden and unexpected resumption at the hands of the Head. This prevents the right of the Lord-Proprietor from lapsing by time. The *khansamah's* decision was reversed without reason given, and the enemies of Karim Baksh sustained their first defeat. They were bold in making their first move so soon. I, Smith, who devote hours that would be better spent on honest money-getting, to the study of my servants, knew they would not try less direct tactics. Karim Baksh slept soundly, over against the drain that carries off the water of my bath, as the enemy conspired.

One night I was walking round the house when the pungent stench of a *hookah* drifted out of the pantry. A *hookah*, out of place, is to me an abomination. I removed it gingerly, and demanded the name of the owner. Out of the darkness sprang a man, who said, 'Karim Baksh!' It was the bearer. Running my hand along the stem, I felt the loop of leather which a *chamar* attaches, or should attach, to his pipe, lest higher castes be defiled unwittingly. The bearer lied, for the burning *hookah* was a device of the groom—friend of the lady in the pink *saree*—to compass the downfall of Karim Baksh. So the second move of the enemy was foiled, and Karim Baksh asleep as dogs sleep, by the drain, took no harm.

Came thirdly, after a decent interval to give me time to forget the Private Services Commission, the *gumnamah* (the anonymous letter)—stuck into the frame of the looking-glass. Karim Baksh had proposed an elopement with the sweeper's wife, and the morality of the *serai* was in danger. Also the sweeper threatened murder, which could be avoided by the dismissal of Karim Baksh. The blear-eyed orphan heard the charge against him unmoved, and, at the end, turning his face to the sun, said: 'Look at me, Sahib! Am I the man a woman runs away with?' Then pointing to the *ayah*, 'Or she the woman to tempt a Mussulman?' Low as was Karim Baksh, the *mussalchi*, he could by right of creed look down upon a she-sweeper. The charge under Section 498, I. P. C., broke down in silence and tears, and thus the third attempt of the enemy came to naught.

I, Smith, who have some knowledge of my subjects, knew that the next charge would be a genuine one, based on the weakness of Karim Baksh, which was clumsiness—phenomenal ineptitude of hand and foot. Nor was I disappointed. A fortnight passed, and the bearer and the *khansamah* simultaneously preferred charges against Karim Baksh. He had broken two tea-cups and had neglected to report their loss to me; the value of the tea-cups was four annas. They must have spent days spying upon Karim Baksh, for he was a morose and solitary boy who did his cup-cleaning alone.

Taxed with the fragments, Karim Baksh attempted no defence. Things were as the witnesses said, and I was his father and his mother. By my rule, a servant who does not confess a fault suffers, when that fault is discovered, severe punishment. But the red *Hanuman*, who grins by the well in the bazar, prompted the bearer at that moment to express his extreme solicitude for the honour and dignity of my service. Literally translated, the sentence ran, 'The zeal of thy house has eaten me up.'

Then an immense indignation and disgust took possession of me, Smith, who have trodden, as far as an Englishman may tread, the miry gullies of native thought. I knew—none better—the peculations of the bearer, the vices of the *khansamah*, and the abject, fawning acquiescence with which these two men would meet the basest wish that my mind could conceive. And they talked to me—thieves and worse that they were—of their desire that I should be well served! Lied to me as though I had been a griff but twenty minutes landed on the Apollo Bunder! In the middle stood Karim Baksh, silent; on either side was an accuser, broken tea-cup in hand; the *khansamah*, mindful of the banished lady in the pink *saree;* the bearer remembering that, since the date of the Private Services Commission, the whisky and the rupees had been locked up. And they talked of the shortcomings of Karim Baksh—the outcaste—the boy too ugly to achieve and too stupid to conceive sin—a blunderer at the worst. Taking each accuser by the nape of his neck, I smote their cunning skulls the one against the other, till they saw stars by the firmamentful. Then I cast them from me, for I was sick of them, knowing how long they had worked in secret to compass the downfall of Karim Baksh.

And they laid their hands upon their mouths and were dumb, for they saw that I, Smith, knew to what end they had striven.

This Administration may not control a revenue of seventy-two millions, more or less, per annum, but it is wiser than—some people.

THE STORY OF A KING

If there be any idle ones who remember the campaign against Peroo, the cow-man's son, or retain any recollection of the great intrigue set afoot by all the servants against the scullion,—if, I say, there be any who bear in mind these notable episodes in my administration, I would pray their attention to what follows.

The *Gazette of India* shows that I have been absent for two months from the station in which is my house.

The day before I departed, I called the Empire together, from the bearer to the *sais*' friends' hanger-on, and it numbered, with wives and babes, thirty-seven souls—all well-fed, prosperous, and contented under my rule, which includes free phenyle and quinine. I made a speech—a long speech—to the listening peoples. I announced that the inestimable boon of local self-government was to be theirs for the next eight weeks. They said that it was 'good talk.' I laid upon the Departments concerned the charge of my garden, my harness, my house, my horse, my guns, my furniture, all the screens in front of the doors, both cows, and the little calf that was to come. I charged them by their hope of presents in the future to act cleanly and carefully by my chattels; to abstain from fighting, and to keep the *serai* sweet. That this might be done under the eye of authority, I appointed a Viceroy—the very strong man Bahadur Khan, *khitmatgar* to wit—and, that he might have a material hold over his subjects, gave him an ounce-phial of cinchona febrifuge, to distribute against the fevers of September. Lastly — and of this I have never sufficiently repented—I gave all of them their two months' wages in advance. They were desperately poor some of them,—how poor only I and the money-lender knew,—but I repent still of my act. A rich democracy inevitably rots.

Eliminating that one financial error, could any man have done better than I? I know he could not, for I took a plebiscite of the Empire on the matter, and it said with one voice that my scheme was singularly right. On that assurance I left it and went to lighter pleasures.

On the fourth day came the *gumnameh.* In my heart of hearts I had expected one, but not so soon—oh, not so soon! It was on a postcard, and preferred serious accusations of neglect and immorality against Bahadur Khan, my Viceroy. I understood then the value of the anonymous letter. However much you despise it, it breeds distrust—especially when it arrives with every other mail. To my shame be it said I caused a watch to be set on Bahadur Khan, employing a tender Babu. But it was too late. An urgent private telegram informed me: 'Bahadur Khan secreted sweeper's daughter. House leaks.' The head of my administration, the man with all the cinchona febrifuge, had proved untrustworthy, and—the house leaked. The agonies of managing an Empire from the Hills can only be appreciated by those who have made the experiment. Before I had been three weeks parted from my country,

I was compelled, by force of circumstance, to rule it on paper, through a hireling executive—the Babu—totally incapable of understanding the wants of my people, and, in the nature of things, purely temporary. He had, at some portion of his career, been in a subordinate branch of the Secretariat. His training there had paralysed him. Instead of taking steps when Bahadur Khan eloped with the sweeper's daughter, whom I could well have spared, and the cinchona febrifuge, which I knew would be wanted, he wrote me voluminous reports on both thefts. The leakage of the house he dismissed in one paragraph, merely stating that 'much furniture had been swamped.' I wrote to my landlord, a Hindu of the old school. He replied that he could do nothing so long as my servants piled cut fuel on the top of the house, straining the woodwork of the verandahs. Also, he said that the *bhisti* (water-carrier) refused to recognise his authority, or to sprinkle water on the road-metal which was then being laid down for the carriage drive. On this announcement came a letter from the Babu, intimating that bad fever had broken out in the *serai*, and that the servants falsely accused him of having bought the cinchona febrifuge of Bahadur Khan, ex-Viceroy, now political fugitive, for the purpose of vending retail. The fever and not the false charge interested me. I suggested—this by wire—that the Babu should buy quinine. In three days he wrote to know whether he should purchase common or Europe quinine, and whether I would repay him. I sent the quinine down by parcel post, and sighed for Bahadur Khan with all his faults. Had he only stayed to look after my people, I would have forgiven the affair of the sweeper's daughter. He was immoral, but an administrator, and would have done his best with the fever.

In course of time my leave came to an end, and I descended on my Empire, expecting the worst. Nor was I disappointed. In the first place, the horses had not been shod for two months ; in the second, the garden had not been touched for the same space of time ; in the third, the *serai* was unspeakably filthy ; in the fourth, the house was inches deep in dust, and there were muddy stains on most of the furniture ; in the fifth, the house had never been opened ; in the sixth, seventeen of my people had gone away and two had died of fever ; in the seventh, the little calf was dead. Eighthly and lastly, the remnant of my retainers were fighting furiously among themselves, clique against clique, creed against creed, and woman against woman ; this last was the most overwhelming of all. It was a dreary home-coming. The Empire formed up two deep round the carriage and began to explain its grievances. It wept and recriminated and abused till it was dismissed. Next morning I discovered that its finances were in a most disorganised condition. It had borrowed money for a wedding, and to recoup itself had invented little bills of imaginary expenses contracted during my absence.

For three hours I executed judgment, and strove as best I could to repair a wasted, neglected, and desolate realm. By 4 P.M. the ship of state had been cleared of the greater part of the raffle, and its crew—to continue the metaphor—had beaten to quarters, united and obedient once more.

Though I knew the fault lay with Bahadur Khan — wicked, abandoned, but decisive and capable-of-ruling-men Bahadur Khan—I could not rid myself of the thought that I was wrong in leaving my people so long to their own devices.

But this was absurd. A man can't spend all his time looking after his servants, can he?

THE GREAT CENSUS

Mowgi was a *mehter* (a sweeper), but he was also a Punjabi, and consequently, had a head on his shoulders. Mowgi was my *mehter*—the property of Smith who governs a vast population of servants with unprecedented success. When he was my subject I did not appreciate him properly. I called him lazy and unclean; I protested against the multitude of his family. Mowgi asked for his dismissal,—he was the only servant who ever voluntarily left the Shadow of my Protection,—and I said: 'O Mowgi, either you are an irreclaimable ruffian or a singularly self-reliant man. In either case you will come to great grief. Where do you intend to go?' 'God knows,' said Mowgi cheerfully. 'I shall leave my wife and all the children here, and go somewhere else. If you, Sahib, turn them out, they will die! For you are their only protector.'

So I was dowered with Mowgi's wife—wives rather, for he had forgotten the new one from Rawalpindi; and Mowgi went out to the unknown, and never sent a single letter to his family. The wives would clamour in the verandah and accuse me of having taken the remittances, which they said Mowgi must have sent, to help out my own pay. When I supported them they were quite sure of the theft. For these reasons I was angry with the absent Mowgi.

Time passed, and I, the great Smith, went abroad on travels and left my Empire in Commission. The wives were the feudatory Native States, but the Commission could not make them recognise any feudal tie. They both married, saying that Mowgi was a bad man; but they never left my compound.

In the course of my wanderings I came to the great Native State of Ghorahpur, which, as every one knows, is on the borders of the Indian Desert. None the less, it requires almost as many printed forms for its proper administration as a real district. Among its other peculiarities, it was proud of its prisoners—*kaidis* they were called. In the old days Ghorahpur was wont to run its dacoits through the stomach or cut them with swords; but now it prides itself on keeping them in leg-irons and employing them on 'remunerative labour,' that is to say, in sitting in the sun by the side of a road and waiting until some road-metal comes and lays itself.

A gang of *kaidis* was hard at work in this fashion when I came by, and the warder was picking his teeth with the end of his bayonet. One of the fettered sinners came forward and *salaamed* deeply to me. It was Mowgi,—fat, well fed, and with a twinkle in his eye. 'Is the Presence in good health and are all in his house well?' said Mowgi. 'What in the world are you doing here?' demanded the Presence. 'By your honour's favour I am in prison,' said he, shaking one leg delicately to make the ankle-iron jingle on the leg-bar. 'I have been in prison nearly a month.'

'What for—dacoity?'

'I have been a Sahib's servant,' said Mowgi, offended. 'Do you think that I should ever become a low dacoit like these men here? I am in prison for making a numbering for the people.'

'A what?' Mowgi grinned, and told the tale of his misdeeds thus:—

'When I left your service, Sahib, I went to Delhi, and from Delhi I came to the Sambhur Salt Lake over there!' He pointed across the sand. 'I was a Jemadar of *mehters* (a headman of sweepers) there, because these Marwarri people are without sense. Then they gave me leave because they said that I had stolen money. It was true, but I was also very glad to go away, for my legs were sore from the salt of the Sambhur Lake. I went away and hired a camel for twenty rupees a month. That was shameful talk, but these thieves of Marwarris would not let me have it for less.'

'Where did you get the money from?' I asked.

'I have said that I had stolen it. I am a poor man. I could not get it by any other way.'

'But what did you want with a camel?'

'The Sahib shall hear. In the house of a certain Sahib at Sambhur was a big book which came from Bombay, and whenever the Sahib wanted anything to eat or good tobacco, he looked into the book and wrote a letter to Bombay, and in a week all the things came as he had ordered—soap and sugar and boots. I took that book; it was a fat one; and I shaved my moustache in the manner of Mahometans, and I got upon my camel and went away from that bad place of Sambhur.'

'Where did you go?'

'I cannot say. I went for four days over the sand till I was very far from Sambhur. Then I came to a village and said: "I am Wajib Ali, Bahadur, a servant of the Government, and many men are wanted to go and fight in Kabul. The order is written in this book. How many strong men have you?" They were afraid because of my big book, and because they were without sense. They gave me food, and all the headmen gave me rupees to spare the men in that village, and I went away from there with nineteen rupees. The name of that village was Kot. And as I had done at Kot, so I did at other villages,—Waka, Tung, Malair, Palan, Myokal, and other places,—always getting rupees that the names of the strong young men might not be written down. I went from Bikanir to Jeysulmir, till my book in which I always looked wisely so as to frighten the people, was back-broken, and I got one thousand seven

'I have said that I had stolen it. I am a poor man. I could not get it by any other way.'

'But what did you want with a camel?'

'The Sahib shall hear. In the house of a certain Sahib at Sambhur was a big book which came from Bombay, and whenever the Sahib wanted anything o eat or good tobacco, he looked into the book and wrote a letter to Bombay, and in a week all he things came as he had ordered—soap and sugar and boots. I took that book; it was a fat one; and I shaved my moustache in the manner of Mahometans, and I got upon my camel and went away from that bad place of Sambhur.'

'Where did you go?'

'I cannot say. I went for four days over the sand till I was very far from Sambhur. Then I came to a village and said: "I am Wajib Ali, Bahadur, a servant of the Government, and many men are wanted to go and fight in Kabul. The order is written in this book. How many strong men have you?" They were afraid because of my big book, and because they were without sense. They gave me food, and all the headmen gave me rupees to spare the men in that village, and I went away from there with nineteen rupees. The name of that village was Kot. And as I had done at Kot, so I did at other villages,—Waka, Tung, Malair, Palan, Myokal, and other places,—always getting rupees that the names of the strong young men might not be written down. I went from Bikanir to Jeysulmir, till my book in which I always looked wisely so as to frighten the people, was back-broken, and I got one thousand seven hundred and eight rupees twelve annas and six pies.'

'All from a camel and a Treacher's Price List?'

'I do not know the name of the book, but these people were very frightened of me. But I tried to take my *takkus* from a servant of this State, and he made a report, and they sent troopers, who caught me,—me, and my little camel, and my big book. Therefore I was sent to prison.'

'Mowgi,' said I solemnly, 'if this be true, you are a great man. When will you be out of prison?'

'In one year. I got three months for taking the numbering of the people, and one year for pretending to be a Mahometan. But I may run away before. All these people are very stupid men.'

'My arms, Mowgi,' I said, 'will be open to you when the term of your captivity is ended. You shall be my body-servant.'

'The Presence is my father and my mother,' said Mowgi. 'I will come.'

'The wives have married, Mowgi,' I said.

'No matter,' said Mowgi. 'I also have a wife at Sambhur and one here. When I return to the service of the Presence, which one shall I bring?'

'Which one you please.'

'The Presence is my protection and a son of the gods,' said Mowgi. 'Without doubt I will come as soon as I can escape.'

I am waiting now for the return of Mowgi. I will make him overseer of all my house.

THE KILLING OF HATIM TAI

Now *Hatim Tai* was condemned to death by e Government, because he had stepped upon his *ihout*, broken his near-hindleg-chain, and punched)or old pursy *Durga Pershad* in the ribs till that 'nerable beast squealed for mercy. *Hatim Tai* is dangerous to the community, and the *mahout's* idow said that her husband's soul would never st till *Hatim's* little, pig-like eye was glazed in e frost of death. Did *Hatim* care? Not he. [e trumpeted as he swung at his pickets, and he ole as much of *Durga Pershad's* food as he could. hen he went to sleep and looked that 'all the to-iorrows should be as to-day,' and that he should :ver carry loads again. But the minions of the aw did not sleep. They came by night and 'anned the huge bulk of *Hatim Tai*, and took)unsel together how he might best be slain.

'If we borrowed a seven-pounder,' began the ubaltern, 'or, better still, if we turned him loose nd had the Horse Battery out! A general in-)ection would be nothing to it! I wonder 'hether my Major would see it?'

'Skittles,' said all the Doctors together. 'He's *ur* property.' They severally murmured, 'arsenic,' strychnine,' and 'opium,' and went their way, 'hile *Hatim Tai* dreamed of elephant loves, wooed nd won long ago in the Doon. The day broke, nd savage *mahouts* led him away to the place of xecution; for he was quiet, being 'fey,' as are)oth men and beasts when they approach the brink)f the grave unknowing. 'Ha, *Salah!* Ha,

Budmash! To-day you die!' shouted the *mahouts*, 'and Mangli's ghost will rode you with an *ankus* heated in the flames of *Put*, O murderer and tun-bellied thief.' 'A long journey,' thought *Hatim Tai*. ''Wonder what they'll do at the end of it.' He broke off the branch of a tree and tickled himself on his jowl and ears. And so he walked into the place of execution, where men waited with many chains and grievous ropes, and bound him as he had never been bound before.

'Foolish people!' said *Hatim Tai*. 'Almost as foolish as Mangli when he called me—the pride of all the Doon, the brightest jewel in Sanderson Sahib's crown—a "base-born." I shall break these ropes in a minute or two, and then, between my fore and hind legs, some one is like to be hurt.'

'How much d'you think he'll want?' said the first Doctor. 'About two ounces,' answered the second. 'Say three to be on the safe side,' said the first; and they did up the three ounces of arsenic in a ball of sugar. 'Before a fight it is best to eat,' said *Hatim Tai*, and he put away the *gur* with a *salaam;* for he prided himself upon his manners. The men fell back, and *Hatim Tai* was conscious of grateful warmth in his stomach. 'Bless their innocence!' thought he. 'They've given me a *mussala*. I don't think I want it; but I'll show that I'm not ungrateful.'

And he did! The chains and the ropes held firm. 'It's beginning to work,' said a Doctor. 'Nonsense,' said the Subaltern. 'I know old *Hatim's* ways. He's lost his temper. If the ropes break we're done for.'

Hatim kicked and wriggled and squealed and his best, so far as his anatomy allowed, to k-jump; but the ropes stretched not one inch. I am making a fool of myself,' he trumpeted. must be calm. At seventy years of age one uld behave with dignity. None the less, these es are excessively galling.' He ceased his iggles, and rocked to and fro sulkily. 'He is ng to fall!' whispered a Doctor. 'Not a bit it. Now it's my turn. We'll try the strych-e,' said the second.

Prick a large and healthy tiger with a corking-, and you will, in some small measure, realise difficulty of injecting strychnine subcutaneously o an elephant nine feet eleven inches and one-f at the shoulder. *Hatim Tai* forgot his dignity d stood on his head, while all the world wondered. told you that would fetch him!' shouted the ostle of strychnine, waving an enormous bottle. 'hat's the death-rattle! Stand back all!'

But it was only *Hatim Tai* expressing his regret at he had slain Mangli, and so fallen into the nds of the most incompetent *mahouts* that he d ever made string-stirrups. 'I was never obed with an *ankus* all over my body before; d I *won't* stand it!' blared *Hatim Tai.* He ood upon his head afresh and kicked. 'Final nvulsion,' said the Doctor, just as *Hatim Tai* ew weary and settled into peace again. After l, it was not worth behaving like a baby. He ould be calm. He was calm for two hours, nd the Doctors looked at their watches and awned.

'Now it's my turn,' said the third Doctor. '*Afim* lao.' They brought it—a knob of Patna opium of the purest, in weight half a seer. *Hatim* swallowed it whole. Ghazipur excise opium, two cakes of a seer each, followed, helped down with much *gur*. 'This is good,' said *Hatim Tai*. 'They are sorry for their rudeness. Give me some more.'

The hours wore on, and the sun began to sink, but not so *Hatim Tai*. The three Doctors cast professional rivalry to the winds and united in ravaging their dispensaries in *Hatim Tai's* behalf. Cyanide of potassium amused him. Bisulphide of mercury, chloral (very little of that), sulphate of copper, oxide of zinc, red lead, bismuth, carbonate of baryta, corrosive sublimate, quicklime, stramonium, veratrium, colchicum, muriatic acid, and lunar caustic, all went down, one after another, in the balls of sugar; and *Hatim Tai* never blenched.

It was not until the Hospital Assistant clamoured: 'All these things Government Store and Medical Comforts,' that the Doctors desisted and wiped their heated brows. ''Might as well physic a Cairo sarcophagus,' grumbled the first Doctor, and *Hatim Tai* gurgled gently; meaning that he would like another *gur*-ball.

'Bless my soul!' said the Subaltern, who had gone away, done a day's work, and returned with his pet eight-bore. 'D'you mean to say that you haven't killed *Hatim Tai* yet—three of you? Most unprofessional, I call it. You could have polished off a battery in that time.' 'Battery!' shrieked the baffled medicos in chorus. 'He's

. enough poison in his system to settle the ole blessed Brıtısh Army!'

'Let me try,' said the Subaltern, unstrapping · gun-case in his dog-cart. He threw a hand-·chief upon the ground, and passed quickly in ınt of the elephant. *Hatım Tai* lowered his ıd slightly to look, and even as he did so the ıerical shell smote him on the 'Saucer of Life' the little spot no bigger than a man's hand ıich is six inches above a lıne drawn from eye to e. 'This is the end,' said *Hatım Tai*. 'I die *Nıwaz Jung* died!' He strove to keep his ɛt, staggered, recovered, and reeled afresh. Then, th one wild trumpet that rang far through the ·ilight, *Hatim Tai* fell dead among his pickets.

'Might ha' saved half your dispensaries if you'd lled me ın to treat him at first,' said the Subaltern, ping out the eight-bore.

A SELF-MADE MAN

Surjun came back from Kimberley, which is Tom iddler's Ground, where he had been picking up ɔld and silver. He was no longer a Purbeah. A ɛal diamond ring sparkled on his hand, and his veed suit had cost him forty-two shillings and xpence. He paid two hundred pounds into the ank; and it was there that I caught hım and ·eated him as befitted a rich man. 'O Surjun, ɔme to my house and tell me your story.'

Nothing loath, Surjun came—diamond ring nd all. His speech was composite. When he ·ished to be impressive he spoke English checkered with the Low Dutch slang of the Diamond Fields. When he would be expressive, he returned to his vernacular, and was as native as a gentleman with sixteen-and-sixpenny boots could be.

'I will tell you my tale,' said Surjun, displaying the diamond ring. 'There was a friend of mine, and he went to Kimberley, and was a firm there selling things to the digger-men. In thirteen years he made seven thousand pounds. He came to me —I was from Chyebassa in those days—and said, "Come into my firm." I went with him. Oh no! I was not an emigrant. I took my own ship, and we became the firm of Surjun and Jagesser. Here is the card of my firm. You can read it: "Surjun and Jagesser Dubé, De Beer's Terrace, De Beer's Fields, Kimberley." We made an iron house,—all the houses are iron there,—and we sold, to the diggers and the Kaffirs and all sorts of men, clothes, flour, mealies, that is Indian corn, sardines and milk, and salmon in tins, and boots, and blankets, and clothes just as good as the clothes as I wear now.

'Kimberley is a good place. There are no pennies there—what you call *pice*—except to buy stamps with. Threepence is the smallest piece of money, and even threepence will not buy a drink. A drink is one shilling, one shilling and threepence, or one shilling and ninepence. And even the water there, it is one shilling and threepence for a hundred gallons in Kimberley. All things you get you pay money for. Yes, this diamond ring cost much money. Here is the bill, and there is the receipt stamp upon the bill—" Behrendt of Dutoitspan Road." It is written upon the bill, and the price was thirteen pounds four shillings. It is a good diamond—Cape Diamond. That is why the colour is a little, little soft yellow. All Cape diamonds are so.

'How did I get my money? 'Fore Gott, I cannot tell, Sahib. You sell one day, you sell the other day, and all the other days—give the thing and take the money—the money comes. If we know man very well, we give credit one week, and if very, very well, so much as one month. You buy boots for eleven shillings and sixpence; sell for sixteen shillings. What you buy at one pound, you sell for thirty shillings—at Kimberley. That is the custom. No good selling bad things. All the digger-men know and the Kaffirs too.

'The Kaffir is a strange man. He comes into the shops and say, taking a blanket, "How much?" in the Kaffir talk—So!'

Surjun here delivered the most wonderful series of clicks that I had ever heard from a human throat.

'That is how the Kaffir asks "How much?"' said Surjun calmly, enjoying the sensation that he had produced.

'Then you say, "No, *you* say," and you say it so.' (More clicks and a sound like a hurricane of kisses.) 'Then the Kaffir he say: "No, no, that blanket your blanket, not my blanket. *You* say."' 'And how long does this business last?' 'Till the Kaffir he tired, and *says*,' answered Surjun. 'And then do you begin the real bargaining?' 'Yes,' said Surjun, 'same as in bazar here. The Kaffir he says, "I can't pay!" Then you fold up blanket, and Kaffir goes away. Then he comes back and says "*gobu*," that is Kaffir for blanket. And so you sell him all he wants.'

'Poor Kaffir! And what is Kimberley like to look at?'

'A beautiful clean place—all so clean, and there is a very good law there. This law. A man he come into your compound after nine o'clock, and you say *vootsac*—same as *nickle jao*—and he doesn't *vootsac*; suppose you shoot that man and he dies, and he calls you before magistrate, he can't do nothing.'

'Very few dead men can. Are you allowed to shoot before saying "*vootsac*"?'

'Oh Hell, yes! Shoot if you see him in the compound after nine o'clock. That is the law. Perhaps he have come to steal diamonds. Many men steal diamonds, and buy and sell without license. That is called Aidibi.'

'What?'

'Aidibi.'

'Oh! "I. D. B." I see. Well, what happens to them?'

'They go to gaol for years and years. Very many men in gaol for I. D. B. Very many men your people, very few *mine*. Heaps of Kaffirs. Kaffir he swallows diamond, and takes medicine to find him again. You get not less than ten years for I. D. B. But I and my friend, we stay in our iron house and mind shop. That too is the way to make money.'

'Aren't your people glad to see you when you come back?'

'My people is all dead. Father dead, mother dead; and only brother living with some children across the river. I have been there, but that is not my place. I belong to nowhere now. They are all dead. After a few weeks I take my steamer to Kimberley, and then my friend he come here and put his money in the Bank.'

'Why don't you bank in Kimberley?'

'I wanted to see my brother, and I have given him one thousand rupees. No, one hundred pounds; that is more, more. Here is the Bank bill. All the others he is dead. There are some people of this country at Kimberley,—Rajputs, Brahmins, Ahirs, Parsees, Chamars, Bunnias, Telis,—all kinds go there. But my people are dead. I shall take my brother's son back with me to Kimberley, and when he can talk the Kaffir talk, he will be useful, and he shall come into the firm. My brother does not mind. He sees that I am rich. And now I must go to the village, Sahib. Good day, sir.'

Surjun rose, made as if to depart, but returned. The Native had come to the top.

'*Sahib!* Is this talk for publish in paper?'

'Yes.'

'Then put in about this diamond ring.' He went away, twirling the ring lovingly on his finger.

Know, therefore, O Public, by these presents, that Surjun, son of Surjun, one time resident in the village of Jhusi, in the District of Allahabad, in the North-West Provinces, at present partner in the firm of Surjun and Jagesser Dubé, De Beer's

Terrace, De Beer's Fields, Kimberley, who has tempted his fortune beyond the seas, owns legally and rightfully a Cape stone, valued at thirteen pounds four shillings sterling, sold to him by Behrendt of Dutoitspan Road, Kimberley. •

And it looks uncommonly well.

THE VENGEANCE OF LAL BEG

This is the true story of the terrible disgrace that came to Jullundri *mehter*, through Jamuna, his wife. Those who say that a *mehter* has no caste, speak in ignorance. Those who say that there is a caste in the Empire so mean and so abject that there are no castes below it, speak in greater ignorance. The *arain* says that the *chamar* has no caste; the *chamar* knows that the *mehter* has none; and the *mehter* swears by Lal Beg, his god, that the *od*, whose god is Bhagirat, is without caste. Below the *od* lies the *kaparia-bawaria*, in spite of all that the low-caste *Brahmins* say or do. A *Teji mehter* or a *Sundoo mehter* is as much above a *kaparia-bawaria* as an Englishman is above a *mehter*. Lal Beg is the *Mehter*-god, and his image is the Glorified Broom made of peacocks' feathers, red cloth, scraps of tinsel, and the cast-off finery of English toilette tables.

Jamuna was a *Malka-sansi* of Gujrat, an eater of lizards and dogs, one 'married under the basket,' a worshipper of Malang Shah. When her first husband was cast into the Lahore Central Gaol for lifting a pony on the banks of the Ravee, Jamuna cut herself adrift from her section of the tribe and let it pass on to Delhi. She believed that the Government would keep her man for two or three days only ; but it kept him for two years,—long enough for a *sansi* to forget everything in this world except the customs of her tribe. Those are never forgotten.

As she waited for the return of her man, she scraped acquaintance with a *mehtranee ayah* in the employ of a Eurasian, and assisted her in the grosser portions of her work. She also earned money,—sufficient to buy her a cloth and food. 'The *sansi*,' as one of their proverbs says, 'will thrive in a desert.' 'What are you?' said the *mehtranee* to Jamuna. 'A *Boorat mehtranee*,' said Jamuna, for the *sansi*, as one of their proverbs says, are quick-witted as snakes. 'A *Boorat mehtranee* from the south,' said Jamuna ; and her statement was not questioned, for she wore good clothes, and her black hair was combed and neatly parted.

Clinging to the skirts of the Eurasian's *ayah*, Jamuna climbed to service under an Englishman —a railway employé's wife. Jamuna had ambitions. It was pleasant to be a *mehtranee* of good standing. It will be better still, thought Jamuna, to turn Mussulman and be married to a real table-servant, openly, by the *mullah*. Such things had been ; and Jamuna was fair.

But Jullundri, *mehter*, was a man to win the heart of woman, and he stole away Jamuna's in the dusk, when she took the English babies for their walks.

'You have brought me a stranger-wife. Why did you not marry among your own clan?' said his grey-haired mother to Jullundri. 'A stranger-wife is a curse and a fire.' Jullundri laughed; for he was a jemadar of *mehters*, drawing seven rupees a month, and Jamuna loved him.

'A curse and a fire and a shame,' muttered the old woman, and she slunk into her hut and cursed Jamuna.

But Lal Beg, the very powerful God of the *mehters*, was not deceived, and he put a stumbling-block in the path of Jamuna that brought her to open shame. 'A *sansi* is as quick-witted as a snake'; but the snake longs for the cactus hedge, and a *sansi* for the desolate freedom of the wild ass. Jamuna knew the chant of Lal Beg, the prayer to the Glorified Broom, and had sung it many times in rear of the staggering, tottering pole as it was borne down the Mall. Lal Beg was insulted.

His great festival in the month of *Har* brought him revenge on Jamuna and Jullundri. Husband and wife followed the Glorified Broom, through the station and beyond, to the desolate grey flats by the river, near the Forest Reserve and the Bridge-of-Boats. Two hundred *mehters* shouted and sang till their voices failed them, and they halted in the sand, still warm with the day's sun. On a spit near the burning *ghât*, a band of *sansis* had encamped, and one of their number had brought in a ragged bag full of lizards caught on the Meean Meer road. The gang were singing over their captures, singing that quaint song of the 'Passing of the *Sansis*,' which fires the blood of all true thieves.

Over the sand the notes struck clearly on Jamuna's ear as the Lal Beg procession re-formed and moved Citywards. But louder than the cry of worshippers of Lal Beg rose the song of Jamuna, the sober *Boorat mehtranee*, and mother of Jullundri's children. Shrill as the noise of the night-wind among rocks went back to the *sansi* camp the answer of the 'Passing of the *Sansis*,' and the *mehters* drew back in horror. But Jamuna heard only the call from the ragged huts by the river, and the call of the song—

'The horses, the horses, the fat horses, and the sticks, the little sticks of the tents *Aho! Aho!*
Feet that leave no mark on the sand, and fingers that leave no trace on the door. *Aho! Aho!*
By the name of Malang Shah; in darkness, by the reed and the rope. . . .'

So far Jamuna sang, but the head man of the procession of Lal Beg struck her heavily across the mouth, saying, 'By this I know that thou art a *sansi*.'

HUNTING A MIRACLE

Marching-orders as vague as the following naturally ended in confusion: 'There's a priest somewhere, in Amritsar or outside it, or somewhere else, who cut off his tongue some days ago, and says it's grown again. Go and look.' Amritsar is a city with a population of one hundred and fifty thousand, more or less, and so huge that a tramway runs round the walls. To lay hands on one particular man of all the crowd was not easy; for the tongue having grown again, he would in no way differ from his fellows. Now, had he remained tongueless, an inspection of the mouths of the passers-by would have been some sort of guide. However, dumb or tongued, all Amritsar knew about him. The small Parsee boy, who appears to run the refreshment-room alone, volunteered the startling information that the 'Priest without the tongue could be found all anywhere, in the city or elsewhere,' and waved his little hands in circles to show the vastness of his knowledge. A booking-clerk—could it be possible that he was of the Arya-Samaj ?—had also heard of the *Sadhu*, and, pen in hand, denounced him as an impostor, a 'bad person,' and a 'fraudulent mendicant.' He grew so excited, and jabbed his pen so viciously into the air that his questioner fled to a *ticca-gharri*, where he was prompted by some Imp of Perversity to simulate extreme ignorance of the language to deceive the driver. So he said twice with emphasis, '*Sadhu ?*' 'Jehan,' said the driver, 'fush-class, Durbar Sahib!' Then the fare thrust out his tongue, and the scales fell from the driver's eyes. '*Bahut accha*,' said the driver, and without further parley headed into the trackless desert that encircles Fort Govindghar. The Sahib's word conveyed no meaning to him, but he understood the gesture; and, after a while, turned the carriage from a road to a plain.

Close to the Lahore Veterinary School lies a cool, brick-built, tree-shaded monastery, studded with the tombs of the pious founders, adorned with steps, terraces, and winding paths, which is known as Chajju Bhagat's Chubara. This place is possessed with the spirit of peace, and is filled by priests in salmon-coloured loin-cloths and a great odour of sanctity. The Amritsar driver had halted in the very double of the Lahore *chubara*—assuring his fare that here and nowhere else would be found the *Sadhu* with the miraculous tongue.

Indeed the surroundings were such as delight the holy men of the East. There was a sleepy breeze through the *pipals* overhead, and a square court crammed with pigeon-holes where one might sleep ; there were fair walls and mounds and little mud-platforms against or on which fires for cooking could be built, and there were wells by the dozen. There were priests by the score who sprang out of the dust, and slid off balconies or rose from cots as inquiries were made for the *Sadhu*. They were nice priests, sleek, full-fed, thick-jowled beasts, undefiled by wood-ash or turmeric, and mostly good-looking. The older men sang songs to the squirrels and the dust-puffs that the light wind was raising on the plain. They were idle—very idle. The younger priests stated that the *Sadhu* with the tongue had betaken himself to another *chubara* some miles away, and was even then being worshipped by hordes of admirers. They did not specify the exact spot, but pointed vaguely in the direction of Jandiala. However, the driver said he knew and made haste to depart. The priests pointed out courteously that the weather was warm, and that it would be better to rest a while before starting. So a rest was called, and while he sat in the shadow of the gate of the courtyard, the Englishman realised for a few minutes why it is that, now and then, men of his race, suddenly going mad, turn to the people of this land and become their priests; as did —— on the Bombay side, and later ——, who lived for a time with the *fakir* on the top of Jakko. The miraculous idleness — the monumental sloth of the place; the silence as the priests settled down to sleep one by one; the drowsy drone of one of the younger men who had thrown himself stomach-down in the warm dust and was singing under his breath; the warm airs from across the plain and the faint smell of burnt *ghi* and incense, laid hold of the mind and limbs till, for at least fifteen seconds, it seemed that life would be a good thing if one could doze, and bask, and smoke from the rising of the sun till the twilight—a fat hog among fat hogs.

The chase was resumed, and the *gharri* drove to Jandiala—more or less. It abandoned the main roads completely, although it was a 'fush-class,' and comported itself like an *ekka*, till Amritsar sunk on the horizon, or thereabouts, and it pulled up at a second *chubara*, more peaceful and secluded than the first, and fenced with a thicker belt of trees. There was an eruption under the horses' feet and a scattering of dust, which presently settled down and showed a beautiful young man with a head such as artists put on the shoulders of Belial. It was the head of an unlicked devil, marvellously handsome, and it made the horses shy. Belial knew nothing of the *Sadhu* who had cut out the tongue. He scowled at the driver, scowled at the fare, and then settled down in the dust, laughing wildly, and pointing to the earth and the sky. Now for a native to laugh aloud, without reason, publicly and at high noon, is a gruesome thing and calculated to chill the blood. Even the sight of silver coinage had no effect on Belial. He dilated his nostrils, pursed his lips, and gave himself up to renewed mirth. As there seemed to be no one else in the *chubara*, the carriage drove away, pursued by the laughter of the Beautiful Young Man in the Dust. A priest was caught wandering on the road, but for long he denied all knowledge of the *Sadhu.* In vain the Englishman protested that he came as a humble believer in the miracle ; that he carried an offering of rupees for the *Sadhu ;* that he regarded the *Sadhu* as one of the leading men of the century, and would render him immortal for at least twelve hours. The priest was dumb. He was next bribed—extortionately bribed—and said that the *Sadhu* was at the Durbar Sahib preaching. To the Golden temple accordingly the carriage went and found the regular array of ministers and the eternal passage of Sikh women round and round the Grunth ; which things have been more than once described in this paper. But there was no *Sadhu.* An old *Nihang*, grey-haired and sceptical —for he had lived some thirty years in a church as it were—was sitting on the steps of the tank, dabbling his feet in the water. 'O Sahib,' said he blandly, 'what concern have you with a miraculous *Sadhu ?* You are not a Poliswala. And, O Sahib, what concern has the *Sadhu* with you ?' The Englishman explained with heat—for fruitless drives in the middle of an October day are trying to the temper — his adventures at the various *chubaras*, not omitting the incident of the Beautiful Young Man in the Dust. The *Nihang* smiled shrewdly : 'Without doubt, Sahib, these men have told you lies. They do not want you to see the *Sadhu ;* and the *Sadhu* does not desire to see you. This affair is an affair for us common people and not for Sahibs. The honour of the Gods is increased ; but *you* do not worship the Gods.' So saying he gravely began to undress and waddled into the water.

Then the Englishman perceived that he had been basely betrayed by the *gharri*-driver, and all the priests of the first *chubara*, and the wandering priest near the second *chubara ;* and that the only sensible person was the Beautiful Young Man in the Dust, and *he* was mad.

This vexed the Englishman, and he came away. If *Sadhus* cut out their tongues and if the great Gods restore them, the devotees might at least have the decency to be interviewed.

THE EXPLANATION OF MIR BAKSH

My notion was that you had been
(Before they had this fit)
An obstacle that came between
Him and ourselves and it.

'That's the most important piece of evidence we've heard yet,' said the king, rubbing his hands. So now let the jury . . .'

'If any one of them can explain it,' said Alice, 'I'll give him sixpence. *I* don't believe there's an atom of meaning in it.'—*Alice in Wonderland*.

This, Protector of the Poor, is the *hissab* (your bill of house-expenses) for last month and a little bit of the month before,—eleven days,—and this, I think, is what it will be next month. Is it a long bill in five sheets? Assuredly yes, Sahib. Are the accounts of so honourable a house of the Sahib to be kept on one sheet only? This *hissab* cost one rupee to write. It is true that the Sahib will pay the one rupee; but consider how beautiful and and how true is the account, and how clean is the paper. Ibrahim, who is the very best petition-writer in all the bazar, drew it up. Ahoo! Such an account is this account! And I am to explain it all? Is it not written there in the red ink, and the black ink, and the green ink? What more does the Heaven-born want? Ibrahim, who is the best of all the petition-writers in the bazar, made this *hissab*. There is an envelope also. Shall I fetch that envelope? Ibrahim has written your name outside in three inks — a very *murasla* is this envelope. An explanation? Ahoo! God is my witness that it is as plain as the sun at noon. By your Honour's permission I will explain, taking the accounts in my hand.

Now there are four accounts—that for last month, which is in red; that for the month before, which is in black; that for the month to come, which is in green; and an account of private expense and dispens, which is in pencil. Does the Presence understand that? Very good talk.

There was the bread, and the milk, and the cow's food, and both horses, and the saddle-soap for last month, which is in green ink. No, red ink—the Presence speaks the truth. It was red ink, and it was for last month, and that was fifty-seven rupees eight annas; *but* there was the cost of a new manger for the cow, to be sunk into mud, and that was eleven annas. But I did not put *that* into the last month's account. I carried that over to *this* month—the green ink. No? There is no account for this month? Your Honour speaks the truth. Those eleven annas I carried thus—in my head.

The Sahib has said it is not a matter of eleven annas, but of seventy-seven rupees. That is quite true; but, O Sahib, if I, and Ibrahim, who is the best petition-writer in the bazar, do not attend to the annas, how shall your substance increase? So the food and the saddle-soap for the cows and the other things were fifty-seven rupees eight annas, and the servants' wages were a hundred and ten—all for last month. And now I must think, for this is a large account. Oh yes! It was in Jeth that I spoke to the *Dhobi* about the washing, and he said, 'My bill will be eleven rupees two pies.' It is written there in the green ink, and that, in addition to the soap, was sixty-eight rupees, seven annas, two pies. All of last month. *And* the hundred and ten rupees for the servants' wages make the total to one hundred and seventy-eight rupees, seven annas, two pies, as Ibrahim, who is the best petition-writer in the bazar, has set down.

But I said that all things would only be one hundred and fifty? Yes. That was at first, Sahib, before I was well aware of all things. Later on, it will be in the memory of the Presence that I said it would be one hundred and ninety. But that was before I had spoken to the *Dhobi*. No, it was before I had bought the trunk-straps for which you gave orders. I remember that I said it would be one hundred and ninety. Why is the Sahib so hot? Is not the account long enough? I know always what the expense of the house will be. Let the Presence follow my finger. That is the green ink, that is the black, here is the red, and there is the pencil-mark of the private expenses. To this I add what I said six weeks ago before I had bought the trunk-straps by your order. And so that is a *fifth* account. Very good talk! The Presence has seen what happened last month, and I will now show the month before last, and the month that is to come—together in little brackets; the one bill balancing to the other like swinging scales.

Thus runs the account of the month before last:—A box of matches three pies, and black thread for buttons three annas (it was the best black thread), *khas-khas* for the *tatties* twelve annas; and the other things forty-one rupees. To which that of the month to come had an answer in respect to the candles for the dog-cart; but I did not know how much these would cost, and I have written one rupee two annas, for they are always changing their prices in the bazar. And the oil for the carriage is one rupee, and the other things are forty-one rupees, and that is for the next month.

An explanation? Still an explanation? *Khuda-ka-kusm!* Have I not explained and has not Ibrahim, who is notoriously the best petition-writer in the bazar, put it down in the red ink, and the green ink, and the black; and is there not the private dispens account, withal, showing what should have been but which fell out otherwise, and what might have been but could not?

Ai, Sahib, what can I do? It is perhaps a something heavy bill, but there were reasons; and let the Presence consider that the *Dhobi* lived at the *ghat* over against the river, and I had to go there—two *kos*, upon my faith!—to get his bill; and, moreover, the horses were shod at the hospital, and that was a *kos* away, and the Hospital Babu was late in rendering his accounts. Does the Sahib say that I should know how the accounts will fall—not only for the month before last, but for this month as well? I do—I did—I will do! Is it my fault that more rupees have gone than I knew? The Sahib laughs! Forty years I have been a *khansamah* to the Sahib-log—from *mussalchi* to mate, and head *khansamah* have I risen (*smites himself on the breast*), and never have I been laughed at before. Why does the Sahib laugh? By the blessed *Imams*, my uncle was cook to Jan Larens, and I am a priest at the Musjid; and I am laughed at? Sahib, seeing that there were so many bills to come in, and that the *Dhobi* lived at the *ghat* as I have said, and the Horse hospital was a *kos* away, and God only knows where the sweeper lived, but *his* account came late also, it is not strange that I should be a little stupid as to my accounts, whereof there are so many. For the *Dhobi* was at the *ghat*, etc. Forty years have I been a *khansamah*, and there is no *khansamah* who could have kept his accounts so well. Only by my great and singular regard for the welfare of the Presence does it come about that they are not a hundred rupees wrong. For the *Dhobi* was at the *ghat*, etc. And I will *not* be laughed at! The accounts are beautiful accounts, and only I could have kept them.

. . . . . .

Sahib—Sahib! Garibparwar! I have been to Ibrahim, who is the best petition-writer in the bazar, and he has written all that I have said—all that the Sahib could not understand—upon pink paper from Sialkot. So now there are the five accounts *and* the explanation; and for the writing of all six you, O Sahib, must pay! But for my honour's sake do not laugh at me any more.

A LETTER FROM GOLAM SINGH

From Golam Singh, Mistri, Landin, Belait, to Ram Singh, Mistri, son of Jeewun Singh, in the town of Rajah Jung, in the tehsil of Kasur, in the district of Lahore, in the Province of the Punjab.

Wah Gooroojee ki futteh.

Call together now our friends and brothers, and our children and the Lambardar, to the big square by the well. Say that I, Golam Singh, have written you a letter across the Black Water, and let the town hear of the wonders which I have seen in Belait. Rutton Singh, the *bunnia*, who has been to Delhi, will tell you, my brother, that I am a liar ; but I have witnesses of our faith, besides the others, who will attest when we return what I have written.

I have now been many days in Belait, in this big city. Though I were to write till my hand fell from my wrist, I could not state its bigness. I myself know that, to see one another, the Sahib-log, of whom there are crores of crores, use the railway dâk, which is laid not above the ground as is the *Sirkar's* railway in our own country, but underneath it, below the houses. I have gone down myself into this rail together with the other witnesses. The air is very bad in those places, and this is why the Sahib-log have become white.

There are more people here than I have ever seen. Ten times as many as there are at Delhi, and they are all Sahibs who do us great honour.

Many hundred Sahibs have been in our country, and they all speak to us, asking if we are pleased.

In this city the streets run for many miles in a straight line, and are so broad that four bullock-carts of four bullocks might stand side by side. At night they are lit with English lamps, which need no oil, but are fed by wind which burns. I and the others have seen this. By day sometimes the sun does not shine, and the city becomes black. Then these lamps are lit all day and men go to work.

The bazars are three times as large as our bazars, and the shopkeepers, who are all Sahibs, sit inside where they cannot be seen, but their name is written outside. There are no *bunnias'* shops, and all the prices are written. If the price is high, it cannot be lowered ; nor will the shopkeeper bargain at all. This is very strange. But I have witnesses.

One shop I have seen was twice as large as Rajah Jung. It held hundreds of shopkeeper-sahibs and *memsahibs*, and thousands who come to buy. The Sahib-log speak one talk when they purchase their bazar, and they make no noise.

There are no ekkas here, but there are yellow and green *ticca-gharries* bigger than Rutton Singh's house, holding half a hundred people. The horses here are as big as elephants. I have seen no ponies, and there are no buffaloes.

It is not true that the Sahibs use the *belaitee punkah* (the thermantidote) like as you and I made for the Dipty Sahib two years ago. The air is cold, and there are neither coolies nor verandahs.

Nor do the Sahibs drink *belaitee panee* (soda-water) when they are thirsty. They drink water—very clean and good—as we do.

In this city there are plains so vast that they appear like jungle; but when you have crossed them you come again to lakhs of houses, and there are houses on all sides. None of the houses are of mud or wood, but all are in brick or stone. Some have carved doors in stone, but the carving is very bad. Even the door of Rutton Singh's house is better carved; but Rutton Singh's house could be put into any fore-court of these *belaitee* houses. They are as big as mountains.

No one sleeps outside his house or in the road. This is thought shameless; but it is very strange to see. There are no flat roofs to the houses. They are all pointed; I have seen this and so have the others.

In this city there are so many carriages and horses in the street that a man, to cross over, must call a police-*wallah*, who puts up his hand, and the carriages stop. I swear to you by our father that on account of me, Golam Singh mistri, all the carriages of many streets have been stopped that I might cross like a Padshah. Let Rutton Singh know this.

In this city for four annas you may send news faster than the wind over four hundred *kos*. There are witnesses; and I have a paper of the Government showing that this is true.

In this city our honour is very great, and we have learned to *shekand* like the *Sahib-logue*. All the *memsahibs*, who are very beautiful, look at us, but we do not understand their talk. These *memsahibs* are like the *memsahibs* in our country.

In this city there are a hundred dances every night. The houses where they *nautch* hold many thousand people, and the *nautch* is so wonderful that I cannot describe it. The Sahibs are a wonderful people. They can make a sea upon dry land, and then a fire, and then a big fort with soldiers—all in half an hour while you look. The other men will say this too, for they also saw what I saw at one of the *nautches*.

Rutton Singh's son, who has become a pleader, has said that the Sahibs are only men like us black men. This is a lie, for they know more than we know. I will tell. When we people left Bombay for Belait, we came upon the Black Water, which you cannot understand. For five days we saw only the water, as flat as a planed board with no marks on it. Yet the Captain Sahib in charge of the fire-boat said, from the first, 'In five days we shall reach a little town, and in four more a big canal.' These things happened as he had said, though there was nothing to point the road, and the little town was no bigger than the town of Lod. We came there by night, and *yet* the Captain Sahib knew! How, then, can Rutton Singh's son say such lies? I have seen this city in which are crores of crores of people. There is no end to its houses and its shops, for I have never yet seen the open jungle. There is nothing hidden from these people. They can turn the night into day [I have seen it], and they never rest from working. It is true that they do not understand carpenter's work, but all other things they understand, as I and the people with me have seen. They are no common people.

Bid our father's widow see to my house and little Golam Singh's mother; for I return in some months, and I have bought many wonderful things in this country, the like of which you have never seen. But your minds are ignorant, and you will say I am a liar. I shall, therefore, bring my witnesses to humble Rutton Singh, *bunnia*, who went to Delhi, and who is an owl and the son of an owl.

AP-KI-DAS, GOLAM SINGH.

THE WRITING OF YAKUB KHAN

From Yakub Khan, Kuki Khel, of Lala China, Malik, in the Englishman's City of Calcutta with Vahbtahn Sahib, to Katal Khan, Kuki Khel, of Lala China, which is in the Khaibar. This letter to go by the Sirkar's mail to Pubbi, and thence Mahbub Ali, the writer, takes delivery and, if God pleases, gives to my son.

Also, for my heart is clean, this writing goes on to Sultan Khan, on the upper hill over against Kuka Ghoz, which is in Bara, through the country of the Zuka Khel. Mahbub Ali goes through if God pleases.

To My Son.—Know this. I have come with the others and Vahbtahn (Warburton) Sahib, as was agreed, down to the river, and the rail-dâk does *not* stop at Attock. Thus the Mullah of Tordurra lied. Remember this when next he comes for food. The rail-dâk goes on for many days. The others who came with me are witnesses to this. Fifteen times, for there was but little to do in the dâk, I made all the prayers from the *niyah* to the *munajat*, and yet the journey was not ended. And at the places where we stopped there were often to be seen the fighting-men of the English, such as those we killed, when certain of our men went with the Bonerwals in the matter of Umbeyla, whose guns I have in my house. Everywhere there were fighting-men; but it may be that the English were afraid of us, and so drew together all their troops upon the line of the rail-dâk and the fire-carriage. Vahbtahn Sahib is a very clever man, and he may have given the order. None the less, there must be many troops in this country; more than all the strength of the Afridis. But Yar Khan says that all the land, which runs to the east and to the west many days' journey in the rail-dâk, is also full of fighting-men, and big guns by the score. Our Mullahs gave us no news of this when they said that, in the matter of six years gone, there were no more English in the land, all having been sent to Afghanistan, and that the country was rising in fire behind them. Tell the Mullah of Tordurra the words of Yar Khan. He has lied in respect to the rail-dâk, and it may be that he will now speak the truth regarding what his son saw when he went to Delhi with the horses. I have asked many men for news of the strength of the fighting-men in this country, and all say that it is very great. Howbeit, Vahbtahn Sahib is a clever man and may have told them to speak thus, as I told the women of Sikanderkhelogarhi to speak when we were pressed by the Sangu Khel, in that night when you, my son, took Torukh Khan's head, and I saw that I had bred a man.

If there be as many men throughout the place as I have seen and the people say, the mouth of the Khaibar is shut, and it were better to give no heed to our Mullahs. But read further and see for what reasons I, who am a Malak of the Kuki Khel, say this. I have come through many cities —all larger than Kabul. Rawal Pindi, which is far beyond the Attock, whence came all the English who fought us in the business of six years gone. That is a great city, filled with fighting-men—four thousand of both kinds, and guns. Lahore is also a great city, with another four thousand troops, and that is one night by the rail-dâk from Rawal Pindi. Amritsar has a strong fort, but I do not know how many men are there. The words of the people who go down with the grapes and the almonds in the winter are true, and our Mullahs have lied to us. Jullundur is also a place of troops, and there is a fort at Phillour, and there are many thousand men at Umballa, which is one night, going very swiftly in the rail-dâk, from Lahore. And at Meerut, which is half a day from Umballa, there are more men and horses; and at Delhi there are more also, in a very strong fort. Our people go only as far south as Delhi; but beyond Delhi there are no more strong Punjabi people—but only a mean race without strength. The country is very rich here, flat, with cattle and crops. We, of the villages of the Khaibar alone, could loot these people; but there are more fighting-men at Agra, and at Cawnpore, and at Allahabad, and many other places, whose names do not stay with me. Thus, my son, by day and by night, always going swiftly in the rail-dâk we came down to this very big city of Calcutta.

My mouth dripped when I saw the place that they call Bengal—so rich it was; and my heart was troubled when I saw how many of the English were there. The land is very strongly held, and there are a multitude of English and half-English in the place. They give us great honour, but all men regard us as though we were strange beasts, and not fighting-men with hundreds of guns. If Yar Khan has spoken truth and the land throughout is as I have seen, and no show has been made to fill us with fear, I, Yakub Khan, tell you, my son, and you, O Sultan Khan! that the English do well to thus despise us; for on the Oath of a Pathan, we are only beasts in their sight. It may be that Vahbtahn Sahib has told them all to look at us in this manner—for, though we receive great honour, no man shows fear, and busies himself with his work when we have passed by. Even that very terrible man, the Governor of Kabul, would be as no one in this great City of Calcutta. Were I to write what I have seen, all our people would say that I was mad and a liar. But this I will write privately, that only you, my son, and Sultan Khan may see; for ye know that, in respect to my own blood, I am no liar. There are lights without oil or wood burning brightly in this city; and on the water of the river lie boats which go by fire, as the rail-dâk goes, carrying men and fighting-men by two and three thousand. God knows whence they come! They travel by water, and therefore there must be yet another country to the eastward full of fighting-men. I cannot make clear how these things are. Every day more boats come. I do not think that this is arranged by Vahbtahn Sahib; for no man in those boats takes any notice of us; and we feel, going to and from every place, that we are children. When that Kaffir came to us, three years agone, is it in thy memory how, before we shot him, we looked on him for a show, and the children came out and laughed? In this place no children laugh at us; but none the less do we feel that we are all like that man from Kafirstan.

In the matter of our safe-conduct, be at ease. We are with Vahbtahn Sahib, and his word is true. Moreover, as we said in the *jirgah*, we have been brought down to see the richness of the country, and for that reason they will do us no harm. I cannot tell why they, being so strong,—if these things be not all arranged by Vahbtahn Sahib,—took any trouble for us. Yar Khan, whose heart has become so soft within him in three days, says that the louse does not kill the Afridi, but none the less the Afridi takes off his upper-coat for the itching. This is a bitter saying, and I, O my son, and O my friend Sultan Khan, am hard upon believing it.

I put this charge upon you. Whatever the Mullah of Tordurra may say, both respecting the matter that *we* know of, which it is not prudent to write, and respecting the going-out in spring against the Sangu Khel, do you, my son, and you, Sultan Khan, keep the men of the Khaibar villages, and the men of the Upper Bara, *still*, till I return and can speak with my mouth. The blood-feuds are between man and man, and these must go forward by custom; but let there be no more than single shots fired. We will speak together, and ye will discover that my words are good. I would give hope if I could, but I cannot give hope. Yar Khan says that it were well to keep to the blood-feuds only; and he hath said openly among us, in the smoking-time, that he has a fear of the English, greater than any fear of the curses of our Mullahs. Ye know that I am a man unafraid. Ye knew when I cut down the Malik of the Sipah Khel, when he came into Kadam, that I was a man unafraid. But this is no matter of one man's life, or the lives of a hundred, or a thousand; and albeit I cursed Yar Khan with the others, yet in my heart I am afraid even as he is. If these English, and God knows where their homes lie, for they come from a strange place, we do not know how strong in fighting-men,—if, O my son, and friend of my heart Sultan Khan, these devils can thus fill the land over four days' journey by this very swift rail-dâk from Peshawar, and can draw white light, as bright as the sun, from iron poles, and can send fire-boats full of men *from the east*, and moreover, as I have seen, can make new rupees as easily as women make cow-dung cakes,—what can the Afridis do?

The Mullah of Tordurra said that they came from the *west*, and that their rail-dâk stopped at Attock, and that there were none of them except those who came into our country in the great fight. In all three things he has lied. Give no heed to him. I myself will shoot him when I return. If he be a Saint, there will be miracles over his tomb, which I will build. If he be no Saint, there is but one Mullah the less. It were better that he should die than take the Khaibar villages into a new blockade; as did the Mullah of Kardara, when we were brought to shame by Jan Larens and I was a young man.

The black men in this place are dogs and children. To such an one I spoke yesterday, saying, 'Where is Vahbtahn Sahib?' and he answered nothing, but laughed. I took him by the throat and shook him, only a little and very gently, for I did not wish to bring trouble on Vahbtahn Sahib, and he has said that our customs are not the customs of this country. This black man wept, and said that I had killed him, but truly I had only shaken him to and fro. He was a fat man, with white stockings, dressed in woman's fashion, speaking English, but acting without courtesy either to the Sahibs or to us. Thus are all the black people in the city of Calcutta. But for these English, we who are here now could loot the city, and portion out the women, who are fair.

I have bought an English rifle for you, my son, better than the one which Shere Khan stole from Cherat last summer, throwing to two thousand paces; and for Sultan Khan an English revolver, as he asked. Of the wonders of this great city I will speak when we meet, for I cannot write them.

When I came from Lala China the tale of blood between our house and the house of Zarmat Shah lacked one on our side. I have been gone many days, but I have no news from you that it is made even. If ye have not yet killed the boy who had the feud laid upon him when I went, do nothing but guard your lives till ye get the new rifle. With a steady rest it will throw across the valley into Zarmat Shah's field, and so ye can kill the women at evening.

Now I will cease, for I am tired of this writing. Make Mahbub Ali welcome, and bid him stay till ye have written an answer to this, telling me whether all be well in my house. My blood is not cold that I charge you once again to give no ear to the Mullahs, who have lied, as I will show; and, above all else, to keep the villages still till I return. Nor am I a clucking hen of a Khuttick if I write last, that these English are devils, against whom only the Will of God can help us.

And why should we beat our heads against a rock, for we only spill our brains :

And when we have the Valley to content us, why should we go out against the Mountain ?

A strong man, saith Kabir, is strong only till he meet with a stronger.

A KING'S ASHES

1888 : On Wednesday morning last, the ashes of the late ruler of Gwalior were consigned to the Ganges without the walls of Allahabad Fort. Scindia died in June of last year, and, shortly after the cremation, the main portion of the ashes were taken to the water. Yesterday's function, the disposal of what remained (it is impossible not to be horrible in dealing with such a subject), was comparatively of an unimportant nature, but rather grim to witness.

Beyond the melon-beds and *chappar* villages that stand upon the spit of sun-baked mud and sand by the confluence of the Jumna and the Ganges, lies a flag-bedizened home of *fakirs*, *gurus*, *gosains*, *sanyasis*, and the like. A stone's throw from this place boils and eddies the line of demarcation between the pure green waters of the Jumna and the turbid current of the Ganges; and here they brought the ashes of Scindia. With these came minor functionaries of the Gwalior State, six Brahmins of the Court, and nine of Scindia's relatives. In his lifetime, the Maharaja had a deep and rooted distrust of his own family and clan, and no Scindia was ever allowed office about him. Indeed, so great was his aversion that he would not even permit them to die in the Luskar, or City of Gwalior. They must needs go out when their last hour came, and die in a neighbouring *jaghir* village which belonged to Sir Michael Filose, one of that Italian family which has served the State so long and faithfully. When such an one had died, Scindia, by his own command, was not informed of the event till the prescribed days of mourning had elapsed. Then notice was given to him by the placing of his bed on the ground,—a sign of mourning,—and he would ask, not too tenderly, 'Which Scindia is dead?'

Considering this unamiable treatment, the wonder was that so many as nine of his own kin could be found to attend the last rites on that sun-dried mud-bank. There was, or seemed to be, no attempt at ceremony, and, naturally enough, no pretence at grief; nor was there any gathering of native notables. The common crowd and the multitude of priests had the spectacle to themselves, if we except a few artillerymen from the Fort, who had strolled down to see what was happening to 'one of them (qualified) kings.' By ten o'clock, a tawdry silken litter bearing the ashes and accompanied by the mourners, had reached the water's edge, where wooden cots had been run out into the stream, and where the water-deepened boats had been employed to carry the press of sight-seers. Underfoot, the wet ground was trodden by hundreds of feet into a slimy pulp of mud and stale flowers of sacrifice; and on this compost slipped and blundered a fine white horse, whose fittings were heavy with bosses of new silver. He, and a big elephant, adorned with a necklace of silver plaques, were a gift to the priests who in cash and dinners would profit by the day's work to the extent of eight or ten thousand rupees.

Overhead a hundred *fakirs'* flags, bearing devices of gods, beasts, and the trident of Shiva, fluttered in the air; while all around, like vultures drawn by carrion, crowded the priests. There were burly, bull-necked, freshly oiled ruffians, sleek of paunch and jowl, clothed in pure white linen; mad wandering mendicants carrying the peacock's feather, the begging bowl, and the patched cloak; salmon-robed *sanyasis* from up-country, and evil-eyed *gosains* from the south. They crowded upon the wooden bedsteads, piled themselves upon the boats, and jostled into the first places in the crowd in the mud, and all their eyes were turned toward two nearly naked men who seemed to be kneading some Horror in their hands and dropping it into the water. The closely packed boats rocked gently, the crowd babbled and buzzed, and uncouth music wailed and shrieked, while from behind the sullen, squat bulk of Allahabad Fort the booming of minute-guns announced that the Imperial Government was paying honour to the memory of His Highness Maharaja Jyaji Rao Scindia, G.C.B., G.C.S.I., once owner of twenty thousand square miles of land, nearly three million people, and treasure untold, if all tales be true. Not fifty yards upstream, a swollen dead goat was bobbing up and down in the water in a ghastly parody on kidlike skittishness, and green filth was cast ashore by every little wave.

Was there anything more to see? The white horse refused to be led into the water and splashed all the bystanders with dirt, and the elephant's weight broke up the sand it was standing on and turned it to a quag. This much was visible, but little else; for the clamouring priests forbade any English foot to come too near, perhaps for fear that their gains might be lessened. Where the press parted, it was possible to catch a glimpse of this ghoulish kneading by the naked men in the boat, and to hear the words of a chanted prayer. But that was all.

THE BRIDE'S PROGRESS

And school foundations in the act
Of holiday, three files compact,
Shall learn to view thee as a fact
Connected with that zealous tract
'Rome, Babylon, and Nineveh.'

The Burden of Nineveh.

It would have been presumption and weariness deliberately to have described Benares. No man, except he who writes a guide-book, 'does' the Strand or Westminster Abbey. The foreigner —French or American—tells London what to think of herself, as the visitor tells the Anglo-Indian what to think of India. Our neighbour over the way always knows so much more about us than we ourselves. The Bride interpreted Benares as fresh youth and radiant beauty can interpret a city grey and worn with years. Providence had been very good to her, and she repaid Providence by dressing herself to the best advantage—which, if the French speak truth, is all that a fair woman can do toward religion. Generations of untroubled ease and well-being must have builded the dainty figure and rare face, and the untamable arrogance of wealth looked out of the calm eyes. 'India,' said The Bride philosophically, 'is an incident only in our trip. We are going on to Australia and China, and then Home by San Francisco and New York. We shall be at Home again before the season is quite ended.' And she patted her bracelets, smiling softly to herself over some thought that had little enough to do with Benares or India—whichever was the 'incident.' She went into the city of Benares. Benares of the Buddhists and the Hindus—of Durga of the Thousand Names—of two Thousand Temples, and twice two thousand stenches. Her high heels rang delicately upon the stone pavement of the gullies, and her brow, unmarked as that of a little child, was troubled by the stenches. 'Why does Benares smell so?' demanded The Bride pathetically. '*Must* we do it, if it smells like this?' The Bridegroom was high-coloured, fair-whiskered, and insistent, as an Englishman should be. 'Of course we must. It would never do to go home without having seen Benares. Where is a guide?' The streets were alive with them, and the couple chose him who spoke English most fluently. 'Would you like to see where the Hindus are burnt?' said he. They would, though The Bride shuddered as she spoke, for she feared that it would be very horrible. A ray of gracious sunlight touched her hair as she turned, walking cautiously in the middle of the narrow way, into the maze of the byways of Benares.

The sunlight ceased after a few paces, and the horrors of the Holy City gathered round her. Neglected rainbow-hued sewage sprawled across the path, and a bull, rotten with some hideous disease that distorted his head out of all bestial likeness, pushed through the filth. The Bride picked her way carefully, giving the bull the wall. A lean dog, dying of mange, growled and yelped among her starveling puppies on a threshold that led into the darkness of some unclean temple. The Bride stooped and patted the beast on the head. 'I think she's something like *Bessie*,' said The Bride, and once again her thoughts wandered far beyond Benares. The lanes grew narrower and the symbols of a brutal cult more numerous. Hanuman, red, shameless, and smeared with oil, leaped and leered upon the walls above stolid, black stone bulls, knee-deep in yellow flowers. The bells clamoured from unseen temples, and half-naked men with evil eyes rushed out of dark places and besought her for money, saying that they were priests—*padris*, like the *padris* of her own faith. One young man—who knows in what Mission school he had picked up his speech?—told her this in English, and The Bride laughed merrily, shaking her head. 'These men speak English,' she called back to her husband. 'Isn't it funny!'

But the mirth went out of her face when a turn in the lane brought her suddenly above the burning-*ghât*, where a man was piling logs on some Thing that lay wrapped in white cloth, near the water of the Ganges. 'We can't see well from this place,' said the Bridegroom stolidly. 'Let us get a little closer.' They moved forward through deep grey dust—white sand of the river and black dust of man blended—till they commanded a full view of the steeply sloping bank and the Thing under the logs. A man was laboriously starting a fire at the river end of the pile; stepping wide now and again to avoid the hot embers of a dying blaze actually on the edge of the water. The Bride's face blanched, and she looked appealingly to her husband, but he had only eyes for the newly lit flame. Slowly, very slowly, a white dog crept on his belly down the bank, toward a heap of ashes among which the water was hissing. A plunge, followed by a yelp of pain, told that he had reached food, and that the food was too hot for him. With a deftness that marked long training, he raked the capture from the ashes on to the dust and slobbered, nosing it tentatively. As it cooled, he settled, with noises of animal delight, to his meal and worried and growled and tore. 'Will!' said The Bride faintly. The Bridegroom was watching the newly lit pyre and could not attend. A log slipped sideways, and through the chink showed the face of the man below, smiling the dull thick smile of death, which is such a smile as a very drunken man wears when he has found in his wide-swimming brain a joke of exquisite savour. The dead man grinned up to the sun and the fair face of The Bride. The flames sputtered and caught and spread. A man waded out knee-deep into the water, which was covered with greasy black embers and an oily scum. He chased the bobbing driftwood with a basket, that it might be saved for another occasion, and threw each take on a mound of such economies or on the back of the unheeding dog deep in the enjoyment of his hot dinner.

Slowly, very slowly, as the flames crackled, the Smiling Dead Man lifted one knee through the light logs. He had just been smitten with the idea of rising from his last couch and confounding the spectators. It was easy to see he was tasting the notion of this novel, this stupendous practical joke, and would presently, always smiling, rise up, and up, and up, and . . .

The fire-shrivelled knee gave way, and with its collapse little flames ran forward and whistled and whispered and fluttered from heel to head. 'Come away, Will,' said The Bride, 'come away! It is too horrible. I'm sorry that I saw it.' They left together, she with her arm in her husband's for a sign to all the world that, though Death be inevitable and awful, Love is still the greater, and in its sweet selfishness can set at naught even the horrors of a burning-*ghât*.

'I never thought what it meant before,' said The Bride, releasing her husband's arm as she recovered herself; 'I see now.' 'See what?' 'Don't you know?' said The Bride, 'what Edwin Arnold says:—

For all the tears of all the eyes
Have room in Gunga's bed,
And all the sorrow is gone to-morrow
When the white flames have fed.

I see now. I think it is very, *very* horrible.' Then to the guide, suddenly, with a deep compassion, 'And will you be—will you be burnt in that way, too?' 'Yes, your Ladyship,' said the guide cheerfully, 'we are all burnt that way.' 'Poor wretch!' said The Bride to herself. 'Now show us some more temples.' A second time they dived into Benares City, but it was at least five long minutes before The Bride recovered those buoyant spirits which were hers by right of Youth and Love and Happiness. A very pale and sober little face peered into the filth of the Temple of the Cow, where the odour of Holiness and Humanity are highest. Fearful and wonderful old women, crippled in hands and feet, body and back, crawled round her; some even touching the hem of her dress. And at this she shuddered, for the hands were very foul. The walls dripped filth, the pavement sweated filth, and the contagion of uncleanliness walked among the worshippers. There might have been beauty in the Temple of the Cow; there certainly was horror enough and to spare; but The Bride was conscious only of the filth of the place. She turned to the wisest and best man in the world, asking indignantly, 'Why don't these horrid people clean the place out?' 'I don't know,' said The Bridegroom; 'I suppose their religion forbids it.' Once more they set out on their journey through the city of monstrous creeds—she in front, the pure white hem of her petticoat raised indignantly clear of the mire, and her eyes full of alarm and watchfulness. Closed galleries crossed the narrow way, and the light of day fainted and grew sick ere it could climb down into the abominations of the gullies. A litter of gorgeous red and gold barred the passage to the Golden Temple. 'It is the Maharani of Hazaribagh,' said the guide, 'she coming to pray for a child.' 'Ah!' said The Bride, and turning quickly to her husband, said, 'I wish mother were with us.' The Bridegroom made no answer. Perhaps he was beginning to repent of dragging a young English girl through the iniquities of Benares. He announced his intention of returning to his hotel, and The Bride dutifully followed. At every turn lewd gods grinned and mouthed at her, the still air was clogged with thick odours and the reek of rotten marigold flowers, and disease stood blind and naked before the sun. 'Let us get away quickly,' said The Bride; and they escaped to the main street, having honestly accomplished nearly two-thirds of what was written in the little red guide-book. An instinct inherited from a century of cleanly English housewives made The Bride pause before getting into the carriage, and, addressing the seething crowd generally, murmur, 'Oh! you horrid people! Shouldn't I like to wash you.'

Yet Benares—which name must certainly be derived from *be*, without, and *nares*, nostrils—is not entirely a Sacred Midden Very early in the morning, almost before the light had given promise of the day, a boat put out from a *ghât* and rowed upstream till it stayed in front of the ruined magnificence of Scindia's Ghât—a range of ruined wall and drunken bastion. The Bride and Bridegroom had risen early to catch their last glimpse of the city. There was no one abroad at that hour, and, except for three or four stone-laden boats rolling down from Mirzapur, they were alone upon the river. In the silence a voice thundered far above their heads: '*I bear witness that there is no God but God.*' It was the mullah, proclaiming the Oneness of God in the city of the Million Manifestations. The call rang across the sleeping city and far over the river, and be sure that the mullah abated nothing of the defiance of his cry for that he looked down upon a sea of temples and smelt the incense of a hundred Hindu shrines. The Bride could make neither head nor tail of the business. 'What is he making that noise for, Will?' she asked. 'Worshipping Vishnu,' was the ready reply; for at the outset of his venture into matrimony a young husband is at the least infallible. The Bride snuggled down under her wraps, keeping her delicate, chill-pinked little nose toward the city. Day broke over Benares, and The Bride stood up and applauded with both her hands. It was finer, she said, than any transformation scene; and so in her gratitude she applauded the earth, the sun, and the everlasting sky. The river turned to a silver flood and the ruled lines of the *ghâts* to red gold. 'How can I describe this to mother?' she cried, as the wonder grew, and timeless Benares roused to a fresh day. The Bride nestled down in the boat and gazed round-eyed. As water spurts through a leaky dam, as ants pour out from the invaded nest, so the people of Benares poured down the *ghâts* to the river. Wherever The Bride's eye rested, it saw men and women stepping downwards, always downwards, by rotten wall, worn step, tufted bastion, riven water-gate, and stark, bare, dusty bank, to the water. The hundred priests drifted down to their stations under the large mat-umbrellas that all pictures of Benares represent so faithfully. The Bride's face lighted with joy. She had found a simile. 'Will! Do you recollect that pantomime we went to ages and ages ago—before we were engaged—at Brighton? Doesn't it remind you of the scene of the Fairy Mushrooms—just before they all got up and danced, you know? Isn't it splendid?' She leaned forward, her chin in her hand, and watched long and intently; and Nature, who is without doubt a Frenchwoman, so keen is her love for effect, arranged that the shell-like pink of The Bride's cheek should be turned against a dull-red house, in the windows of which sat women in blood-red clothes, letting down crimson turban-cloths for the morning breeze to riot with. From the burning-*ghât* rose lazily a welt of thick blue smoke, and an eddy of the air blew a wreath across the river. The Bride coughed. 'Will,' she said, 'promise me when I die you won't have me cremated—if cremation is the fashion then.' And 'Will' promised lightly, as a man promises who is looking for long years.

The life of the city went forward. The Bride heard, though she did not understand, the marriage-song, and the chant of prayers, and the wail of the mourners. She looked long and steadfastly at the beating heart of Benares and at the Dead for whom no day had dawned. The place was hers to watch and enjoy if she pleased. Her enjoyment was tempered with some thought of regret; for her eyebrows contracted and she thought. Then the trouble was apparent. 'Will!' she said softly, 'they don't seem to think much of *us*, do they?' Did she expect, then, that the whole city would make obeisance to young Love, robed and crowned in a grey tweed travelling dress and velvet toque?

The boat drifted downstream, and an hour or so later the Dufferin Bridge bore away The Bride and Bridegroom on their travels, in which India was to be 'only an incident.'

'A DISTRICT AT PLAY'

1887

Four or five years ago, when the Egerton Woollen Mills were young, and Dhariwal, on the Amritsar and Pathankot Line, was just beginning to grow, there was decreed an annual holiday for all the workers in the Mill. In time the little gathering increased from a purely private *tamasha* to a fair, and now all the Gurdaspur District goes a-merrymaking with the Mill-hands. Here the history begins.

On the evening of Friday, the 20th of August, an Outsider went down to Dhariwal to see that *mela*. He had understood that it was an affair which concerned the People only—that no one in authority had to keep order—that there were no police, and that everybody did what was right in their own eyes; none going wrong.

This was refreshing and pastoral, even as Dhariwal, which is on the banks of the Canal, is refreshing and pastoral. The Egerton Mills own a baby railway—twenty-inch gauge—which joins on to the big line at Dhariwal station, so that the visitor steps from one carriage into another, and journeys in state.

Dusk was closing in as the locomotive—it wore a cloth round its loins and a string of beads round its neck—ran the tiny carriage into the Mill-yard, and the Outsider heard the low grumble of turbines, and caught a whiff of hot wool from a shed. (The Mills were running and would run till eleven o'clock that night, because, though holidays were necessary, orders were many and urgent.) Both smell and sound suggested the North country at once,—bleak, paved streets of Skipton and Keighley; chimneys of Beverley and Burnley; grey stone houses within stone walls, and the moors looking down on all. It was perfectly natural, therefore, to find that the Englishmen who directed the departments of the establishment were from the North also; and delightful as it was natural to hear again the slow, staid Yorkshire tongue. Here the illusion stopped; for, in place of the merry rattle of the clogs as the Mill-hands left their work, there was only the soft patter of naked feet on bare ground, and for purple, smoke-girt moors, the far-off line of the Dalhousie Hills.

Presently, the electric light began its work, and a tour over the Mills was undertaken. The machinery, the thousands of spindles, and the roaring power-looms were familiar as the faces of old friends; but the workers were strange indeed. Small brown boys, naked except for a loin-cloth, 'pieced' the yarn from the spindles under the strong blaze of the electric light, and semi-nude men toiled at the carding-machine between the whirring belts. It was a shock and a realisation—for boys and men seemed to know their work in almost Yorkshire fashion.

But the amusement and not the labour of the Mill was what the Outsider had come to see—the amusement which required no policemen and no appearance of control from without.

Early on Saturday morning all Dhariwal gathered itself on the banks of the Canal—a magnificent stretch of water—to watch the swimming-race, a short half-mile downstream. Forty-three bronzes had arranged themselves in picturesque attitudes on the girders of the Railway bridge, and the crowd chaffed them according to their deserts. The race was won, from start to finish, by a tailor with a wonderful side-stroke and a cataract in one eye. The advantage counter-balanced the defect, for he steered his mid-stream course as straight as a fish, was never headed, and won, sorely pumped, in seven minutes and a few seconds. The crowd ran along the bank and yelled instructions to its favourites at the top of its voice. Up to this time not more than five hundred folk had put in an appearance, so it was impossible to judge of their behaviour in bulk.

After the swimming came the greased pole, an

entertainment the pains whereof are reserved for light-limbed boys, and the prizes, in the shape of gay cloths and rupees, are appropriated by heavy fathers. The crowd had disposed itself in and about the shadow of the trees, where one might circulate comfortably and see the local notabilities.

They are decidedly Republicans in Dhariwal, being innocent of *Darbaries*, C.I.E.'s, fat old gentlemen in flowered brocade dressing-gowns, and cattle of that kind. Every one seemed much on a level, with the exception of some famous wrestlers, who stood aside with an air of conscious worth, and grinned cavernously when spoken to. They were the pick of the assembly, and were to prove their claims to greatness on the morrow. Until the Outsider realised how great an interest the Gurdaspur District took in wrestling, he was rather at a loss to understand why men walked round and round each other warily, as do dogs on the eve of a quarrel.

The greasy-pole competition finished, there was a general move in the direction of the main road, and couples were chosen from among the Mill-hands for a three-legged race. Here the Outsider joyfully anticipated difficulty in keeping the course clear without a line of policemen; for all crowds, unless duly marshalled, *will* edge forward to see what is going on.

But the democracy of Dhariwal got into their places as they were told, and kept them, with such slight assistance as three or four self-constituted office-bearers gave. Only once, when the honour of two villages *and* the Mill was at stake in the Tug-of-War, were they unable to hold in, and the Englishmen had to push them back. But this was exceptional, and only evoked laughter, for in the front rank of all—yellow-trousered and blue-coated—was a real live policeman, who was shouldered about as impartially as the rest. More impartially, in fact; for to keep a policeman in order is a seldom-given joy, and should be made much of.

Then back to the Mill bungalow for breakfast, where there was a gathering of five or six Englishmen,—Canal Officers and Engineers. Here follows a digression.

After long residence in places where folk discuss such intangible things as Lines, Policies, Schemes, Measures, and the like, in an abstract and bloodless sort of way, it was a revelation to listen to men who talk of Things and the People—crops and ploughs and water-supplies, and the best means of using all three for the benefit of a district. They spoke masterfully, these Englishmen, as owners of a country might speak, and it was not at first that one realised how every one of the concerns they touched upon with the air of proprietorship were matters which had not the faintest bearing on their pay or prospects, but concerned the better tillage or husbandry of the fields around. It was good to sit idly in the garden, by the guava-trees, and to hear these stories of work undertaken and carried out in the interests of, and, best of all, recognised by, Nubbi Buksh—the man whose mind moves so slowly and whose life is so bounded. They had no particular love for the land, and most assuredly no hope of gain from it. Yet they spoke as though their hopes of salvation were centred on driving into a Zemindar's head the expediency of cutting his wheat a little earlier than his wont; or on proving to some authority or other that the Canal-rate in such and such a district was too high. Every one knows that India is a country filled with Englishmen, who live down in the plains and do things other than writing futile reports, but it is wholesome to meet them in the flesh.

To return, however, to the 'Tug-of-War' and the sad story of the ten men of Futteh Nangal. Now Futteh Nangal is a village of proud people, mostly sepoys, full in the stomach; and Kung is another village filled with Mill-hands of long standing, who have grown lusty on good pay. When the tug began, quoth the proud men of Futteh Nangal: 'Let all the other teams compete. We will stand aside and pull the winners.' This *hauteur* was not allowed, and in the end it happened that the men of Kung thoroughly defeated the sepoys of Futteh Nangal amid a scene of the wildest excitement, and secured for themselves the prize,—an American plough,—leaving the men of Futteh Nangal only a new and improved rice-husker.

Other sports followed, and the crowd grew denser and denser throughout the day, till evening, when every one assembled once more by the banks of the Canal to see the fireworks, which were impressive. Great boxes of rockets and shells, and wheels and Roman-candles, had come up from Calcutta, and the intelligent despatchers had packed the whole in straw, which absorbs damp. This didn't spoil the shells and rockets—quite the contrary. It added a pleasing uncertainty to their flight and converted the shells into very fair imitations of the real article. The crowd dodged and ducked, and yelled and laughed and chaffed, at each illumination, and did their best to fall into the Canal. It was a jovial scuffle, and ended, when the last shell had burst gloriously on the water, in a general adjournment to the main street of Dhariwal village, where there was provided a magic-lantern.

At first sight it does not seem likely that a purely rustic audience would take any deep interest in magic-lanterns; but they did, and showed a most unexpected desire to know what the pictures meant. It was an out-of-door performance, the sheet being stretched on the side of a house, and the people sitting below in silence. Then the native doctor—who was popular with the Mill-hands—went up on to the roof and began a running commentary on the pictures as they appeared; and his imagination was as fluent as his Punjabi. The crowd grew irreverent and jested with him, until they recognised a portrait of one of the native overseers and a *khitmutgar*. Then they turned upon the two who had achieved fame thus strangely, and commented on their beauty. Lastly, there flashed upon the sheet a portrait of Her Majesty the Empress. The native doctor rose to the occasion, and, after enumerating a few of our Great Lady's virtues, called upon the crowd to *salaam* and cheer; both of which they did noisily, and even more noisily, when they were introduced to the Prince of Wales. One might moralise to any extent on the effect produced by this little demonstration in an out-of-the-way corner of Her Majesty's Empire.

Next morning, being Sunday and cool, was given up to wrestling. By this time the whole of the Gurdaspur District was represented, and the crowd was some five thousand strong. Eventually, after much shouting one hundred and seventy men from all the villages, near and far, were set down to wrestle, if time allowed. And in truth the first prize—a plough, for the man who showed most 'form'—was worth wrestling for. Armed with a notebook and a pencil, the Manager, by virtue of considerable experience in the craft, picked out the men who were to contend together; and these, fearing defeat, did in almost every instance explain how their antagonist was too much for them. The people sat down in companies upon the grass, village by village, flanking a huge square marked on the ground. Other restraint there was none. Within the square was the roped ring for the wrestlers, and close to the ring a tent for the dozen or so of Englishmen present. Be it noted that anybody might come into this tent who did not interfere with a view of the wrestling. There were no lean brown men, clasping their noses with their hands and following in the wake of the Manager Sahib. Still less were there the fat men in gorgeous raiment before noted—the men who shake hands 'Europe fashion' and demand the favour of your interest for their uncle's son's wife's cousin.

It was a sternly democratic community, bent on

enjoying itself, and, unlike all other democracies, knowing how to secure what it wanted.

The wrestlers were called out by name, stripped, and set to amid applauding shouts from their respective villages and trainers. There were many men of mark engaged,—huge men who stripped magnificently; light, lean men, who wriggled like eels, and got the mastery by force of cunning; men deep in the breast as bulls, lean in the flank as greyhounds, and lithe as otters; men who wrestled with amicable grins; men who lost their tempers and smote each other with the clenched hand on the face, and so were turned out of the ring amid a storm of derision from all four points of the compass; men as handsome as statues of the Greek gods, and foul-visaged men whose noses were very properly rubbed in the dirt.

As he watched, the Outsider was filled with a great contempt and pity for all artists at Home, because he felt sure that they had never seen the human form aright. One wrestler caught another by the waist, and lifting him breast-high, attempted to throw him bodily, the other stiffening himself like a bar as he was heaved up. The *coup* failed, and for half a minute the two stayed motionless as stone, till the lighter weight wrenched himself out of the other's arms, and the two came down, —flashing through a dozen perfect poses as they fell,—till they subsided once more into ignoble scuffle in the dust. The story of that day's strife would be a long one were it written at length,—how one man did brutally twist the knee of another (which is allowed by wrestling law, though generally considered mean) for a good ten minutes, and how the twistee groaned, but held out, and eventually threw the twister, and stalked round the square to receive the congratulations of his friends ; how the winner in each bout danced joyfully over to the tent to have his name recorded (there were between three and four hundred rupees given in prizes in the wrestling matches alone) ; how the Mill-hands applauded their men ; and how Siddum, Risada, Kalair, Narote, Sohul, Maha, and Doolanagar, villages of repute, yelled in reply ; how the Sujhanpur men took many prizes for the honour of the Sugar mills there ; how the event of the day was a tussle between a boy—a mere child—and a young man ; how the youngster nearly defeated his opponent amid riotous yells, but broke down finally through sheer exhaustion ; how his trainer ran forward to give him a pill of dark and mysterious composition, but was ordered away under the rules of the game. Lastly, how a haughty and most wonderfully ugly weaver of the Mill was thrown by an outsider, and how the Manager chuckled, saying that a defeat at wrestling would keep the weaver quiet and humble for some time, which was desirable. All these things would demand much space to describe and must go unrecorded.

They wrestled—couple by couple—for six good hours by the clock, and a Kashmiri weaver (why are Kashmiris so objectionable all the Province over?) later on in the afternoon, was moved to make himself a nuisance to his neighbours. Then the four self-appointed office-bearers moved in his direction; but the crowd had already dealt with him, and the Dormouse in *Alice in Wonderland* was never so suppressed as that weaver. Which proves that a democracy can keep order among themselves when they like.

The Outsider departed, leaving the wrestlers still at work, and the last he heard as he dived through that most affable, grinning assembly, was the shout of one of the Mill-hands, who had thrown his man and ran to the tent to get his name entered. Freely translated, the words were exactly what Gareth, the Scullion-Knight, said to King Arthur:—

> Yea, mighty through thy meats and drinks am I,
> And I can topple over a hundred such

Then back to the Schemes and Lines and Policies and Projects filled with admiration for the Englishmen who live in patriarchal fashion among the People, respecting and respected, knowing their ways and their wants; believing (soundest of all beliefs) that 'too much progress is bad,' and compassing with their heads and hands real, concrete, and undeniable Things. As distinguished from the speech which dies and the paper-work which perishes.

WHAT IT COMES TO

'Men instinctively act under the excitement of the battlefield, only as they have been taught to act in peace.' . . . These words deserve to be engraved in letters of gold over the gates of every barrack and drill-ground in the country. The drill of the soldier now begins and ends in the Company. . . Each Company will stand for itself on parade, practically as independent as a battery of artillery in a brigade, etc., etc. Vide *Comments on New German Drill Regulations*, in *Pioneer*

SCENE.—*Canteen of the Tyneside Tailtwisters, in full blast. Chumer of B Company annexes the Pioneer on its arrival, by right of the strong arm, and turns it over contemptuously.*

CHUMER.—'Ain't much in this 'ere. On'y Jack the Ripper and a lot about *Ci*-vilians. 'Might think the 'ole country was full of *Ci*-vilians. *Ci*-vilians an' drill. 'Strewth a' mighty! As if a man didn't get 'nuff drill outside o' his evenin' paiper. Anybody got the fill of a pipe 'ere?

SHUCKBRUGH *of B Company* (*passing pouch*).—Let's 'ave 'old o' that paper. Wot's on? Wot's in? No more *new* drill?

CHUMER.—Drill be sugared! When I was at 'ome, now, buyin' my *Times* orf the Railway stall like a gentleman, *I* never read nothin' about drill. There *wasn't* no drill. Strike me blind, these Injian papers ain't got nothin' else to write about. When 'tisn't our drill, it's Rooshian or Prooshian or French. It's Prooshian now. Brrh!

HOOKEY (*E Company*).—All for to improve your mind, Chew. You'll get a first-class school-ticket one o' these days, if you go on

CHUMER (*whose strong point is not education*).—*You*'ll get a first-class head on top o' your shoulders, 'Ook, if you go on. You mind that I ain't no bloomin' litteratoor but . . .

SHUCKBRUGH.—Go on about the Prooshians an' let 'Ook alone. 'Ook 'as a—wot's its name?—fas—fas—fascilitude for impartin' instruction. 'E's down in the Captain's book as sich. Ain't you, 'Ook?

CHUMER (*anxious to vindicate his education*).—Listen 'ere! 'Men instinck—stinkivly act under the excitement *of* the battle-field on'y as they 'ave been taught for to act in peace.' An' the man that wrote that sez 't ought to be printed in gold in our barricks.

SHUCKBRUGH (*who has been through the Afghan War*).—'Might a told 'im that, if he'd come to *me*, any time these ten years.

HOOKEY (*loftily*).—O I bid fair he's a bloomin' General. Wot's 'e drivin' at?

SHUCKBRUGH.—'E says wot you do on p'rade you do without thinkin' under fire. If you was taught to stand on your 'ed on p'rade, you'd do so in action.

CHUMER.—I'd lie on my belly first for a bit, if so be there was aught to lie be'ind.

HOOKEY.—That's 'ow you've been taught. We're allus lyin' on our bellies be'ind every bloomin' bush—spoilin' our best clobber. Takin' advantage o' cover, they call it.

SHUCKBRUGH.—An' the more you lie the more you want to lie. That's human natur'.

CHUMER.—It's rare good—for the henemy.

I'm lyin' 'ere where this pipe is; Shukky's there by the 'baccy-paper; 'Ook is there be'ind the pewter, an' the rest of us all over the place crawlin' on our bellies an' poppin' at the smoke in front. Old Pompey, arf a mile be'ind, sez, 'The battalion will now attack.' Little Mildred squeaks out, 'Charrge!' Shukky an' me, an' you, an' 'im, picks ourselves out o' the dirt, an' charges. But 'ow the *dooce* can you charge from skirmishin' order? That's wot I want to know. There ain't no touch—there ain't no *chello;* an' the minut' the charge is over, you've got to play at bein' a bloomin' field-rat all over again.

GENERAL CHORUS.—Bray-vo, Chew! Go it, Sir Garnet! Two pints and a hopper for Chew! Kernel Chew!

HOOKEY (*who has possessed himself of the paper*).—Well, the Prooshians ain't goin' to have any more o' that. There ain't goin' to be no more battalion-drill—so this bloke says. On'y just the comp'ny handed over to the comp'ny orf'cer to do wot 'e likes with.

SHUCKBRUGH.—Gawd 'elp B Comp'ny if they do that to *us!*

CHUMER (*hotly*).—You're bloomin' pious all of a sudden. Wot's wrong with Little Mildred, I'd like to know?

SHUCKBRUGH.—Little Mildred's all right. It's his bloomin' dandified Skipper—it's Collar an' Cuffs—it's Ho de Kolone—it's Squeaky Jim that I'm set against.

CHUMER.—Well. Ho de Kolone is goin' 'Ome, an' may be we'll have Sugartongs instead.

Sugartongs is a hard drill, but 'e's got no bloomin' frills about 'im.

HOOKEY (*of E Company*).—You ought to 'ave Hackerstone—*e*'d wheel yer into line. Our Jemima ain't much to look at, but 'e knows wot 'e wants to do an' he does it. '*E* don't club the company an' damn the Sargints, Jemima doesn't. 'E's a proper man an' no error.

SHUCKBRUGH.—Thank you for nothin'. Sugartongs is a vast better. Mess Sargint 'e told us that Sugartongs is goin' to be married at 'Ome. If 'e's *that*, o' course 'e won't be no good; but the Mess Sargint's a bloomin' liar mostly.

CHUMER.—Sugartongs won't marry—not 'e. 'E's too fond o' the regiment. Little Mildred's like to do that first; bein' so young.

HOOKEY (*returning to paper*).—'On'y the comp'ny an' the comp'ny orf'cer doin'. what 'e thinks 'is men can do.' 'Strewth! Our Jemima'd make us dance down the middle an' back again. But what would they do with our Colonel? I don't catch the run o' this new trick of company officers thinkin' for themselves.

SHUCKBRUGH.—Give 'im a stickin' plaster to keep 'im on 'is 'orse at battalion p'rade, an' lock 'im up in ord'ly-room 'tween whiles. Me an' one or two more would see 'im now an' again. Ho! Ho!

CHUMER.—A Colonel's a bloomin' Colonel anyway. 'Can't do without a Colonel.

SHUCKBRUGH.—'Oo said we would, you fool? Colonel 'll give his order, 'Go an' do this an' go an' do that, an' do it quick.' Sugartongs 'e salutes an' Jemima 'e salutes an' orf we goes; Little Mildred trippin' over 'is sword every other step. *We* know Sugartongs; *you* know Jemima; an' *they* know *us*. 'Come on,' sez they. 'Come on it is,' sez we; an' we don' crawl on our bellies no more, but *comes* on. Old Pompey has given 'is orders an' we does 'em. Old Pompey can't cut in too with · 'Wot the this an' that are you doin' there? Retire your men. Go to Blazes and cart cinders,' an' such like. There's a deal in that there notion of independent commands.

CHUMER.—There is. It's 'ow it comes in action anywoys, if it isn't wot it comes on p'rade. But look 'ere, wot 'appens if you don't know your bloomin' orf'cer, an' 'e don't know nor care a brass farden about you—like Squeakin' Jim?

HOOKEY.—Things 'appens, as a rule; an' then again they don't some'ow. There's a deal o' luck knockin' about the world, an' takin' one thing with another a fair shares o' that comes to the Army. 'Cordin' to this 'ere (*he thumps the paper*) we ain't got no weppings worth the name, an' we don't know 'ow to use 'em when we 'ave—I didn't mean your belt, Chew—we ain't got no orf'cers; we '*ave* got bloomin' swipes for liquor.

CHUMER (*sotto voce*).—Yuss. 'Undred an' ten gallons beer made out of a heighty-four-gallon cask an' the strength kep' up with 'baccy. Yah! Go on, 'Ook.

HOOKEY.—We ain't got no drill, we ain't got no men, we ain't got no kit, nor yet no bullocks to carry it if we 'ad—where in the name o' fortune do all our bloomin' victories come from? It's a tail-uppards way o' workin'; but where *do* the victories come from?

SHUCKBRUGH (*recovering his pipe from Hookey's mouth*) — Ask Little Mildred — 'e carries the Colours. Chew, are you goin' to the bazar?

THE OPINIONS OF GUNNER BARNABAS

A narrow-minded Legislature sets its face against that Atkins, whose Christian name is Thomas, drinking with the 'civilian.' To this prejudice I and Gunner Barnabas rise superior. Ever since the night when he, weeping, asked me whether the road was as frisky as his mule, and then fell head-first from the latter on the former, we have entertained a respect for each other. I wondered that he had not been instantly killed, and he that I had not reported him to various high Military Authorities then in sight, instead of gently rolling him down the hillside till the danger was overpast. On that occasion, it cannot be denied that Gunner Barnabas was drunk. Later on, as our intimacy grew, he explained briefly that he had been 'overtaken' for the first time in three years; and I had no reason to doubt the truth of his words.

Gunner Barnabas was a lean, heavy-browed, hollow-eyed giant, with a moustache of the same hue and texture as his mule's tail. Much had he seen from Karachi to Bhamo, and, so his bosom friend, McGair, assured me, had once killed a man 'with 'e's naked fistes.' But it was hard to make him talk. When he was moved to speech, he roved impartially from one dialect to another, being a Devonshire man, brought up in the slums of Fratton, nearly absorbed into Portsmouth Dockyard, sent to Ireland as a blacksmith's assistant, educated imperfectly in London, and there enlisted into what he profanely called a 'jim-jam batt'ry.' 'They want big 'uns for the work we does,' quoth Gunner Barnabas, bringing down a huge hairy hand on his mule's withers. 'Big 'uns an' steady 'uns. He flung the bridle over the mule's head, hitched the beast to a tree, and settled himself on a boulder ere lighting an unspeakably rank bazar-cheroot.

The current of conversation flowed for a while over the pebbles of triviality. Then, in answer to a remark of mine, Gunner Barnabas heaved his huge shoulders clear of the rock and rolled out his mind between puffs. We had touched tenderly and reverently on the great question of temperance in the Army. Gunner Barnabas pointed across the valley to the Commander-in-Chief's house and spoke: ''Im as lives over yonder is goin' the right way to work,' said he. 'You can make a man march by reg'lation, make a man fire by reg'lation, make a man load up a bloomin' mule by reg'lation. You can't make him a Blue Light by reg'lation, and that's the only thing as 'ill make the Blue Lights stop grousin' and stiffin'.' It should be explained for the benefit of the uninitiated, that a 'Blue Light' is a Good Templar, that 'grousing' is sulking, and 'stiffing' is using unparliamentary language. 'An' Blue

Lights, specially when the orf'cer commanding is a Blue Light too, is a won'erful fool. You never be a Blue Light, Sir, not so long as you live.' I promised faithfully that the Blue Lights should burn without me to all Eternity, and demanded of Gunner Barnabas the reasons for his dislike.

My friend formulated his indictment slowly and judicially. 'Sometimes a Blue Light's a blue shirker; very often 'e's a noosance; and more than often 'e's a lawyer, with more chin than 'e or 'is friends wants to 'ear. When a man—any man—sez to me "you're damned, and there ain't no trustin' you,"—meanin' not as you or I sittin' 'ere might say "you be damned" comfortable an' by way o' makin' talk like, but official damned—why, naturally, I ain't pleased. Now when a Blue Light ain't *sayin'* that 'e's throwin' out a forty-seven-inch chest hinside of 'isself as it was, an' letting you see 'e thinks it. I hate a Blue Light. But there's some is good, better than ord'nary, and them I has nothing to say against. What I sez is, too much bloomin' 'oliness ain't proper, nor fit for man or beast.' He threw himself back on the ground and drove his boot-heels into the mould. Evidently, Gunner Barnabas had suffered from the 'Blue Lights' at some portion of his career. I suggested mildly that the Order to which he objected was doing good work, and quoted statistics to prove this, but the great Gunner remained unconvinced. 'Look 'ere,' said he, 'if you knows anything o' the likes o' us, you knows that the Blue Lights sez when a man drinks he drinks for the purpose of meanin' to be bloomin' drunk, and there ain't no safety 'cept in not drinking at all. Now that ain't all true. There's men as can drink their whack and be no worse for it. Them's grown men, for the boys drink for honour and glory—Lord 'elp 'em—an' *they* should be dealt with diff'rent.

'But the Blue Light 'e sez to us. "You drink mod'rate? You ain't got it in you, an' you don't come into our nice rooms no more. You go to the Canteen an' hog your liquor there." Now I put to you, Sir, *as* a friend, are that the sort of manners to projuce good feelin' in a rig'ment or anywhere else? And when 'Im that lives over yonder'—out went the black-bristled hand once more towards Snowdon—'sez in a—in a—pamphlick which it is likely you 'ave seen'—Barnabas was talking down to my civilian intellect—'sez "come on and be mod'rate them as can, an' I'll see that your Orf'cer Commandin' 'elps you;" up gets the Blue Lights and sez: "'Strewth! the Commander-in-Chief is aidin' an' abettin' the Devil an' all 'is Angels. You *can't* be mod'rate," sez the Blue Lights, an' that's what makes 'em feel 'oly. Garrn! It's settin' 'emselves up for bein' better men than them as commands 'em, an' puttin' difficulties all round' an' about. That's a bloomin' Blue Light all over, that is. What I sez is give the mod'rate lay a chance. I s'pose there's room even for Blue Lights an' men without aprins in this 'ere big Army. Let the Blue Lights take off their aprins an' 'elp the mod'rate men if they ain't too proud. I ain't above goin' out on pass with a Blue Light if 'e sez I'm a man, an' not an — untrustable Devil always a-hankerin' after lush. But *contrariwise*'—Gunner Barnabas stopped.

'Contrariwise how?' said I.

'If I was 'Im as lives over yonder, an' you was me, an' you wouldn't take the mod'rate lay, an' was a-comin' on the books and otherwise a-misconductin' of yourself, I would say: "Gunner Barnabas," I would say, an' by that I would be understood to be addressin' everybody with a uniform, "you are a incorrigable in-tox-i-cator"' —Barnabas sat up, folded his arms, and assumed an air of ultra-judicial ferocity—'"reported to me as such by your Orf'cer Commandin'. Very good, Gunner Barnabas," I would say. "I cannot, knowin' what I do o' the likes of you, subjergate your indecent cravin' for lush; but I will edgercate you to hold your liquor without offence to them as is your friends an' companions, an' without danger to the Army if so be you're on sentry-go. I will make your life, Gunner Barnabas, such that you will pray on your two bended knees for to be shut of it. You shall be flogged between the guns if you disgrace a Batt'ry, or in hollow square o' the rig'ment if you belong to the Fut, or from stables to barricks and back again if you are Cav'lry. I'll clink you till you forget what the sun looks like, an' I'll pack-drill you till your kit grows into your shoulder-blades like toadstools on a stump. I'll learn you to be sober when the Widow requires of your services, an' if I don't learn you I'll *kill* you. Understan' that, Gunner

Barnabas; for tenderness is wasted on the likes o' you. You shall learn for to control yourself for fear o' your dirty life; an' so long as that fear is over you, Gunner Barnabas, you'll be a man worth the shootin'."'

Gunner Barnabas stopped abruptly and broke into a laugh. 'I'm as bad as the Blue Lights, only t'other way on. But 'tis a fact that, in spite o' any amount o' mod'ration and pamphlicks we've got a scatterin' o' young imps an' old devils wot you can't touch excep' through the hide o' them, and by cuttin' deep at that. Some o' the young ones wants but one leatherin' to keep the fear o' drink before their eyes for years an' years; some o' the old ones wants leatherin' now and again, for the want of drink is in their marrer. You talk, an' you talk, an' you talk o' what a fine fellow the Privit Sodger is—an so 'e is many of him; but there's *one* med'cin' or *one* sickness that you've guv up too soon. Preach an' Blue Light an' medal and teach us, but, for some of us, keep the whipcord handy.'

Barnabas had rather startled me by the vehemence of his words. He must have seen this, for he said with a twinkle in his eye: 'I should have made a first-class Blue Light—rammin' double-charges home in this way. Well, I know I'm speakin' truth, and the Blue Light thinks he is, I s'pose; an' it's too big a business for you an' me to settle in one afternoon.'

The sound of horses' feet came from the path above our heads. Barnabas sprang up.

'Orf'cer an' 'rf'cer's lady,' said he, relapsing

into his usual speech. ''Won't do for you to be seen a-talkin' with the likes o' me. Hutup *kurcha!*'

And with a stumble, a crash, and a jingle of harness Gunner Barnabas went his way.

THE END

Printed by R. & R CLARK, LIMITED, *Edinburgh*.

Milton Keynes UK
Ingram Content Group UK Ltd.
UKHW040140030823
426240UK00002B/13

9 781443 739092